White-Collar Crime
in America

White-Collar Crime in America

Jay Albanese

Professor and Director
Graduate Program in Criminal Justice Administration
Niagara University

PRENTICE-HALL
Upper Saddle River, New Jersey 07458

LIBRARY OF CONGRESS CATALOGING-IN-PUBLICATION DATA

Albanese, Jay S.
    White collar crime in America / Jay S. Albanese
       p. cm.
    Includes index.
    ISBN 0-02-301261-7 (paper)
    1. White collar crimes—United States. I. Title.
HV6783.A49   1995
364.1'68—dc20   94-2292
                                        CIP

Editors: Christine Cardone and Robin Baliszewski
Production Supervisor: Jane O'Neill
Production Managers: Nick Sklitsis and Kurt Scherwatzky
Text Designer: A Good Thing Inc.
Cover Designer: Eileen Burke
Photo Researcher: Clare Maxwell

PRINTED IN THE UNITED STATES OF AMERICA

10 9 8 7 6 5 4 3 2

ISBN 0-02-301261-7

Prentice-Hall International (UK) Limited,London
Prentice-Hall of Australia Pty. Limited, Sydney
Prentice-Hall Canada Inc., Toronto
Prentice-Hall Hispanoamericana, S.A., Mexico
Prentice-Hall of India Private Limited, New Delhi
Prentice-Hall of Japan, Inc., Tokyo
Pearson Education Asia Pte. Ltd., Singapore
Editora Prentice-Hall do Brasil, Ltda., Rio de Janeiro

To my friends and family without whose never-failing love and support this book would have been finished in half the time.

Preface

In the same way that introductory criminal justice texts offer a view of crime and justice as they relate to traditional street crimes, this book does the same for white-collar crimes with two important additions. First, *White-Collar Crime in America* does not merely summarize the existing literature, it *organizes existing work* so that students can understand how the information fits together. Rather than listing and defining various types of white-collar crimes, this book has organized all the various manifestations of white-collar crime into a *coherent typology*. Rather than reiterating many different theories of causation, this book assesses them by type and evaluates their effectiveness in explaining actual cases. The same method of organizing diverse materials for *systematic understanding* is used throughout the book on topics from law enforcement methods to sentencing white-collar offenders.

Everyone is familiar with the term "white-collar crime," but it is puzzling that this phrase does not appear in any criminal code or law. In fact, white-collar crime is a generic term for a wide variety of illegal acts. To compound the confusion, there is no regular national count of its extent, and explanations of its causes are scattered among the criminology and business literature. The effectiveness of enforcement, prosecution, and defense efforts has not been analyzed in a systematic way for a college and university audience. Finally, few proposals to "solve" the white-collar crime problem on a long-term basis have been evaluated in a manner accessible to students. Instead, these ideas are scattered among monographs, government reports, and journal articles that are often never synthesized and do not reach a wide audience.

This book has *six distinct features* that distinguish it from the existing literature:

1. A *definition* and *typology* of white-collar crime that makes clear how white-collar crimes are invariably comprised of one of three types of offenses: crimes of fraud, offenses against public administration, and regulatory offenses.
2. An *estimate of its true nature and extent*, given existing counts and extrapolations of known instances of white-collar crime, as collected in government reports and by individual researchers over the years.

3. A *review of specific theories of causation*, gathered from both the criminological and business literature, together with a new explanation based on ethical principles.

4. An *assessment of the comparative effectiveness of enforcement, prosecution, and defense strategies* in the detection and adjudication of white-collar crime.

5. An *examination of outcomes* of white-collar crime cases to compare traditional fines and prison sentences to more unusual sanctions such as "rehabilitation" for corporations, professional suspensions, civil remedies, and other methods to resolve these cases.

6. A *review of special issues* in white-collar crime, as compared to conventional crime, including the role of *women* in white-collar crime and *organized crime* infiltration of business.

An important distinction of this book is the inclusion of *new material*, based on analyses, conducted by the author, of data, case studies, and the theoretical literature. The incorporation of this new material serves to transmit the important notions that (1) more is unknown about white-collar crime than is known; (2) more and better data, theory, and investigation are required if white-collar crime is to be more effectively controlled; and (3) individuals entering professions in criminal justice or business can have a significant impact on the extent and prevention of white-collar crime in the future.

Pedagogical Features

Several important teaching and learning aids have been employed to enhance understanding of the material in this book: use of many actual case studies, critical thinking questions, and a detailed instructor's resource manual. Case studies are used extensively throughout the book. In every instance, they illustrate points of law, causation, enforcement, prosecution, defense, or sentencing principles, and how they apply to an actual case. These case summaries are designed to develop the *critical thinking* ability of students in evaluating and applying general principles to actual fact situations and, thereby, help make the material come alive for them. Police officers, attorneys, businesspersons, and virtually every other career professional is required to apply the law, principles and procedures, to often difficult real-life situations. The case studies in this book should assist in developing this skill.

An instructor's resource manual for this book is available to instructors. The manual contains several hundred questions drawn from the book for use as exam or review questions. Critical thinking questions are included as well for student evaluation and application of principles to fact situations. These questions can be used as essay questions or as topics for oral or written assignments.

White-collar crime is often seen as a diffused area of study that is difficult to pin down. This book is aimed to draw precise parameters around the subject, its treatment in the justice system, and alternative approaches to dealing with it now and in the future.

Organization of the Book

The remainder of this book distinguishes more fully among the various types of white-collar crimes, examines what is known about their prevalence in American society, and reviews and categorizes prominent explanations of their possible causes. Subsequent chapters also provide an assessment of enforcement, prosecution, defense, and sentencing strategies and outcomes. Insight is also offered into the growth of white-collar crime committed by females and the infiltration of organized crime into legitimate business. Numerous case studies and summaries are provided throughout the book to illustrate how the various principles of law, causation, and procedure are applied in practice.

Chapter 1 defines white-collar crime in specific terms, showing how it can be characterized by a distinct constellation of offenses with similar characteristics. Chapter 2 delineates the boundaries of the crime of conspiracy which lies at the heart of the concept of white-collar crime. Using a plethora of actual case examples, the planning and organizing behind white-collar crimes are fully explained.

Chapter 3 further specifies the nature of the white-collar crimes of theft, using actual court challenges that illustrate the elements of these offenses. Chapter 4 reviews the elements of the four offenses against public administration to make clear their similarities and differences in the context of actual court cases.

Chapter 5 examines the distinctions among the various types of regulatory offenses that constitute the third category of white-collar crime. Chapter 6 reviews what is known about the extent of various forms of white-collar crime in the United States. It will be seen that there is less known about these offenses than there is about less serious forms of criminal behavior.

Chapter 7 analyzes several influential explanations of white-collar crime. Their consequences for prevention strategies are also examined, and a new explanation, based on ethical principles, is described. It is further shown how successful control strategies are most often based on a precise understanding of the causes of the misbehavior.

The investigation techniques, prosecution avenues, and defense strategies peculiar to white-collar crime cases are reviewed in Chapter 8. The role of administrative hearings, consent decrees, and other relevant methods are examined there. An assessment of prosecution tools and defense alternatives in white-collar crime cases is also included.

Chapter 9 provides an analysis of sentences imposed in white-collar crime cases. These outcomes are compared with traditional "street" crimes, as well as with public order offenses. Efforts to employ innovative sentences in white-collar cases are reviewed.

Chapter 10 examines the changing role of women in white-collar crime. It is shown that the nature of female involvement has been dependent on several pivotal factors arising from the growing female presence in the work force.

Chapter 11 provides an innovative look at the growing phenomenon of business infiltration and exploitation by criminals. This has been accomplished in the past by external organized crime elements and, in some cases, by internal business managers. An assessment of this problem, together with an analysis of organized crime prosecutions nationwide that have involved business-type activities, will be presented. A prediction model, designed to forecast businesses susceptible to such infiltration, is included.

Chapter 12 offers five propositions that will define the future of white-collar crime. How these five factors will change the nature, incidence, and response to these crimes is discussed.

Taken together, the chapters of this book will assist students in understanding the nature and complexities of white-collar crime. Indeed, crimes that require organization in their commission also require more systematic inquiry into their nature, causes, and consequences.

Acknowledgments

Writing is a natural outgrowth of reading, and the only way to learn anything reliably is by reading. I acknowledge the work of the many authors cited throughout this book for their attempts to clarify the definition, nature, extent, causes, and response to white-collar crime. It is my hope that this book advances the endeavor another notch or two.

Executive Editor Christine Cardone at Macmillan thought the premise and organization of this book interesting, and she provided the opportunity for me to develop it into its final form. D. Anthony English, editor in chief, and Casey Nicklis, editorial assistant, also provided useful input and assistance along the way. Clare Maxwell did a wonderful job in tracking down my sometimes unusual photo requests. The quick and competent production and editing of Jane O'Neill, production editor, and Sally Ann Bailey, copyeditor, did much to enhance how this book looks and reads.

Several scholars reviewed this book in manuscript form and offered helpful suggestions. The reviewers were Frank E. Hagan, Gary W. Potter, William Clements, James D. Calder, and Ernest L. Cowles. I thank them for their time and insights, and also for their lack of consensus on a number of issues. This divergence was liberating for me, providing the freedom to take a somewhat novel approach to the study of white-collar crime, the boundaries of which are still being debated.

J.S.A.

About the Author

Jay S. Albanese is professor and director of the Graduate Program in Criminal Justice Administration at Niagara University. He received his B.A. from Niagara University and M.A. and Ph.D. from Rutgers University. He was the first Ph.D. graduate from the Rutgers School of Criminal Justice. He is author of seven books, including *Organized Crime in America*, *Dealing with Delinquency*, and *Crime in America: Some Existing and Emerging Issues* (with R. Pursley). Dr. Albanese is president of the Academy of Criminal Justice Sciences for 1995–96.

Contents

White-Collar Crime
in America

CHAPTER 1

The Nature of White-Collar Crime

*Most dangerous criminals are like elephants,
difficult to define but easy to recognise.*
— Lord Justice Lawton (1981)

What Is White-Collar Crime?

The line between accepted, undesirable, and illegal business practices is some-times difficult to draw. There is a constant stream of cases that provoke doubt about the conduct of business and government.

- The Ford Pinto explodes upon low-speed rear-end collisions.
- The space shuttle *Challenger* explodes soon after lift-off, promoting a crit-ical investigation of its design and safety.
- Hundred of homes at Love Canal must be plowed into their foundations due to hazardous waste contamination.
- Corporate executives are charged with making secret payments overseas to sell their products.
- Thousands of women wearing the Dalkon Shield birth control device con-tract pelvic inflammatory disease, and some die.
- The construction industry in New York City is found to be infiltrated to a significant degree by organized crime.
- Government corruption at the highest (and lowest) levels keeps recurring from Watergate to Abscam to HUD to Iran-Contra.
- Corporate misconduct at the highest (and lowest) levels continues unde-terred from insider trading scandals to the savings and loan crisis to the BCCI money bank fraud.
- New, bolder, and more serious business scams of all varieties appear every day.

There are hundreds of well-known cases on the borderland of white-collar crime, and thousands of others we never hear about. Each of the cases just listed will be described in this book in some detail, as will many other lesser known incidents and investigations of white-collar crime. Before we proceed, however, we must be sure to understand where we are going.

Definition of White-Collar Crime

Attempts to explain the deviant and criminal acts of individuals have a long history that cross the boundaries of biology, psychology, sociology, and many other disciplines. The history of explanations of deviance having an organizational base, however, is brief.

Unlike the criminology of individuals, the criminology of organizations (and the individuals *within* those organizations) has gained systematic attention only recently by researchers and policymakers. A primary reason for the belated development of the study of such "organizational," "economic," "professional," or "white-collar" crime is the complexity of organizational behavior. Unlike crimes committed by individuals, it is much more difficult to isolate and ascribe meaningful motives, qualities, and distinguishing characteristics to corporate entities, or to those working within these organizations. As a result, questions remain about the very fundamentals of white-collar crime, including its exact definition.

Much of the confusion over precisely what constitutes white-collar crime can be attributed to Edwin Sutherland's original definition, when he introduced the term as a subject for criminologists in 1939.[1] He refers to crimes by "persons of high social status" that are committed "in the course of" an occupation as types of white-collar crime. Clearly, the acts of individuals are included in this definition. The second part of the definition, however, appears to *omit* individual crimes, such as income tax evasion or credit card fraud, which are usually unconnected with one's occupation. Likewise, occupational thefts committed by *working-class* individuals, such as embezzlement or bribe-taking, also seem to fall outside Sutherland's definition.[2] Sociologist Edwin Lemert claims to have once asked Sutherland whether he meant a specific type of crime, or crime committed by a specific type of person, in his definition of white-collar crime. Sutherland said he was not sure.[3]

There were reasons for his lack of specificity. The comparatively small amount of information available to him in the 1940s and, as Gilbert Geis points out, Sutherland's belief that *all* criminal behavior could be explained by his theory of differential association made definitional precision inconsequential.[4]

Ironically, the debate continues today. Hirschi and Gottfredson argued in 1987 that white-collar crimes are those that occur "in an occupational setting," but two years later, in response to a critique, they claimed that the definition is *not* limited to "crimes committed by employees."[5] Others continue to hold that white-collar crimes are limited to those that are occupationally related. Indeed, as Steffensmeier has suggested, "the meaning of the term white-collar crime is notoriously uncertain."[6] Nevertheless, the term has garnered worldwide recognition and has become part of both popular and scholarly literature everywhere. Sometimes it is referred to in different ways, however, such as "economic" crime or, in the case of the United Nations, "abuse of power," but the concept clearly has been internationalized with remarkably similar terminology.[7]

White-Collar Crime or White-Collar Offender?

Much of this current definitional debate is unnecessary, as it was 50 years ago. It seems arbitrary to distinguish white-collar crime from other forms of crime solely by the kind of person engaging in it. We make no such distinctions about the social position of the mugger, burglar, drug dealer, or rapist, because it is simply not relevant. From Cesare Beccaria forward, the offense, not the offender, has been the unit of analysis for defining crime.[8] The primary problem with offender-based conceptions of white-collar crime is that they can be misleading in focusing on often spurious offender attributes. As Sutherland declared in 1949, the historical bias in studies that focused exclusively on the crimes of the poor (i.e., street crimes) is as significant "as it would be if the scholars selected only red-haired criminals for study and reached the conclusion that redness of hair was the cause of crime."[9]

Likewise, most white-collar crime occurs during the course of one's occupation, but it does not appear to be a *necessary* element in defining white-collar crime. Tax evasion, and many forms of forgery and fraud, are entirely unrelated to one's job, yet they still involve all the attributes of occupationally related crimes of this type. It appears arbitrary to omit nonjob-related frauds from job-related frauds, for example, when the same behaviors, laws, and criminal justice response apply to each.

Planning, Fraud, and White-Collar Crime

Another important factor in distinguishing white-collar crime from other forms of criminal behavior is that it requires *planning and organization* (unlike most street crimes), and also involves trickery (fraudulent representations). That is to say, white-collar crime usually can be distinguished from conventional crimes by its use of advance preparation of some kind, as well as some form of fraud. Fraud often involves a violation of financial trust, using false representations, but trust is not a necessary element of fraud. Many frauds are committed where the victim is merely deceived in a business relationship. There is no trust here beyond the trust we place in others when we hope they will stop at stop signs, not steal our unlocked car, or not rob us as we leave the theater at night. Thus, fraud connotes the *deceptive element* of white-collar crime that distinguishes it from the stealth and force, randomness, and general lack of advance planning that characterize street crimes.

Therefore, taking the best parts of Sutherland's definition, and adding the dimensions noted here, a general definition of white-collar crime would read:

> Planned or organized illegal acts of deception or fraud, usually accomplished during the course of legitimate occupational activity, committed by an individual or corporate entity.

It is important, therefore, to be clear about the behavior in question when discussing white-collar crimes. Whereas conventional crimes (such as robbery, assault, and larceny) can be characterized by the use of force or stealth, white-collar crimes can be characterized by planning and deceit, often exploiting opportunities created by one's occupation.

The typology of white-collar crime to be described here expands on the general definition of white-collar crime offered by Herbert Edelhertz in 1970, because violent acts are not excluded here.[10] Therefore, the categories described in the paragraphs that follow include white-collar crimes that involve violence, such as extortion or certain criminal conspiracies.

Law-Based Versus Offender-Based Definitions

It may be argued that such a law-based typology of white-collar crimes fails to pay adequate attention to the "abuse-of-power" aspect of white-collar crime so prominent in sociological definitions of the term. It is true that many instances of white-collar crime involve an abuse of power, but this does not appear to be a *necessary* condition. To distinguish individual tax evasion for personal reasons from corporate tax evasion for business reasons in this way is arbitrary. While the status of the offender in white-collar crime is often important, it should not be *controlling* in defining the boundaries of white-collar crime.

In fact, it can be argued that abuse of power works in *two* ways: by intent of the offender in a position of power to abuse an official position *or* by an offender without such a position who believes that government or business is abusing *its* power (and uses this belief as a "justification" for the crimes, or as a means to "correct" this abuse). Viewed in this way, both a corrupt government official and a business executive can be classified as white-collar criminals, as would an otherwise powerless private citizen who cheats on his or her income tax return.

The issue is one of legitimacy. Many white-collar crimes are committed as an abuse of trust by those in positions of political or economic power. On the other hand, there are white-collar crimes that involve precisely the same behaviors by relatively powerless people. "Abuse of power" can be defined, therefore, as *either abuse* by the offender of a position of trust or else a *perceived abuse* of political or economic authority by those not holding a position of trust.

The point is that the distinction among corporate, government, and individual frauds is, in fact, irrelevant under law, because the *behaviors* involved are the same. To exclude otherwise identical acts from consideration as white-collar crime, due only to a person's social status (or lack thereof), misses a vital opportunity to understand the true nature and scope of white-collar *criminal behavior* throughout society.

The typology of white-collar crime offered here is broader than past definitions that have excluded violence, limited white-collar crime to occupationally related behaviors, excluded government misconduct, or excluded crimes that do not involve an abuse of an official position by the offender.[11] As Susan Shapiro has argued, it is time to look "beyond the perpetrators' wardrobe and social characteristics" to examine the motivations and methods of their misdeeds.[12]

Types of White-Collar Crime

The manifestations of "white-collar" crime include many different specific types of crimes, although the term itself rarely appears in law. Fortunately, these offenses can be classified into distinct categories, according to the definition just given.

Perhaps the characteristic white-collar crime is *conspiracy*. A conspiracy is an agreement between two or more persons to commit a criminal act or to achieve a noncriminal act by unlawful means. Therefore, conspiracy is essentially the planning of a crime and is considered an inchoate crime, or attempt. Nevertheless, if you conspire with your associates to defraud a company of its assets, for example, it is possible to be convicted of *both* conspiracy *and* fraud. An example is the Long Island Pet Cemetery, where people paid more than $1,000 to have their pets buried in individual graves. In an organized scheme, the owners of the cemetery took this money under false pretenses, burying 250,000 pets in mass graves instead. The owners were sentenced to five years in prison.[13]

A Three-Part Typology

The remaining types of white-collar crimes can be divided into three groups. Like conspiracy, these crimes can be considered white-collar (or organizational) crimes, because they all involve planning and deceit in their commission, and often involve occupational activity. They can be grouped into three categories: white-collar crimes of theft, crimes against public administration, and regulatory offenses.

The white-collar crimes of theft include embezzlement, extortion, forgery, and fraud. *Embezzlement* is the purposeful misappropriation of property entrusted to one's care, custody, or control, to which you are not entitled. In some states, embezzlement is called "misapplication of property" and is included under theft as a type of larceny. The essential element of embezzlement is the violation of financial trust. It is usually punished on the basis of how much money or property is misappropriated. An example is the former police chief in Rochester, New York, who was convicted of stealing $243,000 in police department funds over a three-year period.[14] Similarly, the former Detroit police chief, William Hart, was sentenced to ten years in prison for embezzling $2.6 million from a police fund.[15]

Extortion also involves theft, but it is accomplished in a different manner. Purposely obtaining property from another, with his or her consent, induced by a wrongful use of force or fear or under color of official right, is extortion. Like embezzlement, many states classify extortion as a type of larceny or theft. Extortion is sometimes called blackmail, as in the case of Sol Wachtler, chief judge of the New York State Court of Appeals, who was charged with telling his former lover that he would sell sexually explicit photos of her and her new boyfriend if she did not give him money.[16]

A person who falsely makes or alters an official document with intent to defraud commits the crime of *forgery*. The penalty for forgery is often based on the type of document that is forged. Forgery also includes other offenses that are sometimes defined separately under state law. Counterfeiting, criminal possession of forged instruments, unlawful use of slugs, falsifying business records—all are variations of the crime of forgery. For example, police found 250,000 fake social security cards, green cards, and counterfeit $20 bills in a suspected $8 million operation at a Los Angeles print shop.[17]

Still another type of white-collar crime of theft is *fraud*. To commit fraud, one must purposely obtain the property of another by deception. Fraud encompasses a wide variety of white-collar crimes and is at the heart of the concept of white-collar crime. Together with conspiracy, fraud forms the basis for many organized illegal acts. For example, many states include the separate offenses of bankruptcy fraud, false advertising, issuing a bad check, fraudulent accosting, criminal impersonation, and theft of services as specific types of fraud. Therefore, fraud involves larceny-by-trick or deceit. There are hundreds of variations of fraud that include telemarketing scams, like one in New Jersey, where a company was accused of using a 900-number to charge up to $28 per call for people responding to mail announcing they had won a prize, which turned out to be worthless jewelry.[18]

The second category of white-collar crimes can be called offenses against public administration. The crimes in this category include bribery, obstruction of justice, official misconduct, and perjury. *Bribery* involves the voluntary giving or receiving of anything of value in corrupt payment for an official act, with the intent to influence the action of a public official. The punishment for bribery is usually based on the type of act to be exchanged for the corrupt payment. The more important, or serious, the official act to be performed, the more serious the penalty. Therefore, a judge who accepts a bribe to "fix" a parking ticket will not be punished as severely as will a member of Congress who accepts a payment to influence an official action while in office. Bribery law also works two ways: you can be convicted of bribery *for offering* the corrupt payment as well as *for receiving* it. In South Carolina, for example, 15 legislators and 6 lobbyists were among those caught in a Federal Bureau of Investigation sting operation, where legislators were videotaped taking cash from a lobbyist in exchange for their votes.[19] Seven legislators in Arizona were charged in a similar bribery scandal.[20]

Intentionally preventing a public servant from lawfully performing an official function by means of intimidation is *obstruction of justice*. In the Watergate affair, for example, members of the White House staff refused to cooperate with investigations of alleged wrongdoing, and some were ultimately convicted of purposely concealing relevant information, which was obstruction of justice.

Official misconduct is the unauthorized exercise of an official function by a public official with intent to benefit or injure another. A person who uses an elected office for personal gain, rather than fulfilling his or her duties, is guilty of official misconduct. Such misconduct can result from an act of omission (failure to perform legal duties) or commission (exercising powers in an unauthorized manner). People who use their public office to "fix" tickets, obtain permits without payment, or solicit sex from those without such power are guilty of official misconduct. A police officer was convicted of this crime, when he tried to get the driving records of a woman he was accused of raping.[21]

When someone makes a false statement under oath in an official proceeding, he or she is guilty of *perjury* or false swearing. The punishment for perjury is usually based on the nature of the proceeding. Perjury during a trial or grand jury proceeding, therefore, is usually more serious than is false swearing on an affidavit. John Poindexter, one-time national security advisor to former President Reagan, was convicted of lying to Congress as part of the cover-up in the Iran-Contra affair.[22]

The third category of white-collar crimes is regulatory offenses. These offenses are designed to ensure fairness and safety in the conduct of business. There are literally hundreds of types of regulatory offenses, so they will be referred to here only by area of regulation. In fact, it is possible to group regulatory offenses into five different types: administrative, environmental, labor, and manufacturing violations, as well as unfair trade practices.

Administrative offenses involve the failure to comply with court orders or agency requirements. The failure to keep adequate records, submit compliance reports, or acquire a valid permit, for example, is against the law where these procedures are required. For example, Equifax, a leading credit-reporting agency, settled a case brought by 18 states that alleged it was issuing inaccurate credit reports. The company agreed to make credit reports easier to read, explain to consumers how a credit rating is derived, and resolve disputed reports within 30 days. Another credit-reporting agency, TRW, settled a similar case brought by 19 states.[23]

Environmental violations include emissions or dumping in violation of legal standards. Discharges into the air or water without a permit, failure to treat waste adequately before disposal, and deposit of hazardous waste in a landfill are examples of environmental violations. For example, Rockwell International pleaded guilty to felony charges that it had stored hazardous waste without a permit, in containers that leaked, and permitted leakage into reservoirs outside Denver, Colorado. The company agreed to pay an $18.5 million fine.[24]

Labor violations are discriminatory practices, unsafe exposure, or unfair treatment of employees. These include wage and hour violations, firings without cause, and refusing employment, in addition to more serious offenses, such as in the case of Imperial Food Products. Officials of the company were charged with 25 counts of involuntary manslaughter for locked exits and other safety violations that resulted in the deaths of 25 workers in a fire at its chicken-processing plant in Hamlet, North Carolina.[25]

The manufacture of unsafe products is the essence of *manufacturing violations*. Electric shock hazards, fire hazards, lack of adequate labeling, or failure to provide directions are all manufacturing violations. The Federal Trade Commission found, for example, that Kraft had falsely advertised its Singles® brand cheese slice as containing the calcium of five ounces of milk when, in fact, the level was measurably lower than that.[26]

Unfair trade practices are those that prevent fair competition in the marketplace. Monopolization, price discrimination, price-fixing, and bid-rigging are examples of unfair trade practices. In one case, the state of Florida filed a lawsuit against three infant formula manufacturers, claiming that they conspired to raise the price of baby formula artificially. It was pointed out that formula prices had risen 155 percent, while the price of milk, the primary ingredient, had risen only 36 percent over the same period.[27]

As these offense categories illustrate, regulatory offenses are designed to protect the public from unscrupulous practices of business and government. This category of white-collar crime is very important because white-collar crimes often involve deviations from legitimate business or governmental activity. The penalties for violation of these regulations involve criminal sanctions, and therefore, regulatory offenses are part of the criminal law.

Summary

The preceding summary of so-called white-collar crimes has shown that this type of crime involves a wide range of possible criminal behavior. Table 1.1 provides a summary of the typology presented here. The categories help to distinguish areas of concern in the study of white-collar crime. The crimes involving theft, crimes against public administration, and regulatory offenses illustrate the breadth and complexity required in the investigation, prosecution, and disposition of these cases. Conspiracy is the common characteristic of all three categories of white-collar crime, given the need to plan and/or organize in preparation for these offenses.

Organization of the Book

The remainder of this book distinguishes more fully among the various types of white-collar crimes, examines what is known about their prevalence in American society, and reviews and categorizes prominent explanations of their possible causes. Subsequent chapters also provide an assessment of enforcement, prosecution, defense, and sentencing strategies and outcomes. Insight is also offered into the growth of white-collar crime committed by females and the infiltration of organized crime into legitimate business. Numerous case studies and summaries are provided throughout the book to illustrate how the various principles of law, causation, and procedure are applied in practice.

Chapter 1 defines white-collar crime in specific terms, showing how it can be characterized by a distinct constellation of offenses with similar characteristics.

Chapter 2 delineates the boundaries of the crime of conspiracy that lies at the heart of the concept of white-collar crime. Using a plethora of actual case examples, the planning and organizing behind white-collar crimes are fully explained.

Table 1.1   A Typology of White-Collar Crime

Crimes of Theft	Crimes Against Public Administration	Regulatory Offenses
Embezzlement	Bribery	Administrative violations
Extortion	Obstruction of justice	Environmental violations
Forgery	Official misconduct	Labor violations
Fraud	Perjury	Manufacturing violations
		Unfair trade practices

Chapter 3 further specifies the nature of the white-collar crimes of theft, using actual court challenges that illustrate the elements of these offenses.

Chapter 4 reviews the elements of the four offenses against public administration to make clear their similarities and differences in the context of actual court cases.

Chapter 5 examines the distinctions among the various types of regulatory offenses that constitute the third category of white-collar crime.

Chapter 6 reviews what is known about the extent of various forms of white-collar crime in the United States. It reveals that there is less known about these offenses than there is about less serious forms of criminal behavior.

Chapter 7 analyzes several influential explanations of white-collar crime. Their consequences for prevention strategies are also examined. A new explanation, one based on ethical principles, is described. The discussion also shows how successful control strategies are most often based on a precise understanding of the causes of the misbehavior.

Chapter 8 reviews the investigation techniques, prosecution avenues, and defense strategies peculiar to white-collar crime cases. The role of administrative hearings, consent decrees, and other relevant methods is examined there, and an assessment of prosecution tools and defense alternatives in white-collar crime cases is also included.

Chapter 9 provides an analysis of sentences imposed in white-collar crime cases. These outcomes are compared with traditional "street" crimes, as well as with public order offenses. Efforts to employ innovative sentences in white-collar cases are reviewed.

Chapter 10 examines the changing role of women in white-collar crime. It is shown that the nature of female involvement has been dependent on several pivotal factors arising from the growing female presence in the work force.

Chapter 11 provides an innovative look at the growing phenomenon of business infiltration and exploitation by criminals. This has been accomplished in the past by external organized crime elements and, in some cases, by internal business managers. An assessment of this problem, together with an analysis of organized crime prosecutions nationwide that have involved business-type activ-

ities, is presented. A prediction model, designed to forecast businesses susceptible to such infiltration, is included.

Chapter 12 offers five propositions that will define the future of white-collar
crime. How these five factors will change the nature, incidence, and response to
these crimes is discussed.

Endnotes

1. Edwin Sutherland, "White-Collar Criminality," *American Sociological Review*, 5 (1940), pp. 1–12.
2. Richard Sparks, "White-Collar Crime and the Female Offender," *The Criminology of Deviant Women*, ed. by Freda Adler and Rita Simon (Boston: Houghton-Mifflin, 1979), pp. 181–192.
3. Edwin Lemert, *Human Deviance, Social Problems and Social Control*, 2nd ed. (Englewood Cliffs, NJ: Prentice-Hall, 1972), pp. 43–44.
4. Gilbert Geis, "White-Collar Crime: What Is It?" in *White-Collar Crime Reconsidered*, ed. by Kip Schlegel and David Weisburd (Boston: Northeastern University Press, 1992), pp. 33–35.
5. Travis Hirschi and Michael Gottfredson, "Causes of White-Collar Crime," *Criminology*, 25 (1987), p. 961; and Travis Hirschi and Michael Gottfredson, "The Significance of White-Collar Crime for a General Theory of Crime," *Criminology*, 27 (1989), p. 362.
6. Darrell J. Steffensmeier, "On the Causes of 'White-Collar' Crime: An Assessment of Hirschi and Gottfredson's Claims," *Criminology*, 27 (1989), p. 347.
7. Geis, "White-Collar Crime: What Is It?" p. 36; and Wojciech Cebulak, "White-Collar and Economic Crime: An International Perspective," *International Journal of Comparative and Applied Criminal Justice*, 13 (Winter 1989), pp. 31–40.
8. Cesare Beccaria, *Essay on Crimes and Punishments* (Indianapolis: Bobbs-Merrill, 1963; published originally in 1764).
9. Edwin H. Sutherland, *White-Collar Crime* (New York: The Dryden Press, 1949), p. 9.
10. Herbert Edelhertz, *The Nature, Impact and Prosecution of White-Collar Crime* (Washington, D.C.: U.S. Department of Justice, 1970), pp. 3–5.
11. For examples, see James S. Coleman, *The Criminal Elite*, 2nd ed. (New York: St. Martin's Press, 1989), p. 5; Gary S. Green *Occupational Crime* (Chicago: Nelson-Hall, 1990), p. 13; Gary S. Green, "White-Collar Crime and the Study of Embezzlement," *The Annals*, 525 (January 1993), pp. 95–106; and Albert J. Reiss and Albert D. Biderman, *Data Sources on White-Collar Lawbreaking* (Washington, D.C.: U.S. Government Printing Office, 1980), p. 4.
12. Susan P. Shapiro, "Collaring the Crime, Not the Criminal: Reconsidering the Concept of White-Collar Crime," *American Sociological Review*, 55 (June 1990), p. 363.

13. "Rest in Peace," *USA Today*, September 1, 1992, p. 4.
14. "Ex-Rochester Police Chief Is Guilty of Embezzlement," *The Buffalo News*, February 26, 1992, p. 7.
15. "Chief Sentenced," *USA Today*, August 28, 1992, p. 6.
16. Bethany Kandel, "Top N.Y. Judge Faces Charges," *USA Today*, November 9, 1992, p. 2.
17. "Counterfeit Arrests," *USA Today*, September 26, 1991, p. 3.
18. "Mount Pleasant Suit," *USA Today*, February 28, 1992, p. 8.
19. Joseph Stedino with Dary Matera, *What's in It for Me?* (New York: HarperCollins, 1993); and Mark Mayfield, "S. Carolina Bribery Scandal Widens," *USA Today*, March 21, 1991, p. 4.
20. "Bribery Plea," *USA Today*, February 20, 1991, p. 5.
21. "Albany: Ex-State Trooper," *USA Today*, January 23, 1992, p. 8.
22. Aaron Epstein, "Poindexter Guilty on All Counts," *The Buffalo News*, April 8, 1990, p. 1.
23. "Equifax Settlement," *USA Today*, July 1, 1992, p. 1B.
24. Jana Mazanec, "Rockwell Critics Hail Guilty Plea," *USA Today,* June 30, 1992, p. 3.
25. "Chicken Plant Executives Charged in Deadly Fire," *USA Today*, March 10, 1992, p. 3.
26. "Cheese Biz," *USA Today*, April 7, 1989, p. 3.
27. "Baby Food Companies Fixed Price, Florida Says," *USA Today*, January 4, 1991, p. 3.

Conspiracy: The Characteristic White-Collar Crime

You may think a crime horrible because
you could never commit it. I think it
horrible because I could commit it.
— G. K. Chesterton (1927)

The characteristic white-collar or organizational crime is conspiracy. Conspiracy is, essentially, *preparation* to commit an offense. It is an incomplete, or inchoate, crime. As noted earlier, street crimes commonly occur without planning. White-collar crimes are unique in that they *require* some form of preparation. The crime of conspiracy prohibits persons from preparing to commit illegal acts.

A conspiracy takes place when two or more persons agree to commit a crime, or to carry out a legal act in an illegal manner. Like all criminal acts, conspiracy requires a specific act (actus reus) and a particular state of mind (mens rea). The act requirement is the agreement to commit an illegal act. The state of mind requirement is less clear, but courts have applied conspiracy statutes over the years in such a way as to require something more than the intention to agree with a co-conspirator. Instead, it appears that if the objective of the agreement is to commit a specific crime, the mens rea to follow through with that crime must also be shown.

Nevertheless, a number of questions remain. Is a specific agreement required for conspiracy? If not, how formal must an agreement be to be held liable for the crime? Furthermore, what if a person enters an agreement to commit one crime (such as robbery) but the victim dies in the attempt? Can this person be held liable for conspiracy to commit robbery *and* murder? Can a person withdraw from a conspiracy and escape liability? These, and many other, questions have been resolved through law and court interpretation over a period of years.

Liability Issues

In fact, there are five common issues of liability that arise in conspiracy cases: (1) responsibility for acts of co-conspirators, (2) the type of agreement required, (3) whether an overt act is needed, (4) the extent of participation required, and (5) whether it is possible for independent acts to be joined together as a single conspiracy. Actual court challenges will be used to show how these issues are applied and decided in practice.

In a case decided in 1993, a director of the Greater Boston Police Council (GBPC), Timothy Coogan, was responsible for the purchase and maintenance of a radio communications system for a consortium of metropolitan area law enforcement agencies. The contract for this project was awarded to CES Corporation, headed by Sheldon Yefsky, and its subsidiary, ITS Corporation, headed by Michael Yefsky (Sheldon's son). At some point, Coogan approached the elder Yefsky, proposing to become a paid consultant on the project for ITS. Coogan was not required to submit a time sheet to justify his fee, he never revealed his consulting relationship to the GBPC, and he repeatedly denied having any outside telecommunications consulting activities to the police chief in charge of GBPC.

As police departments were added to the communications system, CES was paid nearly $1 million for its engineering services. Coogan received almost $500,000 from ITS for his services, and CES reimbursed ITS for Coogan's fee.

Coogan, Sheldon, and Michael Yefsky, as well as the financial officer for CES and ITS, were charged with conspiracy to defraud the GBPC. They were convicted, but appealed, arguing the evidence was insufficient for a conviction for conspiracy.

The decision by the U.S. Court of Appeals points to crucial elements of conspiracy. The government must prove the *existence* of a conspiracy, the defendant's *knowledge* of it, and his or her *voluntary* participation in it.[1] To show there was voluntary participation, it must be proved "that the defendant intended to both agree with his co-conspirators and to commit the substantive offense (fraud)."[2] Given the facts of the case, the court held a jury could find that Coogan and the others "grasped an opportunity to make money" from the police communications project. It could conclude that Coogan's open-ended contract with CES and ITS was designed so that CES would "pay him kickbacks to steer work orders to CES" and would charge "inflated fees" for work performed and "completely false" fees for work never done.[3] The convictions were affirmed, because the facts revealed the conspiracy's existence, the defendants' knowledge of it, and their voluntary participation in it. Several other important elements to the crime of conspiracy can be illustrated using other actual cases.

Medical Clinic Kickbacks: A Single Conspiracy?

Hubbell Medical Clinic (HMC) in Detroit served drug addicts by conducting blood-testing and prescribing less addictive drugs to wean addicts off "harder" drugs. As it turned out, the clinic's policy of taking blood from every patient was designed to ensure a profit. The "comprehensive" blood test allowed the testing lab to bill the patient's insurance company up to $650 per test, with the lab realizing a profit of up to $350 for each patient. A portion of this money "was illegally kicked back to HMC and used to operate the clinic."[4] One of the defendants in this case was Dale Dudley, a medical doctor, who was paid $500 in cash weekly "in order to lend a facade of legitimacy to the medical practice at HMC." Dudley did not "meaningfully supervise" the activities at HMC, nor did he obtain the appropriate supervisory license. Instead, physician's assistants actually treated the patients and were told by Dudley "to provide the patients with the controlled substance of their choice."[5] Dudley was ultimately found guilty of a racketeering conspiracy and was sentenced to four years in prison.

Another of the defendants in this case, Charles Hughes, was a registered pharmacist who owned the Sunshine Pharmacy. He filled the illegal prescriptions issued by HMC for codeine. He then "fraudulently billed the patient's insurance company for the medication." Hughes and another pharmacist were also found guilty of racketeering conspiracy and were each sentenced to three years in prison.

All the defendants argued on appeal that there was insufficient evidence to prove a single conspiracy connecting all the participants. This is a fundamental argument in attempting to defeat the government's effort to link the clinic owner, physician, and pharmacists together as part of an illegal enterprise. The U.S. Court of Appeals found that "a reasonable juror could find that the multiple criminal acts committed by defendants ... were elements of a single scheme." The court pointed to the "interdependent relationship" between the illegitimate blood-testing and illegal prescription component. "Without both components," the court reasoned, "the scheme would not have functioned."[6]

Dudley also claimed that he was a "naive doctor" who knew nothing about the blood-for-drugs scheme. He argued that he may have been negligent but that he did not *intend* to commit the crimes charged. The U.S. Court of Appeals rejected his claim, pointing to evidence that Dudley was warned by another physician that he would "jeopardize his credentials" if he affiliated with HMC. Furthermore, he never obtained the required license to supervise the physician's assistants, and he then directed them to exercise their own judgment. Dudley also never filed a required supervisory or emergency treatment plan. The government's medical expert testified that the "over-prescription of Tylenol with codeine and the over-use of comprehensive blood tests were so obvious" that they were easily discovered. In addition, a government wiretap indicated "Dudley was aware of the risks" of his affiliation with HMC.[7] The convictions of all the defendants were affirmed. This case shows how independent acts, linked by a common criminal purpose, can be considered part of a single conspiracy.

An Explicit Agreement?

This case of *U.S. v. Hughes*[8] illustrates another significant element of the crime of conspiracy: no explicit agreement is required for a conspiracy prosecution. As the court held, the defendants' "agreement to participate in the conspiracy may be inferred from their acts."[9] In fact, the courts have recognized that "conspiracies are rarely evidenced by explicit agreements, and must almost always be proven by inferences that may be fairly drawn from the behavior of the alleged conspirators."[10] A 50-year-old case in Buffalo, New York, in which a drug company filled orders for morphine from a South Carolina physician, is illustrative. Although the town in South Carolina had only 2,000 residents, the physician ordered enough morphine for more than 400 doses *per day*. The U.S. Supreme Court affirmed a conviction for conspiracy between the physician and the drug company to illegally distribute a controlled substance. Even though there was no written or oral agreement between the two parties, the Court held, "it can make no difference [that] the agreement was a tacit understanding, created by a long course of conduct and executed in the same way." The Court concluded that "conspiracies, in short, can be committed by mail and by mail-order houses. This is true, notwithstanding [the fact that] the overt acts consist solely of sales, which but for their volume, frequency and prolonged repetition, coupled wholly with the seller's unlawful intent to further the buyer's project, would be wholly lawful transactions."[11] It is clear, therefore, that a conspiratorial agreement does not necessarily require a spoken or written agreement; a tacit understanding, reasonably inferred from the circumstances, is sufficient.

Liability for Co-conspirators?

One of the three remaining elements of the crime of conspiracy, the extent of liability for the acts of co-conspirators, is evident in the case of *U.S. v. Bryser*.[12] Ronnie Bryser and two others, Gerald and Vincent DeGerolamo, acquired two armored car companies for the purpose of stealing the money entrusted to them. They obtained customers to employ their services by falsely representing company ownership and experience. They obtained large insurance policies by making similar false statements about their company. One of their armored car companies, Hercules, became the target of theft when Bryser and the DeGerolamo brothers began to experience financial pressures from high insurance premiums and client account cancellations.

Over a single weekend, Bryser ordered all his drivers to take all their cash to the Hercules vault. This totaled more than $3.7 million. Gerald and Vincent DeGerolamo reprogrammed the alarm system on Saturday, asking the former owner "what type of loss would involve the FBI in an investigation?"[13] The former owner said the loss of federal money "sealed in blue plastic Federal Reserve Bank trays" would result in FBI involvement. The alarm computer system recorded that the alarm system was turned off for less than one hour on Sunday of that weekend. The vault had to be drilled open on Monday, revealing that all the money was gone, except for $190,000 sealed in blue plastic Federal Reserve trays.

The defendants were convicted of conspiracy, theft from interstate shipment, mail fraud, and wire fraud. They were each sentenced to prison terms ranging from six and one-half to ten years in length. The defendants appealed on several grounds, including denial of responsibility for the acts of others involved in the conspiracy. The U.S. Court of Appeals held that, "once a conspiracy is established, the liability of defendants extends to all acts of wrongdoing occurring during the course of and in furtherance of the conspiracy, such as the theft, mail fraud, and wire fraud."[14] It is clear from this case that all participants in a conspiracy are liable for the acts of their co-conspirators, even if conducted without their knowledge. The acts need only be carried out in furtherance of the conspiracy.

As the Court of Appeals held in a 1992 case involving evasion of federal excise taxes on sales of gasoline, a defendant "need not have joined a conspiracy at its inception in order to incur liability for the unlawful acts of the conspiracy committed both before and after he or she became a member."[15] In a cocaine distribution conspiracy case, the court stated this in another way: "a defendant may be guilty of conspiracy even if he or she joined it midway, or played only a minor role in the total scheme."[16]

Conspiracy and Criminal Intention

The state of mind required for conspiracy is judged according to a *reasonableness* standard. In the *Direct Sales* morphine case, for example, the company was held liable because a reasonable party *should have known* what was being done with its morphine sales, even if it really did not. Direct Sales disregarded this substantial and unjustifiable risk of black market sales of its narcotic.

In an earlier case, however, the U.S. Supreme Court responded differently to a similar situation. In the case of *United States v. Falcone*,[17] sugar and yeast were sold to people knowing that they were engaging in a conspiracy to manufacture liquor illegally. The sellers were acquitted in this case, because the Court found they did not purposely further the illegal manufacturing. In the *Direct Sales* case, the Court distinguished its earlier finding by noting that all products "do not have inherently the same susceptibility to harmful and illegal use." The Court went on to say that "the difference is like that between toy pistols or hunting rifles and machine guns. . . . Gangsters, not hunters or small boys, constitute the normal private market for machine guns. So do drug addicts furnish the normal outlet for morphine which gets outside the restricted channels of legitimate trade."

Therefore, it is important for the crime of conspiracy in these cases "that the seller knows the buyer's intended illegal use." It is also necessary to show "that by the sale he intends to further, promote and cooperate in it."[18]

The act requirement for the crime of conspiracy can be summarized as follows: no formal agreement is required, although most jurisdictions require an overt act in furtherance of the conspiracy as evidence of willingness to carry out the planned offense. Of course, at least two people are needed to engage in a conspiracy. One cannot conspire alone under law. Certain crimes, however, *require* two people for their completion. Bribery and adultery are examples. Some states have a so-called "Wharton rule" that disallows a prosecution for conspiracy to commit these crimes, unless more than two persons are involved.

In these jurisdictions, the crime of "attempted" bribery is used when only two parties are involved without a completed act, because there is no increased danger in this situation (which the crime of conspiracy is designed to prevent). Conspiracy is reserved, in those states, for planned offenses involving three or more persons.

The state of mind requirement for conspiracy is somewhat less precise. To establish criminal liability, it is necessary that there be *intention to enter* into some kind of agreement, in addition to the intention *to commit the crime* that is the object of the conspiracy. If you conspire to burglarize my house, it is not a conspiracy under law unless you intended to enter my home unlawfully to commit a crime inside. This is easy to establish in many cases, leading many observers to term conspiracy "the prosecutor's darling," because once there is evidence that two or more persons engaged in a crime, conspiracy can almost always be added as an ancillary charge.[19] This assists prosecutor in plea negotiations. Critics, however, argue that conspiracy can be abused when evidence of an completed crime is impossible, or in cases attempting to restrain free speech or divergent views.[20]

Table 2.1 summarizes the important principles of liability for the crime of conspiracy.

Conspiracy in Conventional Crimes

If conspiracy plays a fundamental role in white-collar crimes, what role does it play in conventional crimes? As the accompanying case illustrates, conspiracy occasionally can be found in traditional crimes as well.

It was discovered that two men, Robert Winslow and Stephen Nelson, were members of an organization known as the Aryan Nations. They traveled from Idaho to Seattle, Washington, with the intention to explode a bomb inside a gay bar. They were arrested after they had bought the parts required for the bomb, but prior to assembling it. The arrest was based on evidence gathered by an undercover informant, who had penetrated the Aryan Nations organization and had accompanied the two men on their trip to Seattle. Winslow, Nelson, and Proctor Baker, a co-conspirator who had remained in Idaho, were convicted of conspiracy to build a pipe bomb involving interstate travel to kill or hurt human beings in violation of federal law. They were also convicted for violating various firearms laws.

Nelson and Baker appealed their convictions arguing there was insufficient evidence. Among other claims, the appellants believed the government had failed to prove beyond a reasonable doubt that there existed "an agreement to engage in" the crimes charged, that "one or more overt acts" were taken to carry out the alleged conspiracy, and that they had "the requisite intent to commit" the crimes charged.[21]

The Court examined the evidence at trial to determine the sufficiency of evidence. The Court found the testimony of the undercover informant, as well as tape-recorded statements of the conspirators, to be convincing. Before they had

Table 2.1   Elements of Conspiracy

1	No formal agreement is required.
2	Liable for acts of co-conspirators.
3	Participation need be only slight.
4	An overt act is required in furtherance of the conspiracy.
5	Independent acts toward a common criminal purpose can be linked together as a single conspiracy.

left for Seattle, Nelson and Winslow discussed obtaining a bomb from Baker. When Baker could not be found, "Nelson actively participated in purchasing the components necessary to build another pipe bomb." Once in Seattle, Nelson "contacted a friend and tried to borrow a drill to use" in assembling the bomb. Baker also made overt actions that indicated a conspiratorial agreement and intent to carry out a crime. The testimony of the undercover informant revealed that Baker had "discussed the effect an explosion from a similar bomb would have on a room full of people." He explained to the others that "in order to kill the most people, a bomb should be placed on a table, or at table level." When the group discussed the number of homosexuals who would be killed by such a bomb, Baker stated "the gravel and nails inside it would be lethal." He also told Winslow that it is best "to buy pipe and pipe caps for the bombs at various stores."[22] Baker also agreed to take the second assembled pipe bomb home with him. The Court of Appeals concluded that once a conspiracy is proved to exist, evidence establishing a defendant's connection with it beyond a reasonable doubt "is sufficient to convict the defendant of knowing participation in the conspiracy," even though the connection may be "slight."[23]

This case illustrates several important elements of the crime of conspiracy: there must be intent to commit the crime planned and an overt action must be taken in furtherance of the conspiracy. Also, conspiracy is not confined to white-collar crimes. As this case demonstrates, conspiracy characterizes any type of *planned* illegal act, although this is much more common in the case of white-collar crimes than it is for conventional crimes (which usually involve very little planning or organization).

Defenses to Conspiracy

There are a number of defenses that can be offered when charged with the crime of conspiracy. These may, or may not, excuse the conduct, depending on the circumstances present. The most common defenses include legal impossibility, mere presence, no knowledge of the conspiracy, involuntary participation, and withdrawal from the conspiracy. Each of these excuses will be examined as it has been presented in actual cases.

Legal Impossibility

In the case of *United States v. Bosch*,[24] the defendant owned and operated an investigation and Hispanic services agency in California. Using his business, he became involved with Colombian drug dealers, providing false paperwork for a fictitious sale of cattle in South America. This enabled the drug dealers to launder income from drug sales through a corporate bank account. Bosch also was found to have helped provide documentation for a marriage contracted solely for immigration purposes and rent an apartment for the dealers, drugs, money, and guns. Bosch was caught when he agreed to provide similar services to an undercover agent of the Internal Revenue Service (IRS) posing as a cocaine dealer.

Bosch was charged with conspiracy to distribute cocaine and other crimes and was convicted. He was sentenced to concurrent seven-year sentences.

On appeal, Bosch argued that he and his son should have their cocaine distribution convictions reversed because the undercover IRS agent never possessed or distributed cocaine. Therefore, it was "legally impossible" for the Boschs to conspire to aid and abet a nonexistent offense.

The U.S. Court of Appeals held that past cases clearly show that the doctrine of legal impossibility is not a defense to the crime of conspiracy.[25] As the court declared, "the conspiracy was complete when the conspirators had agreed to commit the offense and one of them had done an overt act in furtherance of the agreement. The accomplishment of the conspiracy's goal is immaterial to the crime."[26] Here, Bosch agreed to assist in the cocaine distribution conspiracy, and he undertook actions in furtherance of it. It is clear from these cases that legal impossibility is not a defense to a charge of conspiracy.

Is Mere Presence Enough?

The question of mere presence versus active participation in a conspiracy is a matter of degree. It is decided based upon the circumstances present at the time of the defendant's action. In a 1990 case, Charles Binkley was charged with conspiracy to distribute marijuana.[27] Binkley claimed he bought the marijuana from members of the conspiracy for personal use, but that he was not part of the conspiracy itself. He argued, and the U.S. Court of Appeals agreed, that "the purchase of drugs from a conspiracy, without more, does not rise to the level of membership in a conspiracy."[28] Binkley also claimed that his "mere presence" at the scene of the crime or "mere association with the co-conspirators" is insufficient for a conspiracy conviction. Once again, the Court of Appeals agreed.[29]

Nevertheless, mere presence suffices for a conviction, if the circumstances "permit the inference that the presence or act was intended to advance the ends of the conspiracy."[30] In this case, the court found that Binkley's telephone conversations with a drug dealer indicated intent to resell the marijuana he bought, thus advancing the conspiracy. His conviction was affirmed.

Other cases in other courts have reached the same conclusion: the government has the burden to show more than the mere *presence* of the defendant to prove a charge of conspiracy.[31] Therefore, all conspiracy cases must make a showing of how the defendant's conduct knowingly furthered the objective of the conspiracy.

What About Knowledge of the Conspiracy?

Occasionally, a defendant will claim that he or she had no knowledge that a conspiracy ever existed. A person cannot be held liable under these circumstances, unless the prosecution can show the defendant had criminal intentions. In the case of *United States v. Hoffman*,[32] the defendant (an accountant) engaged in a complex series of financial transactions, where he lent money to a Kentucky coal operator who was seriously overdrawn at the bank. The coal operator was in debt beyond the state's lending limit. Hoffman was charged with conspiracy to defraud the United States by conspiring to exceed Kentucky's state lending limits. The U.S. Court of Appeals ruled in this case that Hoffman's role as an accountant, both for the lender and for the borrower, made him privy to the details of the financial transactions. He knew that the borrower was overdrawn, yet he continued to write promissory notes and direct others to write letters of credit for the borrower. The fact that Hoffman did not know of the bank president's intent to defraud the bank is not enough to excuse Hoffman, because his "reckless disregard" of the bank's interests "was equivalent to intent to injure or defraud" the bank as required by law.[33] Hoffman was sentenced to ten years in prison, and his conviction was affirmed. Therefore, lack of knowledge of a conspiracy is a defense only where there are no other circumstances indicating the defendant *should have been* aware.

Voluntary Participation and Withdrawal

Voluntary participation in a conspiracy is also required for liability. If it can be shown that a conspirator participated against his or her will, the conduct is excused. In *United States v. Parekh*,[34] the defendant was charged with conspiracy to misapply funds of a savings and loan association and conspiracy to make false statements to the Federal Home Loan Bank Board. On appeal, Parekh argued that the evidence was insufficient to prove him guilty. The U.S. Court of Appeals found otherwise, declaring that the government met each of its three burdens in proving the charges: "(1) that two or more people agreed to pursue an unlawful objective together; (2) that the defendant voluntarily agreed to join the conspiracy; and (3) that one of the members of the conspiracy performed an overt act to further the objectives of the conspiracy."[35] Indeed, there exists a long series of cases that indicate voluntariness may be raised by the defense, but it must convince the jury that such coercion necessitated participation in the conspiracy.[36]

Withdrawal from a conspiracy is generally not a defense. The only exception to this rule is where the conspirator withdraws and also takes affirmative steps to stop the conspiracy. MMR Corporation was a subcontractor involved in building an electrical generator in Louisiana. It was found at trial that the four companies submitting bids on the construction project had met beforehand and

Table 2.2   Defenses to Conspiracy

---

1   Legal impossibility is not a defense.

2   Mere presence by itself is insufficient for liability.

3   If no reasonable knowledge of the conspiracy's existence can be inferred, it is a defense.

4   Involuntary participation prevents liability.

5   Withdrawal from a conspiracy is generally not a defense.

---

rigged the bidding process. As the court found, "This was nothing new. These companies had been, for several years, rigging bids for large projects throughout the country."[37] The companies involved met at the City Club in Baton Rouge, Louisiana, and discussed "MMR's outstanding obligations on three earlier projects rigged by MMR and Fischbach (another contractor)—Borden Chemical Company, Freeport Uranium Recovery Company, and Strategic Petroleum Reserve." The president of MMR went to the men's room and was followed by a vice president of Fischbach. A deal was worked out where MMR would get a subcontract if Fischbach were permitted to win the bidding.[38]

Fischbach was the eventual low bidder and won the contract for $21.3 million. MMR received a $4.3 million subcontract from Fischbach. MMR and its president were charged with conspiracy to rig bids in violation of the Sherman Anti-Trust Act and with conspiracy to defraud Cajun Electric by arranging the winning bid in advance.

MMR appealed on several grounds, including the fact that it had withdrawn from the conspiracy. The U.S. Court of Appeals recognized that the burden of proving withdrawal is on the defendant. To prove withdrawal, the defendant must take actions "inconsistent with the object of the conspiracy and communicated in a manner reasonably calculated to reach co-conspirators."[39] The court found that MMR's decision not to submit a bid "was hardly inconsistent with the object of the conspiracy." The convictions were affirmed. MMR was fined more than $1 million, and its president was sentenced to six months' imprisonment and fined $103,000.

Table 2.2 summarizes these common defenses to conspiracy charges.

Summary

Conspiracy forms the basis for understanding all types of planned criminal behavior. White-collar crime requires planning by definition; therefore, conspiracy lies at the heart of white-collar crime. This review of five common issues of liability and five common defense issues raised in conspiracy cases illustrates the complexities that white-collar crimes pose for enforcement and prosecution. These issues of enforcement are discussed in greater detail in Chapter 8.

Conspiracy has been addressed at length here because it is the most fundamental of the white-collar crimes. The typology of white-collar crimes presented in Chapter 2 is considered separately by category in the next three chapters. In

CRITICAL THINKING EXERCISE

The scenario that follows describes an actual fact situation, where the courts had to determine whether or not the law of conspiracy applied. Resolution of this scenario requires proper application of the legal principles discussed in this chapter.

THE CASE OF ANTONIO, DEL RAY, AND MIGUEL

Antonio was president of the Hotel and Restaurant Employees Union (HARE) and was a trustee of the union's Culinary Fund. The Culinary Fund was responsible for obtaining a health care provider contract for the union membership. Del Ray was personnel director of the Boor Hotel, whose employees were represented by HARE, and was also a trustee of the union's Culinary Fund. Miguel controlled a health care provider called, "Health'R'Us."

The government charged Antonio, Del Ray, and Miguel with the crime of conspiracy, alleging that Miguel agreed to pay Antonio $100,000 and Del Ray $40,000 for their assistance in Health'R'Us receiving the health care contract for the Culinary Fund. To support this allegation, the government documented that Del Ray was on the payroll of Health'R'Us as a marketing representative (earning the $40,000 just mentioned) during the period when the health care contract was decided. The government also documented that $100,000 was, in fact, paid to Antonio surreptitiously through a third party. Finally, the government alleged that Antonio, Del Ray, and Miguel were all part of a single conspiracy. This was supported by proof that Antonio and Del Ray both attended a meeting in Miguel's home at which the Health'R'Us proposal was discussed. This meeting was the sole overt act with which all three defendants were charged.

Questions

1. Of the elements and defenses to conspiracy explained in this chapter, which apply here?
2. Should Antonio, Del Ray, and Miguel be convicted of conspiracy?
3. Are there other crimes that the defendants may be charged with?

each case, the legal requirements for the necessary acts and criminal intention are specifically delineated, as they form the basis for all enforcement actions, prosecutions, defense strategies, and court decisions involving white-collar crime.

Endnotes

1. See *U.S. v. David*, 940 F.2d 735 (1st Cir. 1991).
2. *U.S. v. Yefsky*, 994 F.2d 885 (1st Cir. 1993).
3. at 891.
4. *U.S. v. Hughes*, 895 F.2d 1135 (6th Cir. 1990) at 1139.
5. Ibid.
6. *U.S. v. Hughes*, at 1141. Note 7.
7. at 1141.
8. 895 F.2d 1135 (6th Cir. 1990).
9. *U.S. v. Hughes*, at 1141.
10. *DeLong Equipment v. Washington Mills Abrasive Co.*, 887 F.2d 1499 (11th Cir. 1989); and *H. L. Moore Drug Exchange v. Eli Lilly & Co.*, 662 F.2d 935, cert. denied, 103 S. Ct. 176 (1982).
11. *Direct Sales Company v. United States*, 63 S.Ct. 1265 (1943).
12. 954 F.2d 79 (2nd Cir. 1992).
13. *U.S. v. Bryser*, 954 F.2d 79 (2nd Cir. 1992) at 82.
14. at 88.
15. *U.S. v. Rea*, 958 F.2d 1206 (2nd Cir. 1992) at 1214.
16. *U.S. v. Andrews*, 953 F.2d 1312 (11th Cir. 1992) at 1318 and *U.S. v. Howard*, 895 F.2d 722 (11th Cir.), cert. denied, 111 S.Ct. 3286 (1990).
17. 311 U.S. 205 (1940).
18. *Direct Sales Company v. United States*, 63 S.Ct. 1265 (1943).
19. Paul E. Dow, *Criminal Law* (Monterey, CA: Brooks/Cole, 1985); and Arnold H. Loewy, *Criminal Law* (St. Paul, MN: West, 1975).
20. Joel Samaha, *Criminal Law*, 2nd ed. (St. Paul, MN: West, 1987); and *Krulewitch v. United States*, 69 S.Ct. 716 (1949) (Jackson concurring).
21. *U.S. v. Winslow, Nelson, and Baker*, 962 F.2d 845 (9th Cir. 1992) at 849.
22. Ibid.
23. Ibid. and also *United States v. Stauffer*, 922 F.2d 508 (9th Cir. 1990) at 514–15.
24. *U.S. v. Bosch*, 914 F.2d 1239 (9th Cir. 1990).
25. *United States v. Everett*, 696 F.2d 596 (9th Cir. 1982), cert. denied, 103 S.Ct. 1498 (1983).
26. *United States v. Reuter*, 536 F.2d 296 (9th Cir. 1976) at 298.
27. *United States v. Binkley*, 903 F.2d 1130 (7th Cir. 1990).
28. at 1133. See also *United States v. Mancillas*, 580 F.2d 1301 (7th Cir.), cert. denied, 99 S.Ct. 361 (1978).
29. Ibid.
30. at 1134. See also *United States v. Xheka*, 704 F.2d 974 (7th Cir.), cert. denied, 104 S.Ct. 486 (1983).
31. *United States v. Hernandez*, 876 F.2d 774 (9th Cir.), cert. denied, 110 S.Ct. 179; and *United States v. Stauffer*, 922 F.2d 508 (9th Cir. 1990).
32. 918 F.2d 44 (6th Cir. 1990).
33. at 46. See also *United States v. Woods*, 877 F.2d (6th Cir. 1989).

34. 926 F.2d 402 (5th Cir. 1991).
35. at 406. See also *United States v. Davis*, 810 F.2d 474 (5th Cir.), cert. denied, 109 S.Ct. 3171 (1989).
36. *United States v. Allison*, 908 F.2d 1531 (11th Cir. 1991), cert. denied, 111 S.Ct. 1681 (1991); and *United States v. Howard*, 895 F.2d 722 (11th Cir. 1990).
37. *United States v. MMR Corporation*, 907 F.2d 489 (5th Cir. 1990) at 492.
38. at 493.
39. at 500; see *United States v. U.S. Gypsum Co.*, 98 S.Ct. 2864 (1978).

CHAPTER

3

Crimes of Fraud

From the least one even to the greatest one,
each one is making unjust gain.
—Jeremiah 8:10

The four white-collar crimes of theft are embezzlement, extortion, forgery, and fraud. Each represents a distinct variation from the common law crime of larceny or theft, yet each corresponds with the definition of white-collar crime offered in Chapter 1. In each case, the objective of the offense is theft. The differences lie in the methods by which the theft is accomplished.

Embezzlement

Embezzlement was first created as a statutory offense in England when the crime of larceny appeared insufficient in certain cases. Larceny originally required that property be taken from another's possession. But what of someone who misappropriates property that he or she lawfully controls but does not possess? For example, you check your car with the valet, and he sells it. You take your dress to the dry cleaner who trades it with someone else for a leather jacket. In both cases, the valet and the dry cleaner lawfully possess your car and dress. Yet they violate the trust you have placed in them. They have not committed larceny, because they have not taken your property without your permission. Rather, they have *converted* it into cash or its equivalent without your consent. For this reason, embezzlement is characterized by the *conversion* or *misappropriation* of property entrusted to someone.

Embezzlement is a heterogeneous offense category, as Gary Green has observed, and can include statutory violations of criminal conversion, larceny, fraud, as well as embezzlement.[1] Nevertheless, the violation of a position of financial trust is necessary for embezzlement, whereas it is not required for other crimes of theft.

Embezzling from a Company You Do Not Work For

An actual case illustrates how the law of embezzlement is applied in practice. Robert Coney worked for an armored car company as a messenger responsible for accepting money and then distributing it. The armored car company had a contract with Minneapolis Federal Reserve Bank to deliver money to other banks. One day, Coney received a bag containing $25,000 to deliver to a local bank. The person responsible for signing out the day's cargo to messengers forgot to have Coney sign for the bag. Coney stole the money.

He was charged with embezzling funds from a Federal Reserve Bank in violation of federal law. On appeal, Coney made the interesting argument that he was not "connected in any capacity" with the Minneapolis Federal Reserve Bank and therefore cannot be charged with embezzling from it.[2]

The U.S. Court of Appeals found that, as an employee of an armored car company contracted to transport the bank's currency, "Coney was personally entrusted with Federal Reserve funds." Therefore, Coney was "clearly connected" to the Minneapolis Federal Reserve Bank in a manner covered by "the broad language" of the statute.[3] The statute was interpreted broadly to correspond with "congressional intent by protecting federally insured lenders from fraud."[4]

The act required for embezzlement, therefore, is conversion or misapplication of property under one's lawful control. The state of mind required is the intention to defraud the owner of property he or she places in someone else's trust. Such a violation of financial trust is prohibited under law due to the increasing complexity of society where many hold the property of others without owning it. The nature of banking, investing, rental property, and, yes, dry cleaning, provides opportunities for theft not covered by simple larceny statutes.

Embezzlement: A Consequence of Financial Management Left to Others

Embezzlement has become more common as financial management becomes farther removed from the individual wage-earner and taxpayer. For example, the director of the Denver Roman Catholic cemetery was sentenced to six years' probation and required to repay $410,000 after pleading guilty to assisting in the theft of cemetery funds.[5] As noted in Chapter 1, the police chief in Rochester, New York, was convicted of embezzling $243,000 in police department funds between 1988 and 1990,[6] while the police chief in Detroit was sentenced to ten years in prison for embezzling $2.6 million from a police fund.[7]

A lawyer in New York City was accused of stealing more than $7 million of his clients' funds.[8] Another lawyer vanished with up to $25 million he allegedly stole from clients. This was believed to be the largest theft by a lawyer ever committed in the United States.[9] A bank officer in Buffalo admitted that he had used bogus documents to obtain loans from his bank to support a restaurant owned by his family.[10] In each of these cases, money turned over to others to manage was misappropriated for unauthorized use.

As organizations grow in size, it is imperative that financial management becomes the province of specialists and higher management. Without proper oversight of their actions, however, abuses can occur unchecked for many years, given the size of the funds and the complexity of the organization.

Sometimes a defendant will claim that he or she had "good faith" intent to return embezzled funds. This is not a defense, however, because it does not negate the criminal intent needed to take the money in the first place.[11] If such a defense were acceptable, one's motives for theft would be dispository in criminal trials. This would work against the objective of punishing knowing violations of law, regardless of objective.

Extortion

Like embezzlement, extortion also involves misappropriation of property. Extortion, however, involves the threat of force. It can be defined as obtaining property from another due to future threats of physical injury, property damage, or exposure to ridicule or criminal charges. Extortion is distinguished from the crime of robbery in that robbery is a form of theft using threats of *immediate* harm. The case of *State v. Harrington*[12] is illustrative.

Linking an Attorney, Adultery, and Extortion

At the time of the alleged offense, John B. Harrington was an attorney working for a law firm in Burlington, Vermont. He was consulted by Mrs. Norma Morin, the wife of the alleged victim, Armand Morin. Mrs. Morin was separated from her husband because of severe physical abuse. Prior to their separation, the Morins owned and operated the Continental 93 Motel in Littleton, New Hampshire, where they also maintained a residential apartment. The net value of their holdings was $500,000. Mrs. Morin told Harrington that her husband had been guilty of numerous marital infidelities with different women at the motel. Mrs. Morin disclosed that she also had been guilty of marital misconduct that Mr. Morin apparently had condoned.

At a subsequent conference with Harrington, a friend of Mrs. Morin's, who accompanied her to the law office, suggested that an effort be made to procure corroborative evidence of Mr. Morin's marital misconduct. At this time a scheme was hatched to procure the services of a girl who would visit the motel in an effort to corroborate Mrs. Morin's allegations of her husband's infidelity. Arguably, this would strengthen Mrs. Morin's position in an eventual divorce proceeding.

The girl was hired and Mr. Morin saw her at the motel. He invited her to join him at his apartment for a cocktail. The girl accepted. Soon after, Harrington and his associates entered the room. With one or more cameras, several photographs were taken of Morin and the girl in bed and unclothed.

The following day, Harrington met with his client, Mrs. Morin, and encouraged her to seek a reconciliation. She claimed it was "too late" for that. Mr. Harrington then dictated a letter that was sent to Mr. Morin. It stated, in part, "basically, your wife desires a divorce, and if it can be equitably arranged, she would prefer that the divorce be as quiet and undamaging as possible." The letter went on to state the conditions for a divorce: Mrs. Morin would relinquish

CRITICAL THINKING EXERCISE

The scenario that follows describes an actual fact situation where the courts had to determine whether or not the law of extortion applied. Answer the questions posed by applying the principles of extortion.

THE CASE OF MONTGOMERY AND BAGS

Montgomery was hired as a driver by Bags Trucking Company. An anonymous telephone call brought to Mr. Bags's attention that Montgomery was an undercover agent for the Department of Transportation (DOT).

Bags checked Montgomery's employment file and found it lacked certain information. He started to panic. Bags confronted Montgomery, who said that he was, indeed, an agent of the DOT. Montgomery also said that Bags Trucking Company was in violation of several DOT regulations.

Bags subsequently contacted someone at the DOT, who informed him that it did not plant undercover agents at trucking companies to discover violations and that Montgomery was not employed by the DOT or by the

her rights to their properties, all alimony would be waived upon receipt of $175,000, and the settlement "would include the return to you of all tape recordings, all negatives, all photographs and copies of photographs that might in any way, bring discredit upon yourself."

If Mr. Morin was unwilling to accept these terms, Harrington stated that the immediate divorce proceeding would commence, and "it would be necessary to allege, in detail, all of the grounds that Mrs. Morin has in seeking the divorce." Harrington also stated that he was "undecided as to advising Mrs. Morin whether or not to file for 'informer fees' with respect to the IRS and the U.S. Customs Service" for his alleged failure to report all his motel income. A copy of one of the photographs taken of Mr. Morin in bed with the girl was enclosed to show that the "cameras and equipment were in full working order."[13]

Harrington was convicted at trial for extortion, and this conviction was reviewed by the Supreme Court of Vermont. The court held that Harrington fulfilled the requirements for extortion in his letter to Mr. Morin.

The court found that the letter, marked "personal and confidential," made "a private accusation of adultery in support of a demand for a cash settlement." The cost of refusal was the "public exposure of incriminating conduct." As the court concluded, "Quite clearly, these veiled threats exceeded the limits of [Harrington's] representation of his client in the divorce action." It concluded that federal government. Bags then contacted the FBI, which taped the next meeting between Montgomery and Bags. At that meeting, Montgomery informed Bags he was facing about $60,000 in fines, but that Montgomery would give Bags Trucking Company a "clean slate" in exchange for $5,000. Bags wrote Montgomery a check for $5,000.

As he left Bags's office, Montgomery told him, "My word is gold and like I say, ya know, if it goes any further than this office we'd both wind up in the federal penitentiary." Montgomery was arrested for attempted extortion.

Questions

1. What legal principles of extortion would argue for conviction?
2. Should Montgomery be convicted?
3. How would you respond to Montgomery's argument that he cannot be convicted of extortion, because Bags was aware Montgomery was not a DOT agent when he paid the $5,000, and therefore he was not induced by fear to pay the money?

the "demand for settlement of a civil action, accompanied by a malicious threat to expose the wrong-doer's criminal conduct, if made with intent to extort payment, against his will, constitutes [extortion]."[14]

Harrington's claim that he was merely looking out for the best interests of his client was rejected by the court. Instead, the court found the evidence to show Harrington's participation in a "preconceived design" that was "willfully contrived" to produce evidence "procured by a temptress hired for that purpose." As the court concluded,

> These factors in the proof are sufficient to sustain a finding that the respondent acted maliciously and without just cause, within the meaning of our criminal statutes. The sum of the evidence supports the further inference that the act was done with the intent to extort a substantial contingent fee to the respondent's personal advantage.[15]

Variations in Extortion Laws

Some states require that the property actually be obtained from the target to complete the crime of extortion. Others, such as the case just reviewed, require only the threat and proof that the defendant *intended* to carry out the threat, placing the victim in fear. The actus reus for extortion, therefore, is the *threat of future harm.* The nature of this threatened harm varies by state, but it includes bodily harm, damage to property, damage to reputation, criminal accusations, or abuse of a public office. The mens rea required for extortion is the specific intent to obtain property through the threatened future actions. As noted in Chapter 1, the chief judge of New York State's highest court was charged in 1992 with extortion in threats he made to a woman. The woman ended an affair with the judge, and he claimed he would sell sexually explicit photos of her and her new boyfriend if she did not give him money.[16] In this case, it was the threat of damage to reputation, rather than the abuse of a public office, that formed the basis for the threat of future harm.

The federal extortion law is called the *Hobbs Act.* For extortion to occur "under color of official right" under this law, or in similar state laws, the prosecution must show the improper payment was induced in return for an explicit promise or act by a *government official.*[17] This understanding does not have to be verbally explicit to be in violation of the law, but the quid pro quo "must be clear and unambiguous," leaving no uncertainty about the terms of the agreement.[18] An example is the mayor of Passaic, New Jersey, who was convicted of extorting $150,000 from contractors wishing to do business with the city.[19] In another case, former West Virginia governor Arch Moore pleaded guilty to taking nearly $600,000 in kickbacks for helping two companies collect $2 million in state funds.[20]

It has also been held that private citizens can be prosecuted for extortion under the "color of official right" prohibitions, when the defendant aids or conspires with public officials to commit extortion. The important factor is whether the victim "reasonably perceives" the defendant exercises control over official decision making.[21]

Forgery

The making of false legal documents or altering of existing documents is forgery. It is distinguished from *uttering*, which involves *passing* forged documents. It is possible, therefore, to be convicted of *both* forging and uttering a false document.

In most states these offenses are felonies, regardless of the value of the falsified document. This is due to the heavy reliance on checks, stocks, bonds, money orders, and credit cards in today's society. Someone who forges a check and then utters it faces prosecution for two separate felonies. Obviously, forgery is viewed as a serious white-collar crime against property. The other unique characteristics of forgery are best demonstrated in an actual case.

"Raised" Bills: Making One Dollar Seem Like Twenty

In an interesting case, Kenneth Brown and David Butler attempted to purchase cigarettes with two "raised" bills at the Mamos Market in Concord, New Hampshire. ("Raised" bills are created by attaching the corners of a genuine $20 bill to a genuine one dollar bill.) The cashier did not notice the first bill, but noticed the second one, when George Washington's picture appeared on an apparent

$20 bill. She called police, and Brown and Butler were arrested. During a search for contraband and weapons, a jail officer discovered two torn $20 bills hidden in Brown's rectal cavity. Each bill had its left side torn off. Brown and Butler were convicted of connecting parts of different bills and uttering an altered note in violation of federal counterfeiting laws.

Brown appealed, arguing that he did not know that the bill passed at the Mamos market had been altered or that he was responsible for its alteration. The U.S. Court of Appeals rejected this argument, because "he concealed two torn twenty dollar bills in a highly incriminating manner." The court found that "a reasonable jury could easily have concluded the torn twenties were used to create the 'raised' bill and therefore that [Brown] was aware the bill was altered when he attempted to pass it."[22]

When Does a Bad Check Become Forgery?

Forgery requires only that some part of the document is forged. Therefore, someone who forges an entire document incurs the same liability as one who forges only the signature. On the other hand, a person who writes out one of his or her own checks for $200, when there is only $50 in the account, is not liable for forgery unless he or she has no intention of depositing the difference.

Consider the facts of *People v. Williams*.[23] Williams presented two checks for deposit to George Tway, a teller for the Bank of America. He knew these checks had been stolen from the mail and the checks were made payable to Louis Levin. Williams told the teller that he wanted to deposit the two checks and that he also wanted to cash a check of his own using the name of Louis Levin. He also said he had no blank checks of his own, although he had ordered some.

Williams was sent to Mrs. George, new accounts clerk at the bank. He showed her the two stolen checks he wanted to deposit (totaling $3,000), as well as a deposit slip that indicated that he was, in fact, Louis Levin. Williams asked Mrs. George for a counter check and received a blank stock check.

Williams returned to Mr. Tway's window and presented the counter check in the sum of $975, payable to cash. The teller requested Williams endorse the check, which he did, signing the name of the victim, Louis Levin.

The check was then taken to the operations officer of the bank for approval. The operations officer attempted to identify Williams. He observed defendant was attempting to make a deposit for $3,000, and at the same time was attempting to cash a counter check for $975, all in the name of a customer, Louis Levin.

The operations officer checked the signature card of Louis Levin, who was the bank's customer, made a telephone call to the authentic Louis Levin, and then called police. Williams was arrested. Williams was convicted of forgery, when it was held that Williams had "made" a false check when he filled out a blank check under the name of someone else.

The actus reus required for forgery is falsification of any part of a legal document. Placing your name on someone else's term paper is not forgery (although it is plagiarism), because the paper generally has no legal significance. Items such as licenses, checks, stocks, passports, and college degrees are legal documents, and therefore, falsification of any part of these is forgery. In addition, the falsification must be sufficient to make the entire document false. A changed amount on a check is not forgery, because the check is still valid. A changed signature, however, invalidates the check. Likewise, checks or other legal documents completed by unauthorized persons constitute forgery as they have no authorization to complete a valid document.

In a recent Georgia case, a check originally written for $5, made to appear to be a cashier's check for $35,000, was ruled to be "counterfeit" under the law. Even though the law requires a document to be falsely made "in its entirety," all essential information on the check was falsified.[24]

Contemporary examples of forgery abound, as the varied forms of noncash documentation in society continue to multiply. "Coupon Connie" Arvidson was sentenced to more than two years in prison in a $2 million scheme where more than 600,000 illegal copies of supermarket coupons were distributed nationwide.[25] Police found 250,000 fake social security cards, green cards, and $20 bills in a raid at a Los Angeles print shop.[26] In New York City, police confiscated more than 155,000 fake tapes of recordings by popular musicians in a counterfeit tape manufacturing operation. The operation was capable of producing up to 5,000 forged tapes a day.[27]

The mens rea for forgery requires the specific intent to defraud someone through the false writing. It is not necessary that anyone in particular is targeted for the fraud; it is merely sufficient that fraud is the objective of the false writing. Finally, the purpose of forgery is usually to obtain money, but it is not an essential element of the crime. One might forge a university degree to obtain a personal advantage, or a letter of recommendation to obtain admission to a law school. Nevertheless, the elements of forgery are fulfilled once the falsification is completed, whether or not the victim is actually tricked or defrauded.

Fraud

The last white-collar crime of theft is fraud. There are many crimes related to fraud, the most common of which is *false pretenses*. The essence of fraud is larceny by trick. That is, possession of property is obtained through a deception. False pretenses occurs when *title* or *ownership* of property is obtained due to reliance on false representations. If you ask to borrow my car for the day, but your actual intention is to sell it and abscond with the money, you have committed the crime of fraud. If you ask me to give you my $500 car, because you know a sucker who will buy it for $5,000, you have engaged in false pretenses when your intention is merely to gain ownership of my car for personal use or sale.

The Limitless Variations of Fraud

Frauds can be very simple, or rather complicated. Simple cases include that of Jeanne Lawson who in 1992 pleaded guilty of cashing her father's railroad retirement checks for 24 years after he had died in 1967.[28] Owners of the Long

Leona Helmsley was convicted of tax fraud by illegally billing personal expenses to her company, evading $1.7 milliion in taxes. She was sentenced to four years in prison, a $7 million fine, and nearly $2 million in restitution. *(Helayne Seidman, UPI/Bettmann)*

Island Pet Cemetery, noted in Chapter 1, were sentenced to five years in prison for charging customers for individual pet burials, but then burying 250,000 pets in mass graves. One couple was awarded $1.2 million in damages after paying nearly $1,100 to have their English sheepdog buried, but later finding the grave empty.[29] This case illustrates that victims of fraud can also recover their losses in civil suits, as well as seeking criminal penalties through criminal complaints. In a highly publicized case, Leona Helmsley was convicted of tax fraud by illegally billing personal expenses to her company, thereby evading $1.7 million in taxes. She was sentenced to four years in prison, a $7 million fine, and nearly $2 million in restitution.[30]

More complex fraud cases include that of Ellis Neder who was sentenced to 12 years in prison for obtaining multimillion-dollar land loans for housing developments that were never built.[31] Neder was also ordered to repay the banks he defrauded $25 million. In another case, John McNamara, a wealthy car dealer, was charged with borrowing $6 billion from 1985 to 1991 for vehicles he never bought. He was alleged to have skimmed $422 million for himself.[32] In still another complex scam, Jerome Hearne got people who normally did not file tax returns to let him use their names and social security numbers on false W-2 forms. He then filed phony tax returns in their names and received immediate "refund-anticipation" loans from banks associated with tax preparers. The government lost $1 million before Hearne was caught, at which time he was sentenced to 15 years in prison and a $300,000 fine.[33]

The BCCI Fraud

In perhaps the most sophisticated fraud of the century, the Bank of Credit and Commerce (BCCI) lent its money to influential people in the Middle East and elsewhere who never repaid the loans. The bank stayed afloat by collecting more and more deposits. When BCCI collapsed, thousands of depositors around the world lost their savings.[34]

BCCI was established in the 1970s in Pakistan, due to a fear of nationalization of banks there. Owned by Pakistani interests, the bank began to buy U.S. banks and hired such prominent people as Clark Clifford and Robert Altman as its American attorneys. BCCI began to open offices in the United States during the early 1980s, and by 1984 it had assets of $16 billion.

Among BCCI's bank acquisitions was a Colombian bank with branches in Medellin and Cali, two notorious centers for cocaine trafficking. In addition, money generated from heroin in the Middle East was alleged to be laundered through BCCI.[35]

BCCI officials were arrested in 1988 for money laundering, and the bank was fined a record $14.8 million in 1990. An external audit by Price Waterhouse uncovered fraudulent transactions, and in 1991, the Federal Reserve formally charged BCCI and its top executives with the illegal takeover of U.S. banks. At the same time, a New York City grand jury indicted BCCI and two executives for fraud, larceny, and money laundering.[36]

In 1993, one BCCI executive was convicted and sentenced to six years in prison, but attorneys Clark Clifford and Robert Altman were acquitted of wrongdoing. The bank itself agreed to plead guilty to money-laundering charges and forfeit a record $550 million in a scandal believed to be the largest financial fraud in history, accounting for losses of at least $15 billion.[37] A British court approved a liquidation plan where BCCI creditors and depositors will receive only 30 to 40 cents on the dollar in compensation.

Can Marriage Be Fraudulent?

The case of *State v. Lambert*[38] illustrates an interesting variation of the crime of false pretenses. Lambert was charged with six counts of theft by fraud arising from relationships he had with six different women, where he obtained varying amounts of money from each on the basis of promises to marry her.

The evidence against Lambert consisted of the testimony of the six complaining women. In one case, Ms. R. met Lambert (using an alias) in a Milwaukee restaurant. Lambert talked of his life, and Ms. R., a 20-year-old hair stylist, "fell in love with him." Later that same evening, Lambert proposed marriage in his car. He said he owned a nightclub in Denver and would show her "a better life." Ms. R. accepted, but asked that they be married the following spring. Lambert did not tell her he was already married.

The following month, Ms. R. gave Lambert $475 because, she testified, "I loved him and wanted to marry him," and he needed the money for a gambling debt. That same month, however, Ms. R. became suspicious and found out through investigation of his license plate number where Lambert lived. When she arrived there, she found Lambert with a woman, who claimed that she was not married or romantically involved with Lambert. In fact, this woman was Jill Lambert, who had been married to Lambert for several years (and is still married to him). Ms. R. requested her money be returned, and ultimately got about $80 back. Lambert testified he had paid back "close to $300." He characterized their relationship as "truly physical" and stated that he had "never offered to marry her."

Ms. M. was a 30-year-old widow living in Chicago. She also had met Lambert at a Milwaukee restaurant. Two days after their meeting, Lambert visited her at home in Chicago and the following day proposed marriage, stating he was moving to Phoenix and would take her with him. She accepted and loaned him $1,700 to help finance a Phoenix "business deal." Two weeks later she gave him another $275. A May wedding date was set that Lambert did not keep. Lambert denied having proposed to Ms. M. or having taken money from her; "it was a physical relationship, that's all."

There was similar testimony from several other women, where marriage was proposed soon after the first meeting, loan(s) were made to Lambert, and he was rarely seen again (except to request more money). At trial, the jury found Lambert guilty on all counts.

Lambert appealed on grounds that three of the women to whom he proposed were already married, so his promises of marriage were void, not fraudulent. The Supreme Court of Wisconsin ruled, however, that "the question in an action for fraud is not whether the victim could legally rely on the fraudulent promises, but rather whether [s]he did reasonably rely on them in surrendering [her] property or funds."[39] In each of these cases, Lambert knew the woman was married and yet persisted. "If Lambert had no intention to perform at the time he made the proposal, fraud was present *in praesenti*."[40]

Therefore, Lambert's convictions were upheld because he falsely promised to marry. He never intended to marry these women, making his promises a false representation of a fact. Because the women reasonably relied on his promises in giving up their property, the second aspect of false pretenses was fulfilled. As a result, the act requirement is the knowing false promise, which is relied upon by the victim to give up ownership of property. The mens rea is the specific intention to obtain property through these false representations.

It is interesting that Lambert's case is not unique. Alfred Barakett, a twice-divorced factory worker, was charged with forgery and fraud, after police discovered he had 80 aliases and allegedly bilked thousands of dollars from 200 women in 28 states.[41]

CRITICAL THINKING EXERCISE

The scenario that follows describes an actual fact situation, where the courts had to determine whether or not the law of fraud applied. Read the facts and answer the questions that follow, using the principles of liability for fraud.

THE CASE OF STEP-ADDER COMPUTER SYSTEMS

Step-Adder was a company in the computer business that was hired by other companies to assess their computer needs and then to identify hardware and software configurations that would best fulfill these needs. Step-Adder developed a multiuser system specifically for law and medical offices. It sold 142 of these systems and immediately began receiving complaints of serious problems with the system.

Step-Adder investigated these problems and referred them to Wise Technology and TAA, its hardware and software suppliers, respectively. The three companies were unable to resolve the problems, and no one was

---

Summary

This chapter has shown that white-collar crimes of theft can be classified into four distinct types: embezzlement, extortion, forgery, and fraud. These crimes have in common the goal of illicit financial gain through deception or, in the case of extortion, threatened use of future coercion. The varieties of this type of white-collar crime are limitless, in the same way that traditional larceny can be carried out in any number of clever ways. This chapter has shown that, despite these many manifestations, each white-collar crime of theft has distinct act and state of mind requirements that distinguish it under law. This enables the student and investigator to isolate the relevant facts that help discriminate the various forms of planned thefts.

Endnotes

1. Gary S. Green, "White-Collar Crime and the Study of Embezzlement," *The Annals*, 525 (January 1993), pp. 95–106.
2. *U.S. v. Coney*, 949 F.2d 966 (8th Cir. 1991).
3. at 967.

willing to take responsibility for them. More than a dozen of Step-Adder's customers filed suit against Step-Adder because of the problems experienced with the system.

Step-Adder then filed a complaint against Wise Technology and TAA, alleging breach of warranty and intentional misrepresentations about the nature of their products. At trial, the co-founder of TAA said he did not know of any programs "completely compatible" with the operating system used by Step-Adder, although TAA's sales representative said its program had "practical compatibility" with the operating system. As it turned out, of course, the TAA was not compatible with the Step-Adder system.

Questions

1. What questions about this case and the elements of fraud are fundamental to assess TAA's representations to Step-Adder about its computer program?
2. Should TAA be held liable for fraud?
3. If Step-Adder, TAA, and Wise technology were to be sued for conspiracy to defraud customers of the computer system, what would have to be proven?

4. See *United States v. Prater*, 805 F.2d 1441 (11th Cir. 1986).
5. "Cemetery Fund Theft," *USA Today*, July 15, 1992, p. 6.
6. "Ex-Rochester Police Chief is Guilty of Embezzlement," *The Buffalo News*, February 26, 1992, p. 7.
7. "Chief Sentenced," *USA Today*, August 28, 1992, p. 6.
8. "New York," *USA Today*, December 10, 1991, p. 9.
9. "Record Theft," *USA Today*, January 23, 1991, p. 7.
10. "Ex-Bank Officer Admits Embezzlement," *The Buffalo News*, July 13, 1991, p. C4.
11. *U.S. v. Basacca*, 936 F.2d 232, cert. denied, 112 S.Ct. 595 (1991); and *U.S. v. Young*, 955 F.2d 99 (1st Cir. 1992).
12. 260 A.2d 692, 1969.
13. Ibid.
14. at 699.
15. at 700.
16. Bethany Kandel, "Top New York Judge Faces Charges," *USA Today*, November 9, 1992, p. 2.
17. *U.S. v. Montoya*, 945 F.2d 1068 (9th Cir. 1991).
18. *U.S. v. Carpenter*, 961 F.2d 824 (9th Cir. 1992).

19. "Mayor Guilty," *USA Today*, November 30, 1992, p. 3.
20. Mimi Hall, "Former W.VA. Governor Admits Extortion Guilt," *USA Today*, April 13, 1990, p. 2.
21. *U.S. v. Marcy*, 777 F.Supp. 1393 (N.D. Ill. 1991); and *U.S. v. McClain*, 934 F.2d 822 (7th Cir. 1991).
22. *U.S. v. Brown*, 938 F.2d 1482, cert. denied, 112 S.Ct. 611 (1991).
23. 96 Cal. R. 291 (Court of Appeals, Second District of California, 1971).
24. *U.S. v. Blakey*, 960 F.2d 996 (11th Cir. 1992).
25. "Coupon Clipper Gets Prison Term," *USA Today*, April 9, 1990, p. 2.
26. "Counterfeit Arrests," *USA Today*, September 26, 1991, p.3.
27. "Tapes Bust," *USA Today*, November 23, 1991, p. 1D.
28. "Federal Fraud," *USA Today*, August 27, 1992, p. 5.
29. "Rest in Peace," *USA Today*, September 1, 1992, p. 9.
30. Bethany Kandel, "No Breaks for Helmsley," *USA Today*, March 19, 1992, p. 2.
31. "Jacksonville," *USA Today*, September 9, 1992, p. 12.
32. Eric D. Randall, "Prosecutors: Car Dealer Set Up Pyramid Scheme," *USA Today*, June 4, 1992, p. 7B.
33. Desiree French, "Scams Flourish in Electronic Filing System," *USA Today*, June 15, 1992, p. 3B.
34. James Ring Adams and Douglas Frantz, *A Full Service Bank: How BCCI Stole Billions Around the World* (New York: Pocket Books, 1992).
35. Jonathan Beaty and S. C. Guymore, *The Outlaw Bank* (New York: Random House, 1993).
36. Mark Potts, Nicholas Kochan, and Robert Whittington, *Dirty Money* (Washington, D.C.: National Press Books, 1993).
37. Sam Vincent Meddis, "BCCI Agrees to Plead Guilty to All Charges," *USA Today*, December 20, 1991, p. 4.
38. 243 N.W.2d 524 (Supreme Court of Wisconsin, 1976).
39. at 530.
40. Ibid.
41. "Sweetheart Case," *USA Today*, January 17, 1992, p. 3.

CHAPTER
4

Offenses Against Public Administration

A friend that you buy with presents will be bought from you.
— *Thomas Fuller (1732)*

There are four offenses against public administration: bribery, obstruction of justice, official misconduct, and perjury. Each of these offenses represents a planned attempt to affect lawful government processes in an illegal manner. Like the white-collar crimes of theft, these four offenses all have the same objective; they differ only in the method by which they accomplish it.

Bribery

Of the four crimes against public administration, bribery is perhaps the most widely understood. Those who voluntarily solicit or accept any benefit in exchange for influencing an official act have engaged in bribery. Both the giver *and* the receiver are liable under the law of bribery, and the act is punished according to the nature of the act influenced.

The federal bank bribery law is an example of *commercial*, as opposed to government-related *official*, bribery. The bank bribery law states that it is prohibited from "corruptly" giving, offering, or promising something of value "with intent to influence or reward" an officer of a bank in connection with a transaction. Actual cases provide an interesting way to illustrate the elements and application of bribery law in practice.

What Is "Corruptly"?

In *U.S. v. McElroy*,[1] it was argued that the term "corruptly" is unconstitutionally vague. The defendants, McElroy and Stedman, headed two different banks, Marble Bank and First Twin Bank, in Vermont. Both McElroy and Stedman sought loans of nearly $1 million to purchase stock in New England banks on margin. McElroy was denied the loan because his financial condition "was already highly leveraged, and his income was insufficient to service his projected

41

debt."[2] This resulted in McElroy and Stedman entering into an agreement where each would give large, unsecured loans from his own bank to the other party for the purpose of stock speculation. Neither reported the loans to their respective boards of directors. The loans were ultimately discovered by Federal Deposit Insurance Company (FDIC) examiners in the course of routine audits, and state and federal bank regulators testified that "both sets of loans were improvident and unwarranted" and "could not be explained on the basis of prudent banking principles."[3]

McElroy and Stedman were each convicted of bribery and sentenced to three years in prison and restitution of nearly $1 million. The U.S. Court of Appeals rejected their claim that the term "corruptly" was too vague to permit a conviction for bank bribery. The court had previously held that "corruptly" is ordinarily understood to mean acts carried out "voluntarily and intentionally" with the "bad purpose" of accomplishing an unlawful act, or lawful act in an unlawful manner. The motive to act corruptly "is ordinarily a hope or expectation of either financial gain or other benefit to oneself or some profit or benefit to another."[4] The term "corruptly" clearly fit the facts in this case because "both men desired large unsecured loans for purposes of speculation; neither could obtain such loans from his own bank without the approval of his board of directors, [and] neither man informed his bank's board of directors of either his own loans from the other bank or the loans to the other defendant." Such an agreement "designed to circumvent" the legal requirements for such loans "fell plainly within the scope" of the term "corruptly."[5]

In a case on a related issue, a shareholder filed suit against General Electric alleging the company made contributions to G.E.'s political action committee (PAC) to assist incumbent members of Congress by providing information that excess contributions might be converted to the officials' personal use under law. It was argued that this exposes G.E. to liability for bribery (and thereby hurts shareholders). The U.S. Court of Appeals explained that because such conversion of funds by members of Congress is lawful, it obviously does not violate any law. Criminal intent under the federal antibribery statute, according to the court, "turns not on what the contributor expects the recipient to do with the money, but rather on what the contributor expects to receive for that money."[6] Therefore, it can be seen that the corrupt intent required for bribery is generally established by the circumstances of the case to determine whether the benefit is made or received for an illegal purpose.

The Link Between Bribery and Extortion: The Case of Newark, New Jersey

Sometimes there is confusion about the distinction between bribery and extortion, because both involve solicitation of some benefit in exchange for a desired action. An interesting case that helps to distinguish bribery from extortion is a well-known municipal corruption case, *United States v. Addonizio*.[7] The prosecution alleged that there existed a conspiracy that included the Mayor of Newark, New Jersey (Hugh Addonizio), certain members of the city government, and a group headed by Ruggiero "Tony Boy" Boiardo, an alleged organized crime fig-

Hugh Addonizio, former mayor of Newark, New Jersey, was convicted of extortion and conspiracy in his handling of city contracts. He was sentenced to 10 years in prison. *(New Jersey Newsphotos)*

ure. The object of the conspiracy was to extort kickbacks from contractors, suppliers, and engineers engaged in public works projects with the city of Newark.

In one instance, Paul Rigo (a contracted engineer for the project) was enlisted by the city to begin plans for a "Southerly Extension of Newark's water supply," which was needed to alleviate a critical water shortage. At a meeting at City Hall attended by the mayor, the director of public works, the city corporation counsel, and Rigo, Rigo informed the mayor that Gallo (a contractor favored by the mayor) did not make the sort of high pressure pipe required for the project and that the contract would have to go to Interpace (Lock Joint Pipe Company). In that case, the mayor said "Tony Boy [Boiardo] better figure out a way to get something out of Lock Joint." The corporation counsel asked, "Will he get enough?" The mayor replied, "If he goes after it, he'll get enough."[8]

Shortly thereafter in a meeting with an Interpace vice president, a friend of the mayor unconnected with city government (Biancone) said that Interpace could participate in the Southerly Extension only if it agreed to pay a 10 percent

CRITICAL THINKING EXERCISE

The scenario that follows describes an actual fact situation, where the courts had to determine whether or not the law of bribery applied. Read the facts and answer the questions that follow, applying the principles of bribery.

THE CASE OF SULLY'S COMPANY

Sully was in charge of job training and finding employment for the disadvantaged and unemployed in Gary, Indiana. He accomplished this as head of a federal employment act called CETA. Rather than awarding government-funded contracts to secure employment through open bidding, however, Sully awarded contracts to his friends and associates.

Sully and his friends decided to form a corporation of their own, called VCR, that would operate the lounge and restaurant in a downtown hotel that local politicians wanted to keep from closing. A number of those

kickback. The vice president refused. A few weeks later, Biancone met with another Interpace executive and again tried to extract an unspecified figure. No commitment was made. Ultimately, Interpace agreed to a payment of 5 percent, or $35,000, to obtain the city contract.

Interpace recognized that its company was the logical supplier, but time was of the essence and Interpace had two factories in the vicinity of the job site. Interpace executives later testified that Mr. Biancone and his group had obvious control over the specifications and the inspectors on the job. They were fearful that if their company took the job, they would be harassed with delays, rejection of product, and such and that their cost would likely far exceed the $35,000 they agreed to pay. They also testified that, although they did not want to pay this money, they did so because of a degree of fear for personal and family safety, and fear for the corporation.[9]

Soon, however, Rigo (the project engineer) began to feel the burden of making the 10 percent (kickbacks). He spoke to the mayor, but to no avail. The mayor informed him that any changes would have to be cleared by Boiardo. (During this conversation the mayor was asked why he had ever left Congress to come into "this mess." Addonizio replied, "Simple. There's no money in Washington, but you can make a million bucks as the mayor of Newark.")

Rigo was later driven to Boiardo's home. Boiardo's response to Rigo's protestations was: "You pay your 10 percent or I'll break both your legs."[10] Rigo employed by various CETA contractors were placed at the lounge and restaurant owned in part by Sully. But some of these supposed employees later testified that they had never actually been put to work or were not employed full time.

Sully was ultimately charged with bribery for his conduct. He argued that he should not be convicted, however, because an element of the crime was missing—he never solicited or received anything of value. Sully claimed he received nothing of value because "he was not an employee of VCR and any political stature or influence he gained [by helping keep the hotel open] is intangible and cannot be considered 'anything of value'" under the bribery statute.

Questions

1. What elements of the crime of bribery are fulfilled by Sully's conduct?
2. Should Sully be convicted of bribery?
3. Can Sully and the CETA contractors he worked with be held liable for conspiracy?

was also informed that the time might come when he would be called upon to collect the payments from the contractors as well. Soon thereafter, Rigo received a contract on the Southerly Extension and began receiving payments thereunder. He remitted 10 percent of these payments periodically to Boiardo through a conduit. Similar kickbacks were paid to municipal officials and their associates on other city contracts as well.

After a jury trial, Mayor Hugh Addonizio, and others, were each sentenced to ten years in prison for extortion and conspiracy. On appeal, the mayor made the interesting argument that to be guilty of extortion, it must be shown that the payments received were induced by threatened interference with "then-existing" contract rights. The mayor claimed that the alleged victims knew well in advance of entering into a city contract that "10 percent was expected of those doing business with the city" and that they agreed to this well before signing a contract. Therefore, it was argued, the payments constituted bribery, rather than extortion, because money was paid to secure *future* contract rights, rather than to protect existing rights.[11]

The U.S. Court of Appeals held that, even accepting the facts as portrayed by the appellants, "the legal propositions set forth cannot be accepted" for two primary reasons. First, "the essence of the crime of bribery is voluntariness, while the essence of the crime of extortion is duress. . . . The court charged that the jury had to find that the defendants had 'wrongfully used actual fear . . . in order to induce (the contractor) to pay them money.' . . . Unless the payments alleged were made under some form of compulsion, there is no crime."[12]

Second, the Court found that ". . . we cannot agree that advance knowledge alone conclusively establishes bribery." A jury is entitled to find that in an effective extortion conspiracy, "potential victims would be aware of the illicit requirements placed upon contractors and would succumb in advance of contracting to the pressure which they knew would be forthcoming." For example, Rigo testified that he agreed to the payments to "protect his financial future in the face of threats from Boiardo," rather than to gain undue influence.[13] As a result, the U.S. Court of Appeals rejected this appeal, and the U.S. Supreme Court denied further review.

It is clear from this case, therefore, that for bribery to occur, there must be a *voluntary* act that is not the result of fear or duress. In addition, both the giver and receiver of a bribe are criminally liable, whereas only the recipient is liable in cases of extortion. In a similar case, U.S. congressman Mario Biaggi was convicted of bribery and extortion for soliciting a payment for his assistance as a public official to obtain the assistance of other public officials for the benefit of a defense contractor called Wedtech. Biaggi had told Wedtech officials that he had "brought up the company to the point it was" and that he "could also destroy it." The issue on appeal was whether the $50,000 payment can constitute *both* a bribe *and* extortion, when part of the money was for lawful purposes. (Biaggi directed Wedtech to retain his son's law firm and to pay the money for the firm's legal services as well as for his own official actions.) The U.S. Court of Appeals held that both charges can stand, because "a valid purpose that partially motivates a transaction does not insulate participants in an unlawful transaction from criminal liability."[14]

Obstruction of Justice

When a person intentionally impairs a lawful government procedure by means of intimidation, or through any independent unlawful act, he or she has engaged in obstruction of justice. One can be held liable for this offense only when there is a *duty* to cooperate, however, and unknowing violations are not punishable under law. Under federal law, one must obstruct a *judicial* function to be held liable for obstruction of justice, although there are separate offenses dealing with obstruction of federal law enforcement agencies.[15] In most states, any interference with a lawful government process meets the act's requirement.

It is not necessary to succeed in the attempt to obstruct justice, as long as the defendant carries out the required act with the necessary intent.[16] In a Nevada case, the defendant made a conditional threat that if he was forced to meet with the Internal Revenue Service (IRS), he would bring a gun and "someone might be shot." The U.S. Court of Appeals held this threatened act (never actually carried out) to constitute obstruction of justice.[17]

The mens rea requirement involves "specific intent" to "corruptly" impede the administration of justice.[18] In a Kansas case, for example, it was found that the felony of interfering with a federal officer in performance of his or her official duties does not require use of actual physical force. Instead, it is sufficient that "there is proof that actual force was threatened and that the defendant acted in such a way as to inspire fear of pain, bodily harm, or death."[19] In a similar way, an antiabortion protestor argued that his sincere religious conviction should negate the mens rea requirement for obstructing justice (or impeding court orders). The federal district court ruled the elements of the offense were fulfilled by his conduct and that the defendant's religious convictions were not relevant.[20]

The Watergate Affair

The Watergate affair provided a fascinating look at how obstruction of justice can take place. The case of *U.S. v. Haldeman, Ehrlichman, and Mitchell*[21] illustrates the elements of this offense and how they apply in practice.

In March 1974 a grand jury in Washington, D.C., returned a 13-count indictment against seven individuals holding positions in the White House. It charged what amounted to "an unprecedented scandal at the highest levels of government," for most of the defendants had held major positions in the Nixon administration. Charged were John N. Mitchell, former attorney general of the United States and later head of the Committee to Re-elect the President (for the 1972 campaign); Harry R. Haldeman, who served as chief of the White House staff; John D. Ehrlichman, once assistant for domestic affairs to the president; together with several others. The crimes charged in the indictment included conspiracy, obstruction of justice, and false statements under oath to the Federal Bureau of Investigation, to a grand jury and to the Senate Select Committee on Presidential Campaign Activities.

At trial, the jury convicted Mitchell, Haldeman, and Ehrlichman of both conspiracy and obstruction of justice as well as perjury. Sentences of imprisonment were imposed on each (two and one-half to eight years), and the convictions were appealed. All the charges derived from attempts to cover up the break-in at Democratic National Committee (DNC) headquarters in the Watergate Office Building in Washington, D.C.

It began in the early morning hours of June 17, 1972, roughly four and a half months before the presidential election, when police discovered five men inside the DNC offices carrying electronic equipment, cameras, and large sums of cash. The five burglars arrested inside the DNC gave aliases to the D.C. police, but within hours of the break-in, G. Gordon Liddy, who had been monitoring the operation from across the street, reported the capture to the Committee to Re-Elect the President's (CREEP) highest officials.

Meanwhile, White House and CREEP files were being "cleansed" of sensitive materials relating to "Operation Gemstone" (as the break-in plan was called) to gather political intelligence. Gordon Strachan performed this function at the White House, under orders from Haldeman to remove anything embarrassing. Mitchell suggested Jeb Magruder (deputy director of CREEP) "have a fire," and he did—destroying the Gemstone documents in his home fireplace.

Seven principals in the Watergate scandal, all of whom resigned from office under pressure, including President Richard Nixon. Several also were convicted of various crimes, including obstruction of justice, and served prison time. *(UPI/Bettmann)*

Mitchell and Ehrlichman each denied to FBI agents that he knew anything about the break-in except what was in the newspapers. On September 14, Mitchell told a grand jury that he was not aware of any clandestine CREEP intelligence program, nor did he know of Liddy's illegal activities. On September 15, the grand jury handed up indictments against the five burglars, plus E. Howard Hunt and Liddy. No one else was implicated.

Hunt and four of the burglars pleaded guilty. Liddy and James McCord insisted on going to trial, although neither took the stand. They were found guilty, and sentencing was set for March 23, 1973. When McCord began to get restless as that date approached (he threatened in a letter to the White House that "all the trees in the forest will tumble"[22]), Mitchell urged that veiled assurances of clemency be extended to him. Ehrlichman agreed, and assurances were delivered to McCord—to no avail, it later developed.

The greatest apparent threat to the conspirators' plans lay in the impending hearings of the Senate Select Committee on Campaign Activities, chaired by Senator Ervin. John Dean (counsel to the president), Haldeman, and Ehrlichman met at Rancho LaCosta in California in mid-February to plot strategy. They worried most about what the break-in defendants might say before the Committee, if granted immunity. Knowing that increasing demands for hush

G. Gordon Liddy, general counsel to the Committee to Re-elect President Nixon, developed and implemented the plan to gather political intelligence, which included the botched break-in of Democratic National headquarters in the Watergate building. It was the attempted cover-up of this unsuccessful burglary that led to the downfall of the Nixon administration. *(UPI/Bettmann)*

money had been made by the burglars, they decided it was essential that Mitchell provide the "hush" money to the burglars.

Dean decided he had to speak with the president directly about the dangers inherent in guaranteeing the continued flow of money. On March 21, 1973, Dean thus told Nixon that there was a "cancer" growing on the presidency in the form of the endless hush money demands. He recounted all that he knew about the origin of the break-in and the subsequent payment of hush money. He guessed that future demands would come to another million dollars. Nixon replied that "You could get a million dollars. And you could get it in cash. I, I know where it could be gotten."[23]

Haldeman, Ehrlichman, and Dean met later that day to discuss possible strategies. They agreed that Mitchell should step forward and take the full blame, thinking the prosecutors and the Senate Committee would thereby be

John Dean, counsel to President Nixon, became the first insider to reveal the involvement of the White House in the Watergate burglary and cover-up in testimony before the U.S. Senate. *(UPI/Bettmann)*

pacified and would press no further. Despite these plans, however, no one had the fortitude to suggest directly to Mitchell that he take full blame and go to jail to save the Nixon presidency. Finally, on March 23, McCord, facing sentencing, had written a letter to Judge Sirica breaking the word that burglar's silence was the result of pressure, that others were involved, and that perjury had been committed. The letter was released to the public at the sentencing hearing that day. Shortly thereafter, Magruder, Dean, and LaRue began to talk to the prosecutors.

Throughout the month of April 1973 Haldeman, Ehrlichman, and Nixon met frequently at the White House trying to decide how to respond to the new developments. They were faced with two primary problems: how to cope with Dean who, as Nixon's counsel, plainly knew a great deal, and how to explain the hush money payments—which were now bound to be revealed to the prosecutors and the public.

Haldeman and Ehrlichman subsequently testified before the Senate Select Committee and placed all the blame on Dean for the break-in cover-up and the hush money. They both claimed that John Dean was the only one in the White House to know of the scheme and the cover-up. John Dean was the first to claim that the president knew of the plan and the hush money from an early stage, which would have been difficult to prove if it were not for the discovery of the tape-recording system in the Oval Office, which was eventually seized, and which confirmed Dean's version of the Watergate cover-up.

After their conviction for obstruction of justice, Haldeman, Ehrlichman, and Mitchell claimed that the judge's instruction to the jury at their trial was defective. They argued that to be liable for obstruction of justice, it is "necessary" or "required" that a person specifically intended it. Haldeman claimed that the court's failure to use the words "necessary" or "required," and its failure to include the phrase "with bad purpose either to disobey or disregard the law," was prejudicial when referring to specific intent needed for obstruction of justice.

The second argument raised by the appellants was that the court's instruction to the jury failed to distinguish specific from general intent. As the court stated,

> appellant criticizes the use both of the "natural and probable consequences" instruction and the instruction to consider "all of the circumstances" as creating the impression "that is was permissible to infer specific knowledge or intent solely on the basis of equivocal criteria, and without regard to the totality of circumstances."[24]

The U.S. Court of Appeals ruled on each of these issues and held that the instructions to the jury were not defective. First, the Court found that in the jury instruction "[s]pecific intent is plainly identified not only as an 'element' of the offense (and therefore 'necessary') but also an "important element." Second the Court found that instructing the jury to consider "all of the circumstances" was clearly proper.

> Except in extraordinary circumstances, criminal intent cannot be proved by direct evidence; it is therefore not only appropriate but also necessary for the jury to look at "all of the circumstances" in determining specific intent. . . . The instruction in question was therefore both proper and beneficial to the appellants, since it cautioned the jury against fixating on one or two isolated circumstances as evidence of intent.[25]

As a result, the convictions of Haldeman, Ehrlichman, and Mitchell for obstruction of justice were affirmed, and the U.S. Supreme Court denied further review. President Nixon resigned from office and was later pardoned by President Ford without having been indicted or convicted of any crime.

It is clear from the Watergate case that the intention behind actions must usually be inferred from the circumstances. In white-collar crimes, criminal intention can be difficult to establish, although in the Watergate case the evidence was overwhelming, beginning with the burglars' testimony, the money trail of the funds used to buy their silence, John Dean's testimony, and the secret tape recordings made by Richard Nixon in the Oval Office.

The Iran–Contra Scandal

Ironically, the 1980s version of Watergate, the Iran–Contra scandal, resulted in the indictment and conviction of a number of members of the Reagan administration. White House aide Oliver North, national security advisor John Poindex-

John Poindexter, national security advisor to President Ronald Reagan (background), was charged in a scheme to divert profits from Iranian Arms sales to the Nicaraguan Contras in violation of a Congressional ban. Nine former Reagan administration officials pleaded guilty or were convicted in this scheme. Many were pardoned by President George Bush in January 1993 during his last month as President. *(UPI/Bettmann)*

ter, and others engaged in a scheme to divert profits from Iranian arms sales to the Nicaraguan Contras. Nearly $4 million ultimately was diverted to the Contras, violating a congressional ban on such activity during the 1980s.[26]

The participants in the scheme were charged with lying and withholding information from Congress and federal investigators in their investigation of these secret U.S. arms sales to Iran and aid to the Nicaraguan Contra rebels. Nine former administration staff members pleaded guilty or were convicted by 1992.[27] Caspar Weinberger, Reagan's former Defense secretary and the highest-ranking official charged, was indicted in mid-1992.[28] Before he went to trial, Weinberger, and several other implicated officials, were pardoned by President Bush in January 1993, while Bush served his last month as president.

To be held liable for obstruction of justice, there must be some attempt to impair, prevent, or interfere with a lawful government procedure where there is a duty to cooperate. Furthermore, as the Watergate case demonstrated, a per-

CRITICAL THINKING EXERCISE

The scenario that follows describes an actual fact situation, where the courts had to determine whether or not obstruction of justice applied. Read the facts and answer the questions that follow, applying the elements of obstruction of justice.

THE CASE OF BIZZARRO

Bizzarro was a fire inspector for the City of Chicago responsible for enforcing the fire code at various retail establishments. He was charged with accepting payoffs from businesses that had applied for liquor, food, and amusement licenses. Bizzarro would advise the business owners of needed repairs to comply with the fire code and then would demand a payoff in place of, or in addition to, the repairs.

After his arrest, Bizzarro was brought to appear before a grand jury seeking to indict him on these charges. Another fire inspector, Muffy, was known by Bizzarro to be cooperating with the government as a witness. Muffy was seated outside the grand jury room, waiting to testify, when Bizzarro saw him and used "hand gestures mimicking the slashing of a throat and the threat of a gun."

Questions

1. What elements of the crime of obstruction of justice are fulfilled by Bizzarro's actions?
2. Are Bizzarro's actions sufficient for conviction for obstruction of justice?

son must *intentionally* obstruct the government procedure, and this is to be inferred after considering "all of the circumstances." As the U.S. Court of Appeals summarized in 1992, the essential elements of obstruction of justice are two: "that defendant had knowledge or notice of a pending proceeding, and that defendant acted corruptly with specific intent to obstruct or impede the proceeding or due administration of justice."[29]

Perjury alone is not sufficient to constitute obstruction of justice. To justify both charges it must be shown that the false testimony somehow "infects" the process to constitute an obstruction by "corruptly endeavoring to obstruct, impede, or influence due administration of justice." In one case it was found that false testimony before a grand jury was sufficient for conviction for obstruction of justice only if the false statements have the effect of "blocking off the flow of information to the grand jury," thereby obstructing the adjudication process.[30] In another case, a defendant asked a witness to testify falsely on his behalf.[31] This also constitutes obstruction of justice, because it fulfills all the elements of the crime.

Official Misconduct

An offense related to obstruction of justice is official misconduct. If a public servant knowingly performs an unauthorized official act, or fails to perform a legal duty, with intent to receive a benefit or injure or deprive another, the act or omission constitutes official misconduct. It is a requirement that the unauthorized official act or omission is *known* to be unauthorized, and that the personal benefit to be obtained is not necessarily money.

Pistol Permits for Sex

The case *People v. Dunbar*[32] illustrates how the elements of this offense are applied in practice. James Dunbar was an attorney and confidential clerk to a Schenectady county court judge in New York. He agreed to issue a pistol permit to Neil Cuomo only if Cuomo's friend, Grace Zwack, would have sexual relations with him.[33]

Dunbar was convicted at trial, but he appealed on grounds that "only the County Judge may decide and determine the eligibility for pistol permits and that judgment, undertaken by anyone else, i.e., Mr. Dunbar, was unauthorized." Dunbar argued, therefore, that he could not be held liable for official misconduct because he had no authority to act in any official capacity with regard to pistol permits. His demands for sex were unrelated to his position as court clerk, Dunbar claimed, so his misconduct was not done in his "official" capacity.

The appellate court held that it was true that no defendant "could be convicted simply for arrogating to himself the proper powers of a County Judge." Nevertheless, the "record contains a memorandum from the County Judge, put in evidence by the defense, granting Dunbar complete control of issuing pistol permits, so the defendant had at least *de facto* power to issue or withhold such permits."[34]

To hold Dunbar liable in this case it would be necessary for the jury "to decide whether the defendant made the alleged offer to Grace Zwack and whether he wrote the letter denying the Cuomo application and, if [so], whether he did it because she had refused his proposition, and if so, whether such act related to his office and was an unauthorized exercise of his official functions, knowingly committed by him."[35] The appellate court found these conditions were established at trial and affirmed his conviction. As a penalty, Dunbar was disbarred.

It is clear from this case that only public officials, or those acting in such a capacity, can be held liable for official misconduct. In addition, the authorized act must be knowing (not mistaken) and intentional (not accidental).

HUD and Other Cases of Political Corruption

Official misconduct is closely related to bribery although many types of official misconduct do not involve bribery and some types of bribery do not involve government officials. Alabama Governor Guy Hunt was indicted in 1992 on charges that he took $200,000 from political funds for personal use.[36] Although this fulfills the elements of bribery, it also constitutes official misconduct because it involves an unauthorized official act by a public servant. Likewise, the misuses of funds by Detroit police chief William Hart and ex-Kentucky State senator John Hall are examples of official misconduct for personal financial gain.[37]

Criminal conduct by government officials becomes official misconduct only when it involves an unlawful exchange for an "official" act. There were nine people indicted in the HUD probe that involved charges of influence peddling and cronyism at the Department of Housing and Urban Development (HUD) during the Reagan administration.[38] In these cases it was alleged that HUD officials misused their positions for personal benefit and for the benefit of friends.

In 1993, Deborah Gore Dean, a top HUD official during the Reagan administration, was convicted of 12 felony counts of defrauding the government, receiving payoffs, and lying to Congress. She was accused of funneling $66 million in HUD funds to selected developers.[39]

Nearly 10 percent of Arizona's state legislators were indicted in 1991 for accepting money after agreeing to vote for legalized gambling in the state.[40] In South Carolina, 15 current and former state legislators, 6 lobbyists, and 1 state agency director were indicted for accepting cash in exchange for their promise to vote for parimutuel gambling.[41] In both cases, a videotaped "sting" operation was used to record the corrupt exchanges.

In Chicago, five government officials were indicted on charges ranging from fixing zoning cases to manipulating murder trials. During the 1980s, Operation Greylord in Chicago resulted in convictions of nearly 100 judges, lawyers, and others on charges that they fixed primarily minor offenses such as drunken driving cases.[42] It can be seen from these cases that public officials are certainly not immune from the temptation to exploit their offices for personal advantage.

Perjury

Perjury is intentional false swearing under oath at an official proceeding. As shown earlier in the Watergate case, perjury occurred when Haldeman, Ehrlichman, and Mitchell testified falsely to the FBI, to the Senate Select Committee, and before a grand jury investigating the cover-up. Therefore, there are many forums to commit perjury, in addition to false swearing at a trial. *People v. Tyler*[43] involved the testimony of a New York State Supreme Court judge regarding his relationship with a known gambling figure.

Mistaken Versus Intentional False Statements

A grand jury began investigating the relationship of Judge Andrew Tyler to various gambling figures. One of these gamblers was Raymond Marquez, known as "Spanish" Raymond, said to be head of one of the largest illegal gambling operations in New York City. Marquez had been convicted of federal and state gambling laws and was recently released from prison. The perjury charges against Judge Tyler involved a single meeting with Marquez.

Three police officers were engaged in a surveillance of Judge Tyler and they testified before the grand jury and at trial that Tyler "met Marquez and his wife near Lincoln Center in Manhattan. They drove about ten blocks in Tyler's automobile to Patsy's Restaurant on West 56th Street and remained there for over an hour. Upon leaving, Tyler and Marquez allegedly spoke for 10 minutes, while Mrs. Marquez sat in Tyler's car. Tyler then drove the two back to where their own automobile was garaged."[44]

Judge Tyler was questioned before the grand jury on two occasions about Marquez. On the first occasion he claimed that he knew Marquez as a man who had been convicted "some years ago for policy" in a case that had "something to do with gambling." When asked if he had spoken to Marquez since Tyler had become a judge, the defendant (Judge Tyler) denied communicating with him. At a second appearance before the grand jury, after speaking with his wife who had "refreshed his recollection," Judge Tyler recalled his meeting with Marquez.

> A: I saw him on an occasion when he was with his wife on 58th Street in Manhattan.
>
> Q: When was that?
>
> A: I couldn't fix the dates. Probably somewhere around May . . .
>
> Q: Can you describe that in any more detail, that meeting or encounter or whatever it was on 56th Street?
>
> A: Yes. it was outside of Patsy's Restaurant. I think that's where it was. . . . That was on the street. Then they walked into Patsy's and I walked into Patsy's . . .
>
> Q: Did you have a drink alone?
>
> A: No. He and his wife sat down.
>
> Q: How long did that take?
>
> A: About 10 or 15 minutes.
>
> Q: What happened then?
>
> A: I got up and left.
>
> Q: And they remained in the place?
>
> A: I believe so.[45]

Judge Tyler was subsequently convicted for three counts of perjury in the first degree for lying about seeing Marquez "for the first time" in front of Patsy's Restaurant, for testifying that the meeting "had lasted about 10 to 15 minutes," and for saying that he had "left Marquez inside the premises" when he left the restaurant.

The Perjury Trap

Tyler challenged his conviction on two grounds. First, he argued that no attempt was made to establish that the meeting with Marquez was pertinent to the grand jury investigation of official misconduct. Second, the burden is on the prosecution to demonstrate that he testified falsely intentionally, rather than by mistake. In essence, Tyler was claiming that the prosecution set a "perjury trap" for him by tripping him up on details that were not relevant to the charge of official misconduct.

This appeal ultimately reached New York State's highest court, the Court of Appeals, which ruled on both of Tyler's arguments.

> The questioning . . . was an unmitigated effort to trap the witness on minor outward details of a single meeting with a reputed criminal figure. There was no attempt to establish that the meeting was pertinent to a proper substantive goal of grand jury investigation. The meeting might well have been a chance encounter at which the former lawyer chatted with his ex-client. Or it might have been planned to discuss matters inappropriate between one now a judge and the other a convicted gambler, even if he were a former client. . . . The prosecutor evinced minimal or no interest in establishing the materiality of the meeting. Almost as if he were conducting only a quiz to test memory or recall . . .[46]

With regard to the second issue, the Court of Appeals also agreed with Tyler's contention. To find that Tyler's assertion that he first met Marquez "outside of Patsy's Restaurant was knowingly false, and not just a lapse in memory," some effort must be made to stimulate Tyler's recollection. If the meeting "were no more than a benign but questionable socializing between a former lawyer and client, details would not likely be remembered or easily recalled." The prosecution has an "inescapable burden" to demonstrate that the witness "is testifying falsely intentionally, rather than mistakenly."[47] These considerations led the Court of Appeals to dismiss the indictment, due to its reliance on "trapping" a witness on minor details, rather than establishing whether the details were material to the case.

A valid perjury charge, therefore, must contain several elements. It must involve *intentional* false swearing under oath, rather than mistaken testimony. As is true of all elements of a crime, the burden is on the prosecution to prove this. Second, the testimony must be *material* to the proceeding. As the Court concluded in the case just reviewed, "false answers to questions limited to peripheral details of time and place may not support a prosecution for perjury."[48]

Truthful answers are an ultimate defense to charges of perjury. But even if an answer is true, but "arguably misleading," it is the prosecutor's obligation to pin down the witness on a specific point.[49] In a criminal case, of course, a defendant does not have to testify against himself or herself, but if the defendant chooses to testify, it must be truthful, even if it is incriminating. A U.S. congressman was convicted of perjury for giving false testimony regarding his contact with other government officials in a fraud case.[50] As the U.S. Court of Appeals has held, "no criminal defendant enjoys a constitutional privilege to testify falsely."[51]

Endnotes

1. *U.S. v. McElroy*, 910 F.2d 1016 (2nd Cir. 1990).
2. at 1019.
3. at 1020.
4. at 1021 and *United States v. Brunson*, 882 F.2d 151 (5th Cir. 1989).
5. at 1021–2.
6. *Stern v. General Electric*, 924 F.2d 472 (2nd Cir. 1991) at 478.
7. *U.S. v. Addonizio*, 451 F.2d 49, cert. denied, 92 S.Ct. 949 (1972).
8. at 56.
9. at 57.
10. Ibid.
11. at 72–3.
12. at 77–78.
13. at 73.
14. *U.S. v. Biaggi*, 909 F.2d 662 (2nd Cir. 1990), at 683.
15. *U.S. v. Tham*, 960 F.2d 1391 (9th Cir. 1991); see also 18 U.S.C.A. Sec. 1503.
16. *U.S. v. Sprecher*, 783 F.Supp. 133 (1992); and 18 U.S.C.A. Sec. 1505.
17. *U.S. v. Price*, 951 F.2d 1028 (1991).
18. See *Melton v. City of Oklahoma City*, 879 F.2d 706 (1989).
19. *U.S. v. Cooley*, 787 F.Supp. 977 (1992); and 18 U.S.C.A. Sec. 111.
20. *U.S. v. Cooley*, 787 F.Supp. 977 (1992).
21. *U.S. v. Haldeman*, 559 F.2d 31, cert. denied, 97 S.Ct. 2641 (1977).
22. at 57.
23. Ibid.
24. at 115.
25. at 115–116.
26. Michael A. Ledeen, *Perilous Statement: An Insider's Account of the Iran-Contra Affair* (New York: Scribner, 1988).
27. Sam Vincent Meddis, "Reagan May Be Ultimate Target," *USA Today*, June 17, 1992, p. 3.
28. Sam Vincent Meddis, "Weinberger Indicted in Iran-Contra," *USA Today*, June 17, 1992, p.1.
29. *U.S. v. Neal*, 951 F.2d 630 (5th Cir. 1992).
30. *U.S. v. Barfield*, 781 F.Supp. 754 (1991); 18 and U.S.C.A. Sec. 1503.
31. *U.S. v. Brown*, 948 F.2d 1076 (8th Cir. 1991).
32. *People v. Dunbar*, 58 A.2d 329, 396 NYS.2d 720 (1977).
33. at 330.
34. at 331.
35. at 330–331.
36. Gary Fields, "Alabama's Gov. Hunt Indicted," *USA Today*, December 29, 1992, p. 3.
37. "Police Scandal," *USA Today*, May 8, 1992, p. 3; and "Kentucky Corruption," *USA Today*, May 6, 1992, p. 3.

38. "HUD Scandal," *USA Today*, August 21, 1992, p. 10.
39. "Ex-HUD Aide Guilty on 12 Felony Counts," *USA Today*, October 27, 1993, p. 7.
40. Sally Ann Stewart, "New Tarnish on Arizona's Image," *USA Today*, February 13, 1991, p. 6.
41. Joseph Stedino with Dary Matera, *What's in It for Me?* (New York: Harper, 1993); and Mark Mayfield, "S. Carolina Bribery Scandal Widens," *USA Today*, March 21, 1991, p. 3.
42. Kevin Johnson, "5 Indicted in Chicago Crime Probe," *USA Today*, December 20, 1990, p. 3; and *U.S. v. Hogan*, 886 F.2d 1497 (7th Cir. 1989).
43. *People v. Tyler*, 46 NYS.2d 251, 385 NE.2d 1224 (1978).
44. at 255.
45. at 252.
46. at 261.
47. at 262.
48. at 260.
49. *U.S. v. Boone*, 951 F.2d 1526 (1991).
50. *U.S. v. Biaggi*, 705 F.Supp. 790 (1988).
51. *U.S. v. McDonough*, 959 F.2d 1137 (1st Cir. 1992).

CHAPTER 5

Regulatory Offenses

*A criminal is a person with predatory instincts who
has not sufficient capital to form a corporation.*
— *Howard Scott*

There are five types of regulatory offenses that are distinct from the crimes of theft and against public administration described thus far.[1] Although these offenses are often committed with the ultimate goal of financial advantage, these violations usually occur *in preparation* for the commission of white-collar crimes of theft.

Regulatory offenses are designed to ensure fairness and safety in the conduct of business or politics. They are a type of white-collar crime most often applied to corporate entities rather than to individuals acting without corporate knowledge or support.

Each type of regulatory offense will be described, and examples will be provided. Because there are literally thousands of possible regulatory violations, it serves no purpose to list them all individually. An indication of their nature and purpose, together with examples of their scope, will serve to illustrate their importance in the study of white-collar crime.

Administrative Violations

The first type of regulatory offense is administrative violations. These involve a failure to comply with court orders or regulatory agency requirements. Examples are the failure to submit compliance reports with the appropriate agency, failure to obtain a permit when one is necessary, and failure to keep adequate records as required by law. It can be seen that many of these violations are offenses of *omission* rather than of commission.

E. F. Hutton's Check Kiting

An example of administrative offenses is provided in the case of E. F. Hutton. The company violated rules of the Securities and Exchange Commission (the regulatory agency of publicly held corporations) by misusing the "float" time between when a check is deposited and when it clears. According to the U.S. Department of Justice, "The essence of the charges was that Hutton obtained the interest-free use of millions of dollars by intentionally writing checks in excess of the funds it had on deposit in various banks."[2] The misuse of this "float" time was a regulatory offense for which E. F. Hutton paid a $2 million fine, plus $750,000 in litigation costs, after pleading guilty to 2,000 charges of mail and wire fraud. In this case, it can be seen that although the ultimate goal was financial advantage (through fraud), regulatory offenses were committed to conduct the frauds.

Insider Trading

Other cases of administrative offenses include the many instances of "insider trading" in the stock market. Dennis Levine, an investment banker with Drexel Burnham Lambert, Inc., made $12.6 million by trading stock and investing money on tips about the activities and performance of certain companies not yet available to the public. This is considered "insider trading," and it is a regulatory offense inasmuch as it denies investors equal opportunity to invest funds based on public information. Dennis Levine settled the civil charges filed by the Securities and Exchange Commission by paying $11.5 million and a $362,000 fine. He was also sentenced to two years in prison for the related crimes of perjury and fraud that evolved from this scheme.[3] Kidder, Peabody, and Company agreed to pay a record $25.3 million to settle insider trading charges.[4] In 1992, Kidder, Peabody agreed to pay an additional $165 million to settle one of the last remaining insider trading suits from the 1980s.[5] A continuing investigation by the U.S. attorney in New York City produced additional violators, as many of those caught provided information to regulatory agencies and prosecutors in exchange for reduction of possible criminal charges.

Michael Milken was sentenced to ten years in prison for his role in the marketing of otherwise legal "junk bonds" by fixing the trading process through insider trading. Milken cheated clients by trading on confidential information for his own gain, manipulating securities prices to make huge fees, and stealing his clients' securities.[6] Along with Ivan Boesky, who was sentenced to three years in prison, Milken was charged with illegal stock trading.[7] There was a $1.3 billion settlement of the more than 150 lawsuits against him in 1992. Milken must contribute $900 million to this settlement, and former employees and insurers of Drexel Burnham Lambert must contribute an additional $400 million.[8] Ivan Boesky was assessed a $100 million fine in his case, and another investor, Fred Lee, was fined $25 million to settle insider trading charges.[9] Prudential Securities must pay at least $371 million to settle charges it defrauded 320,000 investors in selling securities, a settlement second in size only to that of Drexel Burnham Lambert.[10]

Other Variations of Administrative Violations

David McCloud was the third aide to U.S. Senator Chuck Robb to plead guilty to charges of conspiracy to falsely report expenses during a federal political campaign. He was sentenced to four months' probation and was fined $10,000

Ivan Boesky was sentenced to three years in prison for illegal "insider trading" of stocks using nonpublic information. He also was assessed a $100 million fine. *(UPI/Bettmann)*

for involvement with illegal eavesdropping on the cellular phone conversations of Virginia Governor Douglas Wilder.[11] General Electric agreed to pay $69 million in penalties and plead guilty to fraud charges resulting from a defense procurement scandal involving the sale of jet engines and the diversion of funds meant for Israel.[12] Nine supervisors at Eastern Airlines were charged with falsifying repair records in Atlanta. Nine others were charged at New York's Kennedy Airport eight months earlier.[13]

Administrative violations can also result in charges for other white-collar crimes. An investor, Paul Bilzerian, was charged with misrepresenting the source of funds used to purchase stock and secretly accumulating stock using another name.[14] These are administrative violations regulated by the Securities and Exchange Commission. Bilzerian was also charged with several crimes, however, including conspiracy, fraud, and making false statements. This is because his false statements to the Securities and Exchange Commission also fell within the scope of the federal conspiracy and fraud statutes. He was convicted of these crimes and was sentenced to four years in prison and a $1.5 million fine.

Environmental Violations

Emissions or dumping in violation of legal standards constitute environmental offenses. These offenses involve discharges into the air, land, or water in excess of legal limits; failure to treat waste adequately; or the unlawful disposal of hazardous waste.

Creating Environmental Crimes

There are numerous other examples of these violations, many of which were created after the passage of the federal Resource Conservation and Recovery Act in 1976. This law permitted the Environmental Protection Agency (EPA) to issue standards for the emission of toxics into the land, air, and water. In a similar way, the Nuclear Regulatory Commission (NRC) has established standards for the handling of nuclear materials. Violations of these standards are considered environmental offenses that can involve both civil and criminal penalties.

Many states have enforcement agencies analogous to the EPA and NRC that enforce state environmental regulations that are sometimes more strict than those on the federal level. The case at Love Canal is perhaps the best-known example of an environmental problem. Hooker Chemical buried toxic waste in the ground during the 1950s. The city of Niagara Falls bought the land later and, despite warnings from Hooker, built a school and homes on the site. Because the EPA was not established until 1970, there were no environmental regulations at that time, but a protracted trial is underway in an effort to compensate the state for its clean-up efforts and the victims for their exposure to the leaking chemicals. A detailed case study of the Love Canal case is presented in Chapter 6. Perhaps the most deleterious impact of environment cases, therefore, is the fact that the harm they create often is not manifested for many years after the act.

Air, Land, and Water Violations

Environmental violations can also entail charges for other types of white-collar crimes, depending on the circumstances. Consider the case of Raymond Brittain, public utilities director for the city of Enid, Oklahoma. He directed the supervisor of the Enid waste water treatment plant to falsify 18 monthly discharge monitoring reports, as well as the supporting laboratory records.[15] He was charged not only with misdemeanor counts of discharging pollutants into the water in violation of the Clean Air Act, but he was also charged with 18 felonies for his false statements to the U.S. government. These perjured statements violated federal criminal law, and Brittain's convictions were affirmed by the U.S. Court of Appeals.

Eastman Kodak pleaded guilty to illegally disposing of hazardous waste in Rochester, New York. The company was fined $2.15 million and paid another $1 million in civil fines.[16] Rockwell International Corporation pleaded guilty to four felony counts of hazardous waste violations, as well as violations of the

Animal recovery crews pick up dead sea otters recovered from Green Island in Prince William Sound after the Exxon-Valdez oil tanker ran aground in Alaska, creating the worst oil spill in U.S. history. *(J. David Ake, UPI/Bettmann)*

Clean Water Act, after it admitted to storing hazardous wastes without a permit in containers that leaked and that resulted in seepage to reservoirs.[17] Rockwell agreed to pay an $18.5 million fine. In 1993, the EPA proposed $20 million in fines for 30 companies in 17 states for improperly burning hazardous waste.[18]

Labor Violations

Discriminatory practices, unsafe exposure, or unfair treatment of employees are examples of labor violations. These offenses involve the exploitation of employees by an employer. Wage and hour violations, firings without cause, and refusing employment are some specific violations of labor laws. The federal regulatory agencies responsible for monitoring labor violations are the Department of Labor (Wage and Hour Division), Equal Employment Opportunity Commission, the Occupational Safety and Health Administration, and the National Labor Relations Board.

Corporate Murder?

In 1985, for example, executives from Film Recovery Systems, Inc., were sentenced for their failure to protect employees from cyanide fumes. Cyanide was used to strip the silver from X-ray film for recycling. Employees were not provided with adequate protective gear or ventilation from the toxic cyanide fumes, which resulted in the death of an employee. Three company executives were convicted of murder and each sentenced to 25-year prison terms. The murder convictions of corporate officials were believed the first in the history of the United States in a job-related death.[19] A case study of the Ford Pinto case is presented in Chapter 9 and illustrates a related incident, where Ford Motor Company was charged with criminal homicide for manufacturing a car it knew to be unsafe. Although murder is obviously a criminal offense unto itself, numerous regulations relating to the fair and safe treatment of employees were violated in the case of Film Recovery Systems.

Protecting Workers from Injury and Exploitation

In the typical case, of course, employees do not die from corporate misconduct. More often, they are injured, demoted, fired, or otherwise not treated fairly. Labor offenses are designed to help curtail unfair treatment of employees. For example, the parent company of 69 Jack-in-the-Box Restaurants in California and Hawaii was fined $125,000 for 397 child labor law violations.[20] Most of the violations involved teenagers working more hours than is permitted by law.

Union Carbide Corporation was fined $1.37 million by the Occupational Health and Safety Administration for 221 health and safety violations in its West Virginia plant. According to the U.S. secretary of labor, "We found employees without respirators being asked to detect the presence of deadly gas by sniffing the air after alarms indicated a leak. We used to use canaries for that."[21] Three officials from Imperial Food Products were charged with 25 counts of involuntary manslaughter, when its chicken processing plant in North Carolina caught fire killing 25 people and injuring another 56 workers. The company was fined more than $800,000 for safety violations.[22] A Phillips Petroleum chemical planted exploded, killing 23 workers in Pasadena, Texas. It had been cited for 19 safety violations prior to the explosion.[23]

S. A. Healy Company was fined $750,000 for safety violations that resulted in the deaths of three workers in a sewer tunnel explosion.[24] The tragedy was blamed on methane gas. The U.S. Labor Department proposed a record $5 million in fines against 500 coal mine operators in 16 states who were charged with repeatedly tampering with coal dust samples that are used to gauge a miner's risk of black lung disease.[25] A New York jury awarded $91 million to the families of 45 workers injured or killed by exposure to asbestos at electric-generating plants.[26]

A worker at Boeing Corporation was awarded $1.2 million for a repetitive motion injury she suffered while operating a microfilm machine by pushing a button several thousand times a day. She can no longer work due to nerve damage to her hands.[27] This award was believed to be one of the first where a worker won a damage award from a jury for a repetitive-strain injury. It is clear from these cases that oversight is required to ensure that minimum health and safety standards are met and that workers are not endangered thereby.

Manufacturing Violations

The manufacture of unsafe products is the essence of all manufacturing violations. In most cases, the unsafe product is the result of improper cost-cutting measures or shortcuts that result in injury to the consumer. Three federal agencies are responsible for enforcing manufacturing offenses.

The Consumer Product Safety Commission monitors products for chemical, electric shock, and fire hazards. The National Highway Traffic Safety Administration oversees the safe manufacture of automobiles. This includes monitoring of mechanical and electrical equipment, as well as performance standards. The Food and Drug Administration makes and enforces regulations regarding the safe contents, packaging, and labeling of products designed for human consumption. For drugs, it makes sure the products perform as advertised and are tested properly prior to marketing.

The IUD and Silicone Implants

An example of problems experienced with a manufactured product is the intrauterine contraceptive device (IUD). In 12 years on the market, there were 775 cases filed against the manufacturer, G. D. Searle & Company, for injuries to users. The IUD has been associated with serious pelvic infections. In four injury trials alone, the manufacturer spent more than $1.5 million in successful defenses of its product. Costs were so high and cases so numerous, however, that G. D. Searle announced in 1986 that it was discontinuing its manufacture of the product.[28] This is despite the fact that Food and Drug Administration approval of the device remains in effect. In 1992, a woman was awarded $43,700 in one of the first cases decided after many women rejected settlements from a trust fund to compensate those injured by the Dalkon Shield intrauterine birth control device.[29] This has become one of the largest product liability cases in the United States. A detailed case study of the Dalkon Shield is provided in Chapter 10.

In 1993, a proposed $4.75 billion settlement was reached for women suffering complications from silicon breast implants. An estimated 1 to 2 million women have had these implants, and a significant number have suffered from hardening breasts, implant leaks, and ruptures. Some physicians and women have claimed a link between these implant problems and autoimmune diseases, such as arthritis and lupus.

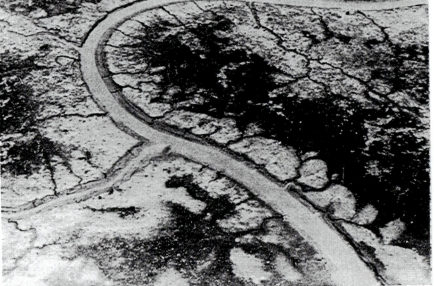

Photographs illustrate the effects of chemical herbicides on mangrove forests in Vietnam. Above is an aerial view of an unsprayed forest 60 miles from Saigon. Below is a herbicide-treated forest nearby. Nearly 250,000 Vietnam veterans and their families sued seven chemical companies that manufactured Agent Orange, a defoliant, for injuries suffered ranging from birth defects to cancer. The class action suit was settled for $200 million to be distributed to disabled veterans, their families, and survivors of deceased veterans. *(UPI/Bettmann)*

The settlement will be funded over a 30-year period by implant manufacturers, insurance companies, physicians, and others involved in implant surgery. Dow-Corning was the largest manufacturer of implants before it stopped in 1992. The company has approximately 6,800 pending lawsuits against it for breast implant complications.[30]

Agent Orange and Other Cases

Another well-known case involving allegations of manufacturing violations was the Agent Orange case. Nearly 250,000 Vietnam veterans and their families sued seven chemical companies that manufactured Agent Orange, a defoliant, for injuries suffered ranging from birth defects to cancer. In 1985, the class-action suit was settled for $200 million to be distributed over ten years to disabled veterans, their families, and survivors of deceased veterans.[31]

Manufacturing violations can range from comparatively minor to those that are lethal. Perrier agreed to drop claims that the French bottled-water product is "natural" in a settlement with the Federal Trade Commission.[32] The producers of Cisco "fortified" wine (which is 20 percent alcohol) agreed to redesign the bottle and market the beverage differently, after confusion with 4 percent alcohol wine coolers caused deaths from alcohol poisoning.[33]

In another case, New York State came to an agreement with 12 automobile manufacturers for $100 million in refunds to car owners. This is one of the largest refunds by automakers in U.S. history and was initiated under New York's "Lemon law." All state residents who were forced to pay for repairs after the warranty expired, but before 24 months or $18,000, are entitled to compensation.[34]

Unfair Trade Practices

The last category of regulatory offenses is unfair trade practices. These include practices that prevent fair competition in the marketplace. Monopolization, price discrimination, price-fixing, and bid-rigging are examples of unfair trade practices.

Price-fixing

Misleading advertisements draw the most attention in this area, although in recent years there was a well-publicized case of price-fixing. In 1985, Exxon Corporation was ordered to pay the largest fine in U.S. history (more than $2 billion) for overpricing Texas crude oil during the energy crisis of the 1970s. Exxon overcharged customers by nearly $1 billion by selling "old" oil as if it were "new" oil, priced $5 to $6 more per barrel.[35] Eleven other firms and 39 refineries pleaded guilty or no contest in similar "daisy chain" schemes, totaling another $2 billion in settlements.[36]

Upstate Milk Cooperatives, Inc., in New York was ordered to pay nearly $1 million in fines and restitution. It pleaded guilty to rigging the price of milk sold to schools. It was the 58th dairy cooperative charged in an investigation of the milk industry.[37]

General Electric Corporation pleaded guilty in 1985 for defrauding the Air Force on a nuclear warhead contract. Through violation of various labor laws, such as altering work records and submitting time cards for work not done, General Electric was charged with 108 counts of overbilling the U.S. government. The company was fined $1.04 million.[38]

Misconduct in the Marketplace

Abbott Laboratories, American Home Products, and Bristol-Myers Squibb were charged in 1991 with conspiring to drive up the price of infant formula. These three companies control 95 percent of the U.S. market and have raised prices 155 percent since 1979, while the main ingredient, milk, has increased only 36 percent in price over the same period.[39]

Eastman Kodak was ordered to pay Polaroid Corporation more than $900 million for infringing on Polaroid's patents on instant photography.[40] This violated the principles of fair competition in the marketplace, when Kodak used a patented (legally protected) idea of Polaroid and attempted to use it to market a virtually identical product.

Summary

Regulatory offenses provide a mechanism by which corporate conduct can be controlled. Administrative, environmental, labor, and manufacturing offenses, together with unfair trade practices, summarize the types of misconduct that regulatory agencies are designed to prevent. Unfortunately, significant cases of large-scale corporate misconduct continue to emerge. The investigative and prosecution problems presented by regulatory offenses are presented in Chapter 7. The next chapter will summarize the extent to which all the various kinds of white-collar crime occur.

CASE STUDY

Case studies are used throughout the book to illustrate points of law, causation, and criminal justice procedures. Read this case study carefully, and then answer the questions that follow it, applying the principles from this chapter and from earlier sections of the book.

The Lockheed Incident
Where Bribery, Extortion, and Regulatory Offenses Meet[41]

It was April 13, 1976, when the U.S. Securities and Exchange Commission filed a complaint against Lockheed Aircraft Corporation and its two senior executives alleging that Lockheed had violated the Securities Exchange Act by not

The Lockheed L-1011 Tristar was developed in the early 1970s as an "airbus" to carry more than 250 passengers in a cabin more than 20 feet wide. Airbuses like these, also developed by Boeing and McDonnell-Douglas, helped to reduce the cost of flying. It was questions raised about the marketing of this aircraft to foreign airlines that resulted in the Foreign Corrupt Practices Act. *(UPI/Bettmann)*

disclosing that (1) payments of at least $25 million had been made to foreign government officials, (2) secret funds were used for these payments, and (3) financial records were altered to conceal the payments. Lockheed signed a "consent decree" that same day agreeing, without admitting any wrongdoing, to a permanent injunction enjoining it from any activities of this kind in the future. This complaint by the Securities and Exchange Commission (SEC) was the result of over a year of investigation, which was preceded by an extensive investigation by the United States Senate.

The discovery of these payments by Lockheed, and other corporations, grew out the Watergate scandal, which uncovered evidence of illegal corporate contributions to President Richard Nixon's reelection campaign. The overseas payments made by corporations drew more concern, however, due to their possible effect on international trade and U.S. foreign policy.

The result of these investigations was the Foreign Corrupt Practices Act of 1977, which makes it a crime for U.S. companies to "bribe" a foreign official to obtain or maintain sales contracts abroad. Companies violating this prohibition face a maximum fine of $1 million, and individuals acting on behalf of companies face a maximum fine of $10,000 and five years' imprisonment. Fines imposed on individuals cannot be paid directly or indirectly by the company. The act also requires publicly held corporations to maintain strict accounting standards and prohibits falsification of accounting records under the threat of criminal penalties.

When Lockheed, and other corporations, made these payments to foreign officials during the 1960s and early 1970s, there was no law prohibiting them

Table 5.1 Lockheed Corporation's Payments in Japan

Payment No.	Payment Amount	Recipient
1	500 million yen ($1.7 million)	Prime Minister Kekuei Tanaka
2	500 million yen	Kenji Osano, influential businessman
3	120 million yen	Six different Japanese politicians
4	120 million yen	Officials of Marubeni (trading company)

from doing so. As a result, the Foreign Corrupt Practices Act applies only to payments made *after* 1977. Therefore, the complaint against Lockheed alleged only violations of SEC accounting and reporting rules, which, in 1976, were subject only to civil fines. Nevertheless, the Foreign Corrupt Practices Act refers specifically to foreign "bribes," and it is this characterization of foreign corporate payments that caused, and continues to confound, efforts to regulate business conduct abroad.

Prosecution and Defense

The Securities and Exchange Commission in its civil complaint against Lockheed claimed that a number of administrative violations had occurred and possibly commercial bribery as well. The president of Lockheed, A. Carl Kotchian, declared from the start, however, that the payments were not made as bribes:

> When in August, 1972, I was requested by Mr. Okubo to make a pledge of 500 million yen [almost $1.7 million] to the office of Japan's Prime Minister, I at once expressed doubt saying, "Couldn't Marubeni [the Japanese trading company representing Lockheed] pay this out of its commission?" However, when I was told that I must make the pledge of 500 million yen or we would not be successful, I was convinced that our competitors were doing the same thing; that is to say, I thought the pledge of money was like admission to a ball game. And if you didn't pay the admission, you were not even qualified to participate in the game—your product would not even be considered. . . . Such was our conclusion; so the payment of money was not an offensive, but rather a defensive, strategy to defend ourselves in the game of international trade.[42]

This payment of 500 million yen was to be the first of four separate demands for money by the Japanese during Lockheed's efforts to sell its L-1011 Tristar aircraft. The payments are summarized in Table 5.1.

Kotchian's version of these payments in Japan has been supported through several subsequent inquiries. Journalistic accounts of Lockheed's experience in Japan have generally reported that Lockheed did not offer money to the Japanese but, rather, the Japanese demanded the payments from Lockheed.[43]

Outcome

Trials of the Japanese officials who received the Lockheed payments began during the late 1970s, but Japanese adjudication proceeds slowly (hearings are often held only a few days a week and long recesses are common). Convictions

Table 5.2 Outcome of Japanese Trials in Lockheed Case

Offender	Conviction	Sentence
Kekuei Tanaka	Bribery	4 years in prison and 500 million yen fine
T. Enomoto (K. Tanaka's secretary)	Violation of foreign exchange laws	1 year in prison
Kenji Osano	Perjury	1 year in prison
T. Hashimoto	Bribery	2.5 years suspended
T. Sato	Bribery	2 years suspended
H. Hiyama	Conspiracy to bribe	2.5 years in prison
T. Okubo	Conspiracy to bribe	2 years in prison
H. Ito	Conspiracy to bribe	2 years in prison

did not occur until the 1980s, resulting ultimately in the conviction of former Prime Minister Tanaka in late 1983. Interestingly, the Japanese trials resulted directly from Lockheed's admissions during the U.S. Senate investigation in 1975, and A. Carl Kotchian's testimony was admitted into evidence in several Japanese trials.[44]

The results of the Lockheed case in Japan can be assessed, now that the trials are over. (Refer to Table 5.2.)

There were a total of 16 Japanese officials indicted in the Lockheed case, and 15 of them have been found guilty. The remaining defendant had his trial postponed indefinitely due to poor health. Most of the offenders appealed their convictions, a process that can take as long as ten years in Japan.[45] In any event, it appears that several conclusions can be drawn from the outcome of the Lockheed case in Japan.

First, it appears that A. Carl Kotchian's account of Lockheed's payments in Japan was accurate. The transcripts of the Japanese trials confirm that Lockheed's payments were solicited by the Japanese and were not offered simply as bribes by the corporation. As the prosecution pointed out in the Tanaka case,

> Okubo [executive director of Marubeni Company, Lockheed's Japanese trading representative] met and talked with Kotchian in his office of the Tokyo branch. He advised Kotchian of the following according to instructions from Hiyama. "Tomorrow Hiyama is going to visit the prime minister and ask his assistance. It is necessary to make a promise of presenting him 500,000,000 yen in Japanese currency in order to succeed with our sales to All Nippon Airways." He also explained to him, "In a large transaction like that involving aircraft 500,000,000 is an average sum, and the promise of presenting money is a custom in making such a deal."[46]

Similarly, it was Okubo who said, "If you do, Mr. Kotchian, three things, you will definitely succeed in selling the Tristar [aircraft]." When Kotchian asked what the money was for, he was told, "to give $300,000 (90 million yen) to Mr. Wakasa and also to make payments to six politicians."[47] These are just two of the four separate incidents of requests for money from Lockheed during the Tristar sales effort in Japan.

Second, it can be seen that the failure to distinguish between the crimes of bribery and extortion is a significant omission. Bribery involves a voluntary giving or receiving of money in corrupt payment for an official act, with the intent to influence the action of a public official. The Japanese clearly fulfilled these requirements in their solicitation of money from Lockheed. Technically, Lockheed also would be liable for bribery only if it could be shown that their representatives knew that such payments were used for corrupt purposes, rather than as an accepted business practice in aircraft sales in Japan.

If Lockheed's payments were made in response to extortionate demands, however, it would not be liable for bribery. Extortion entails purposely obtaining property from another, with his consent, that is induced by a wrongful use of force or fear or under color of official right. A strong case can be made, based on the actions of the Japanese officials, that Lockheed was wrongfully induced to make the payments. Rather than a "voluntary" giving of money, as required for the crime of bribery, it appears that Lockheed would not have made the payments if it were not for the insistence of the Japanese officials. As Lockheed President Kotchian indicated,

> such disbursements [all occurred prior to 1977 and] did not violate American laws. . . . Secondly, I should like to emphasize that the payments to the so-called "high Japanese government officials" were all requested by Mr. Okubo and were not brought up from my side. . . . Finally, I want to make it clear that I never discussed money matters with Japanese politicians, government officials, or airline officials. Except for Tanaka and Fukunga, I did not meet any Japanese politicians. . . . The only people with whom money was discussed were Mr. Okubo of Marubeni and Mr. Kodama, our confidential consultant.[48]

Both the convictions of the Japanese officials for soliciting illicit payments, and the U.S. Justice Department's decision not to prosecute Lockheed officials for misconduct (after a three and a half year investigation), lend support to the notion that Lockheed was wrongfully induced to make payments, rather than guilty of voluntarily offering bribes.[49]

Third, the legislative outcome of the Lockheed affair, the Foreign Corrupt Practices Act of 1977, has not accomplished what it was intended to do. Furthermore, this is a fact that should have been anticipated prior to its enactment.

The U.S. General Accounting Office (GAO), the investigative arm of Congress, has evaluated the impact of the Foreign Corrupt Practices Act. The GAO conducted a questionnaire survey of 250 American multinational corporations randomly selected from the *Fortune* 1000 list of the largest U.S. industrial firms. The firms were questioned about the effects of the act's accounting and anti-bribery provisions. To validate these findings, the GAO randomly selected 27 companies from its sample for site visits. The documentation necessary to assess the credibility of the respondents' answers to the objective questions was reviewed.

The results of the GAO's evaluation of the accounting and antibribery provisions of the Foreign Corrupt Practices Act were critical. The act's accounting provisions were found to be so ambiguous that the GAO recommended that the criminal penalties for violations be repealed.

> The accounting provisions call for management judgement covering diverse and oftentimes complex recordkeeping and internal control systems. The provisions, even with additional guidance from SEC on compliance, will, by their nature, still require highly subjective determinations. We view the fear of criminal reprisals for errors and control weaknesses that are not related to improper payments as a reason that companies may incur unnecessary compliance costs, and we, therefore, believe that the criminal penalties should be repealed.[50]

The antibribery provisions of the act have also been difficult to interpret. The GAO discovered several serious consequences of this ambiguity.

> Uncertainty about what constitutes compliance with the anti-bribery provisions may have caused U.S. businesses to forego [sic] legitimate export opportunities. Companies, particularly those which have reported a decrease in overseas business, have significant problems interpreting the anti-bribery provisions. A Justice Department guidance program has yet to alleviate this uncertainty, and it is doubtful it will in its present format. The program has been criticized by some government officials as inadequate and has been used only nominally by business.[51]

These problems with the provisions of the Foreign Corrupt Practices Act have resulted in several proposals for reform. Beginning as early as 1979, there have been legislative efforts to clarify the act, relax its provisions, and even abandon it altogether.[52] These initiatives have had both vehement supporters and critics. The reformers point to the problems confirmed by the GAO report: the act has incurred large compliance costs, has hurt U.S. international business, and has become unenforceable due to the difficulties of prosecuting cases involving the actions of foreign officials in their own countries.[53] On the other hand, critics of these reform efforts claim that the law has not resulted in large losses of U.S. business overseas, the United States should uphold "moral standards" abroad, and U.S. foreign policy interests would be damaged if foreign payments were permitted.[54]

None of the efforts to change the law has yet been successful. As it turns out, the law has been rendered ineffective by the SEC and Justice Department policy of lax enforcement.[55] After six years, the U.S. Department of Justice had brought only 11 prosecutions under the Foreign Corrupt Practices Act, and most of these arose from a single case begun during the late 1970s.[56]

Case Study Questions

1. With which kinds of regulatory offenses was Lockheed corporation charged?
2. Why is the distinction between bribery and extortion important in the Lockheed case?
3. Why has the Foreign Corrupt Practices Act been ineffective?
4. Is there a better way to prevent this kind of corporate behavior in the future?

CRITICAL THINKING EXERCISE

The facts that follow describe an actual case involving the Foreign Corrupt Practices Act, a legislative result of the Lockheed incident. Read the facts of the case, and answer the questions that follow, applying the principles of the Foreign Corrupt Practices Act.

THE CASE OF NAPCO IN NIGER

Richard Leebo was vice president of NAPCO International, a Minnesota company that sold military aerospace equipment worldwide. NAPCO entered into in an agreement with a German contractor, Darnear, to supply parts to maintain aircraft owned by the Niger government. Ironically, the aircraft to be serviced were C-130 cargo planes, the largest airplanes in the world, which are manufactured by Lockheed Corporation.

Leebo and a Darnear representative then flew to Niger to obtain approval from the president of Niger for this maintenance contract. While in Niger, Leebo met with Captain Ali, who was chief of maintenance for the Niger Air Force. Ali testified later that Leebo told him that "some gestures" would be made if he helped to get the contract approved. With the assistance of Ali's cousin Bark, who was the first consular for the Niger Embassy in Washington, D.C., Leebo opened a bank account in Minnesota in a variation of the name of Bark's girlfriend and deposited $30,000 which Bark spent and shared with Ali.

Endnotes

1. Marshall B. Clinard and Peter C. Yeager, *Corporate Crime* (New York: The Free Press, 1983), p. 112.
2. Jon Friedman, "Hutton's Next Step: Takeover?" *USA Today*, May 5, 1986, p. 1B; and Kathy Rebello, "The Rise and Fall of Dennis B. Levine," *USA Today*, June 6, 1986, p. 4B.
3. Dennis B. Levine with William Hoffer, *Inside Out* (New York: Berkley, 1992); and David Poulson, "Inside Trader Starts Serving Time Today," *USA Today*, April 6, 1987, p. 1B.
4. James Sterngold, "Kidder, Peabody Agrees to Settle Insider Charges for $25.3 Million," *The New York Times*, June 5, 1987, p. 1.
5. Donna Rosato, "Case Settled," *USA Today*, October 12, 1992, p. 1D.
6. James Stewart, *Den of Thieves* (New York: Simon & Schuster, 1991).

Bark returned to Niger to be married, and Leebo offered to pay for the airline tickets for his honeymoon as a gift. Leebo paid for the tickets, which cost $2,000, by charging them to NAPCO's Diner's Club account. Shortly thereafter, the third of a series of contracts was approved in the amount of $1.5 million.

To sell military equipment abroad, the contractor must certify that "no rebates, gifts or gratuities have been given contrary to United States law to officers, officials, or employees" of the Niger government. Leebo was charged with violating the Foreign Corrupt Practices Act concerning NAPCO's purchase of the airline tickets for the honeymoon and the related false statement count.

Questions

1. The Foreign Corrupt Practices Act is violated if there is sufficient evidence to establish that payments (in this case the honeymoon tickets) were given to obtain or retain business. Is this the case here?
2. Leebo argued that he did not act "corruptly," as required by the Foreign Corrupt Practices Act, in buying the airline tickets. "Corruptly" means the gift or payment "must be intended to induce the recipient to misuse his official position." Is this the case here?
3. Explain why it can be difficult to distinguish "accepted" business practice from bribery under the Foreign Corrupt Practices Act.

7. Jesse Kornbluth, *Highly Confident: The Crime and Punishment of Michael Milken* (New York: William A. Morrow, 1992).
8. James Kim, "FDIC OKs Milken Settlement," *USA Today*, March 10, 1992, p. 1B; and David Craig, "$500 Million Payout Won't Break Milken," *USA Today*, February 19, 1992, p. 2B.
9. "Lee to Settle with SEC for $25M," *USA Today*, August 3, 1989, p. 1B.
10. Eric D. Randall, "Prudential to Pay $361 Million in Fraud Case," *USA Today*, October 22, 1993, p. 1B.
11. "Aide Sentenced," *USA Today*, July 28, 1992, p. 3.
12. "GE Apologizes," *USA Today*, July 30, 1992, p. 4, and Steven Pearlstein, "'Reformed' GE Faces Spotlight of Scandal," *The Buffalo News*, July 21, 1992, p. D8.
13. "Eastern Charges," *USA Today*, February 14, 1991, p. 5; and Doug Carroll, "Eastern, 10 Execs Charged," *USA Today*, July 26, 1990, p. 2B.

14. *U.S. v. Bilzerian*, 926 F.2d 1285 (2nd Cir. 1991); and Beth Belton, "Bilzerian: 4 Years, $1.5M Fine," *USA Today*, September 28, 1989, p. 1.
15. *U.S. v. Brittain*, 931 F.2d 1413 (10th Cir. 1991), at 1415.
16. "Kodak Fined $2 Million in Waste Case," *USA Today*, April 6, 1990, p. 1B.
17. Jana Mazanec, "Rockwell Critics Hail Guilty Plea," *USA Today*, April 1, 1992, p. 3.
18. Rae Tyson, "EPA Proposes $20 Million in Fines for Waste-Burners," *USA Today*, September 29, 1993, p. 3.
19. Nancy Frank, *Crimes Against Health and Safety* (Albany, NY: Harrow and Heston, 1985), p. 22; and "Employee Murder: 3 Get 25 Years," *USA Today*, July 2, 1985.
20. "San Francisco," *USA Today*, August 15, 1990, p. 8.
21. Cheryl Mattox Berry, "Carbide Safety Hit at Home," *USA Today*, April 2, 1986, p. 1.
22. "Chicken Plant Execs Charged in Deadly Fire," *USA Today*, March 10, 1992, p. 3; see also Rae Tyson and Mark Mayfield, "Experts Cite 10,500 Deaths Every Year," *USA Today*, September 5, 1991, p. 1.
23. "Blast Probe," *USA Today*, November 7, 1989, p. 3.
24. "Safety Fine," *USA Today*, March 22, 1991, p. 3.
25. "Coal-Tampering Case," *USA Today*, April 5, 1991, p. 3.
26. "Asbestos Verdict," *USA Today*, August 16, 1991, p. 3.
27. Julia Lawlor, "Jury Gives RSI Award," *USA Today*, August 24, 1992, p. 1B; see also Tim Friend, "A Rise in Pain from Repetitious Work," *USA Today*, July 30, 1990, p. 5D.
28. Peg Loftus, "The IUD Suffers Another Setback," *USA Today*, April 3, 1986, p. 4D.
29. "Dalkon Shield War," *USA Today*, July 1, 1992, p. 3.
30. Judith Schroer, "Implant Settlement: $4.7 Billion," *USA Today*, September 10, 1993, p. 1.
31. Carolyn Pesce, "Agent Orange Cash Settlements to Be Half What Vets Expected," *USA Today*, May 29, 1985, p. 3.
32. "Consent Decrees," *USA Today*, March 13, 1991, p. 3.
33. Ibid.
34. "Sweet N.Y. Car Deal: $100M for 'Lemons,'" *USA Today*, October 15, 1990, p. 3.
35. John Reilly, "Exxon Fined $2 Billion for Overcharges," *USA Today*, July 2, 1985, p. 1.
36. U.S. Senate Subcommittee on Oversight and Investigation of the Committee on Investigation and Commerce, *Hearings*, 97th Cong., 1st sess. (Washington, D.C.: U.S. Government Printing Office, 1981).
37. "Upstate Milk Cooperatives," *USA Today*, September 15, 1993, p. 6.
38. "GE Fined $1.04 Million for Defense Fraud," *USA Today*, May 14, 1985, p. 1.

39. "Baby Food Companies Fixed Price, Florida Says," *USA Today*, January 4, 1991, p. 3.
40. David Craig, "Award Lifts Cloud from Kodak," *USA Today*, October 15, 1990, p. 3B.
41. Adapted from Jay S. Albanese, "The Lockheed Foreign Payments Case 10 Years Later: Bribery or Extortion?" *International Journal of Comparative and Applied Criminal Justice*, 9, no. 1 (Spring 1985), pp. 111–118; and in Karlhans Liebl, ed., *Internationale Forschungsergebnisse Auf Dem Gebiet Der Wirtschaftskriminalitat* [International Results of Research in Economic Crime] (Freiburg, Germany: Centaurus-Verlagsgesellschaft, 1987).
42. A. Carl Kotchian, *Rikkiedo Jiken* [Lockheed Incident] (published in Japan, 1976), pp. 231, 236.
43. David Boulton, *The Grease Machine* (New York: Harper & Row, 1978); Robert Shaplen, "The Lockheed Incident I and II," *The New Yorker*, January 23 and 30, 1978; and Anthony Sampson, *The Arms Bazaar* (New York: Bantam, 1978).
44. "Tokyo Hears Statements on Lockheed," *The New York Times*, February 15, 1979, p. D9.
45. Steve Lohr, "Tanaka Is Guilty in Bribery Trial," *The New York Times*, October 12, 1983, p. 1.
46. "Transcript of Tanaka Trial," *Asahi Journal*, February 11, 1977, pp. 41–42.
47. "Prosecutor's Opening Statement at Trial of Hashimoto et al. in Tokyo District Court," *Asahi Journal*, February 18, 1977, pp. 93–94; Kotchian, *Rikkiedo Jiken* [Lockheed Incident], p. 195; Boulton, *The Grease Machine*, p. 248; Sampson, *The Arms Bazaar*, p. 266; and Shaplen, "The Lockheed Incident I and II," p. 73.
48. Kotchian, *Rikkiedo Jiken* [Lockheed Incident], pp. 231–232.
49. Wendell Rawls, "U.S. Drops Inquiry on Lockheed Aides," *The New York Times*, February 16, 1979, p. 1.
50. U.S. Comptroller General, *Impact of Foreign Corrupt Practices Act on U.S. Business* (Washington, D.C.: U.S. General Accounting Office, 1981), p. 35.
51. Ibid., p. 47.
52. Philip Taubman, "Carter Unit Recommends Easing of Bribery Law," *The New York Times*, June 12, 1979, p. D1; Philip Taubman, "Bribe Law Defended in Congress," *The New York Times*, June 13, 1979, p. D7; "Senate Eases Foreign Bribery Law," *The New York Times*, November 24, 1981, p. D1; and Jeff Gerth, "Easing of Bribery Law Under Fire," *The New York Times*, April 30, 1984, p. D4.
53. Mark B. Feldman, "To Be Principled in a Cynical World, Within Limits," *The New York Times*, June 28, 1981, p. E5; and Jeff Gerth, "White House Seeks Eased Bribery Act," *The New York Times*, May 21, 1981, p. 1.

54. Philip Taubman, "Second Look at Bribery Law," *The New York Times*, June 17, 1979, p. E5; Karen M. Lissakers, "Again, Why Congress Barred Bribery Abroad," *The New York Times*, June 18, 1982; and "Japanese Morality and Ours," *The New York Times*, October 14, 1983, p. 30.
55. Jeff Gerth, "U.S. Eases Inquiries on Bribery," *The New York Times*, January 14, 1981, p. D4; and Jeff Gerth, "White House Seeks Eased Bribery Act," *The New York Times*, May 21, 1981, p. 1.
56. Jeff Gerth, "Easing of Bribery Law Under Fire," *The New York Times*, April 30, 1984, p. D4.

The Extent of White-Collar Crime

*Most men only commit great crimes because
of their scruples about petty ones.*
— Cardinal de Retz (1718)

The extent of white-collar crime is more difficult to establish than one might think. In the United States there are only two regularly collected sources of national criminal statistics: victimization surveys and the Uniform Crime Reports.

Assessing the True Extent

Victimization surveys are conducted each year and involve interviews with a representative sample of 60,000 households encompassing 120,000 citizens across the country. Unfortunately, they provide no assistance in determining the extent of white-collar crime because they collect information only about the crimes of rape, robbery, assault, burglary, larceny, and motor vehicle theft.

The Uniform Crime Reports, on the other hand, collect information on all crimes reported to the police each year. These crimes include criminal homicide, rape, robbery, assault, burglary, larceny, motor vehicle theft, and arson. Although none of these crimes is characteristically a white-collar crime, the UCR also collects information for 19 other offenses. For these crimes, however, there are no data on incidents known to the police; only arrests for these offenses are reported. Arrests will always underestimate the true extent of any crime, simply because a large number of offenders are never caught.

Arrest Trends

Among the 19 additional offenses recorded by the Uniform Crime Report are the white-collar crimes of embezzlement, forgery and counterfeiting, and fraud. Trends in arrests for these crimes are summarized in Table 6.1.

Arrests are a measure of police activity, rather than criminal activity, so we must be cautious in how we interpret these data. Nevertheless, it is not unlikely that a high correlation exists between offenses known to police and arrests for these crimes. This is because one is not likely to report crimes such as

Table 6.1 White-Collar Crime Arrests (Number and Rate per 100,000)

Offenses	1970	1980	1990
Forgery/counterfeiting	43,833/28.9	72,643/34.9	74,393/38.4
Fraud	76,861/50.7	261,787/125.7	279,776/144.6
Embezzlement	8,172/5.4	7,885/3.8	12,055/6.2

Source: Compiled from Federal Bureau of Investigation, *Crime in the United States* (Washington, D.C.: U.S. Government Printing Office, published annually).

embezzlement, forgery, and fraud until you know you have been victimized, and once you know, you often have a good idea of who victimized you. Therefore, it can be reasonably assumed that reported crimes for these offenses often result in arrests. Without knowing the number of these crimes that were reported, however, it is impossible to know *how close* the numbers of reported crimes are to the number of arrests.

As Table 6.1 indicates, there has been an increase in the number of arrests for all three white-collar crimes considered by the Uniform Crime Reports. The *numbers* of arrests by themselves may provide a misleading picture of arrest trends, however, because simple increases in the population of the United States would lead one to expect an increase in the extent of these crimes and, therefore, to an increase in arrests. As a result, an examination of arrest *rates* (per 100,000 people) for these crimes is a more reliable indicator of arrest trends because it accounts for population growth and, therefore, provides an estimate of personal risk. If the rate per 100,000 increases, it means the *proportion* of those being arrested for these crimes is increasing in society—thereby increasing personal risk.

Trends in arrest rates for the white-collar crimes of embezzlement, forgery, and fraud from 1970 to 1990 can be assessed from the data in Table 6.1. For example, the arrest rate for forgery has increased from 28.9 arrests per 100,000 citizens to 38.4 in the past two decades. This is an increase of 33 percent. Similarly, the arrest rate for fraud has increased from 50.7 per 100,000 to 144.6—an increase of 185 percent. Arrests for the crime of embezzlement have increased more modestly, at a rate of 15 percent during the past 20 years—from 5.4 per 100,000 to 6.2. Again, it is important to keep in mind that these are *arrest* statistics and not *crime* statistics. However, for an extremely large increase in the arrests rate, such as for the crime of fraud, it must be assumed that either enforcement strategies have changed drastically, there has been a precipitous rise in the rate of reports to the police, or else there are many more people committing frauds.

The Extent of Regulatory Offenses

It is unfortunate, but the Uniform Crime Reports' statistics are the only regularly collected white-collar crime figures that currently exist. No agency systematically collects information about the extent of conspiracy, extortion, bribery, perjury, or other white-collar crimes. Regulatory offenses, however, are monitored by many agencies charged with controlling certain types of activity in business and industry. The Environmental Protection Agency, for example, collects information on illegal pollution, dumping, and other environmental violations. The Food and Drug Administration gathers information on violations of packaging, labeling, and health violations involving food and drugs. Unfortunately, no one ever gathers all this information together to examine trends or emerging problem areas.

Only three comprehensive efforts in this regard have ever been attempted. In 1949, Edwin Sutherland examined the extent of regulatory violations among certain types of businesses and industry. In 1978, Goff and Reasons investigated corporate crime in Canada. In 1979, Marshall Clinard headed an investigation that updated Sutherland's pioneering effort in this area.

Sutherland surveyed 70 of the largest corporations in the United States at that time, which consisted largely of manufacturing corporations. He gathered information on the decisions of courts and administrative commissions against these corporations, covering the entire lifespan of each one (which averaged 45 years). The 70 corporations were involved in a total of 980 violations of laws prohibiting restraint of trade, misrepresentation in advertising, infringements of patents and copyrights, unfair trade practices, rebates, and other violations. Each of the 70 corporations had at least 1 or more violations against it, and the average number of violations per corporation was 14. In addition, 60 percent of these corporations had been convicted in criminal court with an average of four convictions each.[1] It is clear from Sutherland's investigation that corporate violations are common and that many engage in this behavior repeatedly.

Goff and Reasons investigated the 50 largest corporations in Canada covering a 21-year period. Every corporation was found to have committed at least one violation with an average of three violations each. The most common types of offenses were unfair trade practices and false advertising.[2]

In 1979, Marshall Clinard et al. updated Sutherland's survey with an even more exhaustive analysis of regulatory violations by corporations. Clinard and his colleagues collected information on all initiated and enforcement actions against 582 of the largest corporations in the United States by 24 different federal regulatory agencies. Therefore, the scope of this survey was much broader than that of both Sutherland and Goff and Reasons. Clinard collected this information only for cases in a single year, however (those arising during 1975–1976), rather than surveying the corporation's life history as Sutherland had. Due to the vast increase in the number of regulatory offenses that have been introduced since the 1940s, Clinard included many offenses that were not illegal in Sutherland's day. Examples of these offenses would include environmental violations, product safety violations, employment discrimination, and many others.

A total of 1,863 federal actions were initiated against the 582 corporations in 1975–1976. Like Sutherland, and Goff and Reasons, most of the corporations surveyed by Clinard were manufacturing corporations, and most of the offenses

Table 6.2   Surveys of Corporate Crime

Surveys of Corporate Crime	Sutherland (1949)	Goff & Reasons (1978)	Clinard (1979)
No. of corporations	70 largest in United States	50 largest in Canada	582 largest in United States
Time span covered	Average 45 years (corp. life span)	21-year period	1-year period
Offenses	All had 1 (av.=14)	All had 1 (av.=3)	60% had 1 (av.=4)
Most common offenses	Unfair trade and labor offenses	Unfair trade and false advertising	Manufacturing and environmental offenses

discovered were of this type. Environmental offenses took a close second, however. Clinard found that more than 60 percent of the corporations he investigated had at least one enforcement action initiated against them during the 1975–1976 period. In addition, 90 percent of corporations in the motor vehicle, drug, and oil refining industries violated the law at least once (and accounted for nearly half of all the violations discovered). The types of offenses committed were largely in the manufacturing, environmental, and labor areas, which accounted for over three-fourths of all actions against the corporations. There was an average of 4.2 actions completed against those corporations that violated the law at least once.[3] Table 6.2 summarizes the results of the three largest surveys of corporate crime.

It can be seen from all three investigations that organizational crimes on the part of corporations are quite common. Furthermore, this conclusion holds true even though none of these investigations involved a search for *all* possible types of corporate crimes. They limited themselves to certain types of regulatory offenses and court decisions. Until greater effort is devoted to collecting information about the true extent and trends in the commission of organizational forms of criminal behavior, it will remain extremely difficult to gauge the success of strategies designed to prevent its occurrence.

Other Indicators of White-Collar Crime

Other, less comprehensive, indicators of the extent of white-collar crime are complaint and conviction statistics, and other data describing criminal justice system activity. For example, the number of appointed or elected public officials convicted in federal, state, or local courts for offenses involving abuse of their office totaled 44 nationwide in 1970. By 1990, that number had risen to 1,084.[4] The number of federal criminal antitrust suits filed in federal court tripled between 1960 and 1982, as did the number of mail fraud complaints to the U.S. Postal Service.[5]

As one might expect, given the savings and loan bank scandal of recent years, investigations by the Federal Bureau of Investigation in this area have increased dramatically. The number of failed financial institutions under investigation rose from 202 in 1986 to 670 in 1991, a threefold increase. The number of convictions where the loss was $100,000 or more also rose from 533 in 1986 to 986 in 1991.[6]

Counterfeiting operations suppressed by the U.S. Secret Service rose from 78 in 1980 to 148 in 1991, a 90 percent increase.[7] Arrests by the U.S. Postal Inspection Service have increased from 5,358 to 13,513 in ten years, a 250 percent increase.[8]

On the other hand, arrests for forgery, fraud, embezzlement, bribery, and other fraud-related crimes in a sample of six states showed only a 1.3 percent increase between 1983 and 1988.[9] Cases initiated by the Internal Revenue Service Criminal Investigation Division for tax fraud have declined by 10 percent in the last decade.[10]

Similar to arrest statistics in the Uniform Crime Reports, these indicators of official activity are not reliable measures of crime,[11] but they do provide, at minimum, an indication of growing concern about the seriousness of white-collar crime. It is difficult to distinguish, however, trends that result from changes in criminal activity from those that result from changes in staffing levels, agency priorities, and the discretion of prosecutors.

The Impact of White-Collar Crime

A major problem with these selective and sporadic counts of white-collar crimes and arrests is that they implicitly suggest that white-collar crime is not as serious as conventional crimes (which we take exhaustive measures to count accurately). This implicit assumption is not true, of course, using any available indicator.

The Costs of White-Collar Crime

Estimated economic losses from street crimes run about $10 billion per year, according to the UCR, but the losses from white-collar crime are approximately $200 billion, or 20 times as high.[12] Likewise, there are approximately 20,000 criminal homicides in the United States each year, but another 14,000 workers are killed on the job, and a further 2 million are injured at work due to dangerous working conditions. Furthermore, it is estimated that 100,000 workers die each year from illnesses resulting from health and safety violations by corporations.[13]

In a review of job-related accidents, James Messerschmidt found more than one-third were the direct result of employer safety violations.[14] Schraeger and Short had a similar finding in a study of industrial accidents.[15] As Kappeler, Blumberg, and Potter conclude, "all the violent crime, all the property crime, all the crime we concentrate our energy and resources on combatting is less of a threat, less of a danger, and less of a burden to society than the crime committed by corporations [and] white-collar crime."[16]

Victims of White-Collar Crime

White-collar crime victims, historically, have drawn comparatively little concern. This is due to the immediate contact between offender and victim in street crimes, making issues of injury, blame, punishment, and compensation more straightforward. Victims of white-collar crimes, on the other hand, rarely know when they have been victimized, injury is often spread among many others, and the harm can occur years after the illegal act. These circumstances serve to work against the immediacy of white-collar crime victimization.

Several notorious cases in recent years have done much to enhance the visibility and concern over victims of white-collar crime. Toxic dumping at Love Canal, Ford Pinto explosions, injuries caused by the Dalkon Shield, many large-scale financial frauds, and other cases described in this book have served to publicize the problem and to raise a groundswell of support on behalf of victims of these incidents. Unfortunately, this concern has translated into very little action. Walsh and Schram noted how victims of white-collar crime cases often are subjected to blame for their own victimization.[17] The Dalkon Shield case, summarized in Chapter 10, provides an example of this phenomenon. Complaining victims often get little satisfaction for their trouble. "Callous indifference" to complainants, and "bureaucratic," "slow," and "disorganized" responses from government or corporate officials appear to be the norm, even given the heightened awareness of white-collar crime in recent years.[18] Perhaps the most important lesson learned from notorious cases of white-collar crime is that they "produce far more destruction and cost than conventional crime."[19] In addition, white-collar crimes diminish faith in a free economy, trust in government, and erode public morality.[20]

The future for victims of white-collar crime is not clear. Although public perceptions of the seriousness of white-collar crime are high, they are not uniform. Studies in both the United States and Canada show white-collar crime ranked as very serious when it involves violence and physical impact, but consensus for other white-collar offenses varies.[21] Existing victim compensation programs deal primarily with victims of street crimes and usually have far more legitimate claims than they do funds. White-collar victims generally have little other recourse, unless a court settlement provides for victim compensation and the corporation remains solvent. The case study of Love Canal in this chapter graphically illustrates the problems faced by victims and how effective remedies are not imminent.

Summary

This chapter has presented what little is known about the extent, seriousness, and impact of white-collar crimes on victims. There is a surprisingly small amount of systematic information on the extent of the problem. Cases of misconduct appear regularly, but the extent to which these cases are the exception to the rule is not clear. Until both the public and the government see white-collar crime as a problem of equal significance to conventional crimes, we will not achieve a comprehensive understanding of the extent of the problem. Our ability to launch and gauge intervention and prevention strategies will suffer as a result.

CASE STUDY

Several case studies are presented in this book to illustrate issues of law, causation, and adjudication. The case that follows demonstrates why the answers to simple questions, such as the nature, extent, and responsibility for white-collar violations, are rather complex. Read the case carefully, and answer the questions that follow it, applying the principles from this chapter and from earlier sections.

Love Canal
Problems in Understanding the Nature, Extent, and Responsibility for Corporate Actions

It was 1894 when William T. Love began digging a canal that he hoped would join the Niagara River to Lake Ontario by circumventing Niagara Falls. Because direct-current power was the only way to generate electricity at the time, William Love believed that his proposed canal would spur the development of a model city whose cheap hydroelectric power would make it an ideal site for industry.

Before Love's canal was very far along, however, an electrical engineer, Louis Tesla, developed a practical way of producing alternating-current electricity. Because alternating current could be transmitted over great distances, it was no longer necessary for industry to be located near a water supply to generate cheap electricity. This breakthrough caused Love's backers to desert his project, and the Love Canal property was sold at a public auction in 1910.

In 1940, Hooker Chemical Company bought part of the Love Canal site and used it to dump chemical wastes from 1947 to 1952. As it turned out, the 12-acre trench that Love left behind was an ideal spot to bury wastes.

> The company considered the old canal bed, 3 meters deep and 18 meters wide, an excellent disposal site because it was dug into a layer of clay, a material through which liquids flow slowly, if at all. In some places, Hooker dug deeper to increase the amount of waste it could deposit there. In all, about 20,000 metric tons of waste in old metal drums was buried and then covered with clay that previously had been removed from the site. The clay created a sealed "vault" that was expected to hold the chemicals securely.[22]

Evidence has also been found indicating that the U.S. Army used the site to dump wastes during this period.[23] In 1953, Hooker sold the Love Canal property to the Niagara School Board for one dollar. The deed contained a waiver of responsibility for any injuries that might result from the buried chemicals.

Nearly 1,000 families were evacuated from the Love Canal neighborhood near Niagara Falls, New York, due to high levels of hazardous waste detected there. Several hundred homes in the "inner rings" nearest the former dumpsite were bulldozed into their foundations and covered over. *(UPI/Bettmann)*

The fact that the deed included a disclaimer of Hooker's responsibility for any injury was certainly a factor in the widespread perception that Hooker had tricked the Niagara School Board. A look at the final paragraph of the deed, however, leads to a somewhat different conclusion.

> Prior to the delivery of this instrument of conveyance, the grantee herein has been advised by the grantor that the premises above have been filled, in whole or in part, to the present grade level thereof with waste products resulting from the manufacturing of chemicals by the grantor at its plant in the City of Niagara Falls, New York, and the grantee assumes all risk and liability incident to the use thereof. It is therefore understood and agreed that, as a part of the consideration for this conveyance and as a condition thereof, no claim, suit, action or demand of any nature whatsoever shall ever be made of the grantee, its successors or assigns, for injury to a person or persons, including death resulting therefrom, or loss of or damage to property caused by, in connection with or by reason of the presence of said industrial wastes. It is further agreed as a condition hereof that each subsequent conveyance of the aforesaid lands shall be made subject to the foregoing provisions and conditions.

As this portion of the deed indicates, Hooker appeared to be honest in its description of the property. Contrary to popular opinion, Hooker acknowledged the fact that chemical "waste products" were buried there that could cause "injury" or "death." This accurate description of the property is preceded by the company's disclaimer, which is common in property sales. At the end of the paragraph, however, Hooker adds that "each subsequent conveyance" of the property must include the warning that potentially dangerous chemicals are buried there. Therefore, Hooker was apparently concerned that if the school board, or subsequent owners, resold the land, innocent third parties might be unaware of the potential hazard.

Furthermore, as investigative journalist Eric Zuesse was to discover later, Hooker also made sure that school board representatives actually inspected the site before buying it.

> Hooker had escorted them to the canal site and in their presence made eight test borings into the protective clay cover that the company had laid over the Canal, and into the surrounding area. At two spots, directly over Hooker's wastes, chemicals were encountered four feet below the surface. At the other spots, to the sides of the Canal proper, no chemicals showed up.
>
> So whether or not the School Board was of a mind to inspect the Canal, Hooker had gone out of its way to make sure that they *did* inspect it and that they did see that *chemicals* lay buried in that Canal.[24]

It is also interesting to note that Hooker's sale of the canal property was not entirely voluntary. Niagara School Board records indicate that plans for building the 99th Street School on the Love Canal site were developed two years before it was purchased. In addition, the school board had threatened to condemn the property and seize it under eminent domain if Hooker refused to sell it.[25] Placed in this position, Hooker attempted, unsuccessfully, to sell it only if the canal site was used as a park.

> Hooker wanted to require that the donated premises "be used for park purposes only, in conjunction with a school building to be constructed upon premises "in proximity to" them. And it wanted the Board to agree that, should the property ever cease serving as a park, title to it would revert to Hooker. Instead of these restrictions, which the Board rejected, the company had to settle for the liability provisions and warnings in the last paragraph of the deed hammered out in meetings between Hooker and Board representatives.[26]

The attorney for the school board also wrote a letter to the board, warning them that the deed places liability upon the school board for any damages that arise from the canal property. In spite of this warning, however, the school board unanimously accepted the deed to Love Canal in May 1963 and built the 99th Street School on the site.

Hooker provided additional evidence of its concern over the use of the Love Canal property in 1957. In that year, the Niagara School Board, which was in financial difficulty, considered selling some of the unused canal property to developers who planned to build homes. Once again, Hooker strongly resisted the use of the land in this manner. A letter from Hooker's vice president and general counsel to the school board president in November 1957 expressed this concern.

It is our feeling that even though great care might be taken at this time in the construction of buildings on the property that as time passes the possible hazards might be overlooked with the result that injury to either persons or property might result. It is our primary purpose in calling these facts to your attention to avoid the possibility of any damage to any one or to any one's property at any time in the future and we feel that the only way that this can be assured is by using only the surface of the land. We still feel very strongly that the subsoil conditions make it very undesirable and possibly hazardous if excavations are to be made therein and urge most strongly that arrangements be made to use the property for the purposes intended, since we also feel that additional park or recreational facilities in this area are very desirable.[27]

Hooker's plea was successful this time, and the school board's tie vote defeated the resolution to sell the property to developers.

The victory was a hollow one, however, because late in 1957, and again in 1960, the city of Niagara Falls installed sanitary and storm sewers 10 feet below the surface of a new street that was to be paved across the middle of the canal site. Placed on gravel beds, these sewers probably violated the waste storage area and allowed for the escape of chemicals.

In 1960, the school board donated the canal property north of the school to the city of Niagara Falls and, in 1961, auctioned the southern portion for $1,200 to a private citizen. In 1972, the city ordered the owner to do something about the "strong chemical odors permeating from the ground surface," and after spending $13,000 on the property, he sold it to a friend for $100.[28] Following several seasons of above-average precipitation, serious health problems began to appear.

It was August 2, 1978, when the New York State Health Commissioner, acting on studies finding a very high incidence of cancer and other diseases, declared a health emergency at the Love Canal site. The commissioner recommended that children under the age of 2, as well as pregnant women, be evacuated from homes in the area and that the 99th Street School remain closed in September.

Five days later, President Carter declared the Love Canal site a federal disaster area, and the state of New York began to buy nearly 240 abandoned homes at a cost of $10 million. In August 1979, the Niagara School Board voted to close a second area school due to chemical contamination.

The problems at Love Canal continued in 1980 when further tests of area residents by the EPA were said to reveal genetic damage that could result in cancer and birth defects.[29] These findings led President Carter to declare a second federal emergency in May 1980, which resulted in the evacuation of an additional 710 families.

In 1982, tests conducted by New York State found dioxin (a chemical that has been linked to cancer, birth defects, and disorders of the nervous system) in abandoned homes in the Love Canal neighborhood to be "among the highest ever found in the human environment."[30] A few days later, the EPA released its report claiming that only the houses of the "inner rings" closest to the former canal site were uninhabitable and that families could move back into the other homes. The controversy was rekindled, however, when it was found that only 4 of the EPA's 11 consultants would say they "absolutely" supported this position. Six said they did not support the conclusion at all.[31] In late 1982, the 226 homes on the "inner rings" were bulldozed into their foundations and covered over.

Legal Issues

On December 20, 1979, the U.S. Department of Justice initiated a $124.5 million civil suit against Hooker Chemicals and Plastics Corporation charging it with dumping chemical wastes at four different sites in Niagara Falls. On April 28, 1980, the New York State attorney general filed a $635 million lawsuit against Occidental Petroleum Corporation and its subsidiary (Hooker Chemical) charging them with responsibility for the problems and cleanup at Love Canal.

Given the facts of the case, it is not clear that Hooker acted irresponsibly in its handling on the Love Canal property. If responsibility is to be properly assessed, it appears that the school board and the city of Niagara Falls failed to act cautiously, or to follow warnings, regarding the use of the former canal site. Interestingly, both the federal and state suits are against Hooker rather than the city or the school board. (The city and board are named in the suits, but only to ensure their cooperation with any remedial measures that may be ordered on their property.) Perhaps the most important reason for the continuing legal entanglement surrounding Love Canal, therefore, is the fact the lawsuits may be misdirected.

The avenues for legal action in cases like Love Canal are surprisingly limited. It was not until 1976 when Congress passed the Resource Conservation and Recovery Act (RCRA) that legislation was available to protect land, food, and drinking water from environmental pollution. Subtitle C of RCRA regulates the identification, transportation, generation, disposal, and inspection of hazardous wastes. Violators of the provisions are liable (when violations are not corrected within a specified period) for civil penalties of up to $25,000 per day of noncompliance, as well as revocation of their waste permit. Persons who knowingly transport, dispose, or falsely represent any document relating the hazardous waste are subject to criminal fines of up to $25,000 per day of violation, as well as imprisonment for up to one year. A second conviction subjects the offender to penalties of up to $50,000 per day and two years' imprisonment.

Although the RCRA was passed in October 1976, and the EPA was required to administer regulations to implement Subtitle C within 18 months, the EPA did not do so for 4 years. Following a suit against the EPA by two environmental groups, a federal judge set new dates for implementation in 1979. It was November 1980, however, before the EPA implemented the first of its regulations under RCRA, much to the dismay of the U.S. Senate, which found the EPA's justifications for the delay as "lacking in merit."[32] The EPA regulations now require handlers of hazardous wastes to register with the EPA and to comply with a reporting system that tracks the movement of wastes from their generation to their disposal.

Prosecution and Defense

Numerous problems exist that preclude effective prosecution of hazardous waste violators, regardless of the defendant charged. First, and most significant, is the lack of knowledge of the true risk and long-term effects of exposure to various types of hazardous chemicals. As the General Accounting Office has explained,

> The scientific data base is deficient in dealing with hazardous waste problems. Current sampling and analytical methods are not standardized or validated.... EPA's ability to assess the risks posed by hazardous waste dumpsites is also deficient. Little is known concerning how far and how fast wastes may move from dump sites to affect the populace and how long wastes may persist in hazardous forms.... Without fairly quick, inexpensive methods to identify hazards and assess risks, it will become increasingly difficult for EPA to manage the problem. Setting priorities for site investigations, undertaking enforcement actions, and determining appropriate cleanup measures depend upon knowledge that the scientific community cannot sufficiently provide at this time.[33]

A second problem is that the EPA does not know what resources are required to investigate suspected violations, nor is it sure of the number of sites that must be investigated. The incredibly high rate of discovery of new hazardous waste sites has compounded the problem.

> Since 1979 EPA has increased it efforts and resources to investigate and evaluate hazardous waste sites. These efforts, however, have not enabled EPA to perform work at thousands of sites that must be investigated and evaluated. Over 3,400 sites existing at December 31, 1980, had not had preliminary assessments performed or final strategy determinations made.
>
> EPA's fiscal year 1981 budget projected that funding would be sufficient to perform initial investigations on 500 sites and full investigations at 70 sites. At the end of 1980, EPA was identifying new potential hazardous waste sites at a rate of over 400 per month.[34]

Finally, litigation is time consuming and expensive, and the possibility of harm is often difficult to prove, thereby limiting prosecutions.

In December 1980, however, after being overwhelmingly approved by Congress, President Carter signed into law the Comprehensive Environmental Response, Compensation and Liability Act of 1980, which established a $1.6 billion "superfund" to be administered by the EPA to clean up sites such as Love Canal. Nearly 90 percent of this money was to be raised through an excise tax on chemical companies. In addition, this legislation allows the government to sue to recover money spent from the fund, and it makes those illegally disposing hazardous substances liable to pay for the clean-up. The existence of this fund allows the EPA to clean up waste sites first, and then to recover the costs from those responsible later. The superfund also allows the government to clean-up sites where the violator is unknown, no longer exists, is unable to pay for the clean-up, or declares bankruptcy. Further, it provides funds for a program of investigation and enforcement actions against environmental law violators.

Although the superfund has provided some immediate relief in providing for clean-ups prior to court settlements, several serious prosecution problems remain.

> Although EPA's enforcement activities are attempting to force companies to clean up hazardous waste sites, this is only a partial solution. By showing "potential" harm, EPA decreases time and money for litigation, though substantial evidence is still required to sustain risk or harm arguments, and may obtain some timely relief by settling out of court. However, with current resource levels, EPA estimated that only 40 to 50 enforcement actions a year could be filed, while the number of sites with enforcement potential is ever increasing.
>
> The superfund legislation will aid EPA in taking more timely and effective clean-up action at more sites than is now possible. Although the legislation provides $1.6 billion over the next five years, it is difficult to say how many sites can be acted upon because of varying factors, such as costs of clean-up at individual sites and how often payments from the fund will be reimbursed from responsible parties. If EPA is forced to go to court for this reimbursement, past experience has shown that court cases have been limited by both the resources needed to pursue cases and the time it takes to ultimately resolve them.[35]

As a result, an alternative must be found to the slow and resource-consuming problems of hazardous waste litigation.

Outcome

According to the EPA, nearly 57 million tons of hazardous wastes are produced each year by industries across the country. Further, these corrosive, flammable, or toxic wastes do not include radioactive waste products, which are monitored by the Nuclear Regulatory Commission (which has not yet come up with a permanent disposal method for radioactive waste). Clearly, an effective prevention strategy designed to stop the illegal generation, transportation, or disposal of these wastes will not be modest.

The "superfund" legislation does not allow individuals to sue the fund for damages caused by exposure to toxic wastes. Victims can, individually, sue a company for damages, but as one commentator has noted, "such lawsuits are usually very expensive and can go on for years."[36] This is because individuals must generally pursue compensation under the provisions of common law.

Under common law, an individual can initiate a civil suit in hazardous waste cases using several different strategies, including negligence (where the responsible party should have been aware of a substantial and unjustifiable risk), strict liability (where the nature of the activity, i.e., toxic waste dumping, has a great possibility for harm and those engaged in it are criminally liable for legal violations whether or not they had intent), nuisance (knowingly or recklessly creating or maintaining a condition that endangers the health or safety of others), or trespass. To successfully invoke any of these claims, however, it is necessary for the damaged party to (1) locate the source of the hazard, (2) quantify its presence, (3) establish its migration from the source to the damaged property or person, (4) demonstrate the defendant's responsibility for it, and (5) provide evidence of a link between the hazard and the damage suffered. This is an incredibly difficult burden of proof for any individual, which is expensive, time consuming, and, in some cases, impossible.

> Faced with this tremendous burden of proof, individuals may be discouraged from pursuing legal relief for health damages from hazardous waste. The likelihood of adequate relief is dim because such litigation may take years, providing the scientific–technical evidence is expensive, civil procedures cannot provide immediate relief, delays may lead to inadequate out-of-court settlements, total damages may be greater than the polluter's ability to pay, workers' compensation laws cannot apply since there is no clear-cut cause–effect link, some injuries may take decades to manifest themselves, and state laws may apply a statute of limitation which would put a time limit on liability.[37]

This is an especially significant problem because in cases such as Love Canal, where the responsibility may lie with a governmental body, who can citizens sue to recover damages? Governments obtain their money through taxes, so a successful claim will likely be recovered through tax increases. Therefore, when governmental bodies become defendants, citizens can only sue "themselves" inasmuch as they are the source of the government's assets. This situation makes the inability of citizens to sue the superfund for damages an especially serious problem.

Unfortunately, the legacy of the Love Canal disaster continues more than 15 years after its discovery. In 1983, the EPA discovered a "significant migration of chemicals" beyond a proposed containment wall and declared a "total review" was needed of their 1982 determination of habitability.

In 1988, ten years after the health emergency was first declared, the New York State health commissioner said three-fourths of the Love Canal area was now safe to live in, but the rest of the neighborhood may never be safe. To that point, the total cost for clean-up and evacuation of 717 families was $250 million.[38] Then in, 1989, resettlement of the Love Canal neighborhood was delayed due to toxic chemicals found in an area thought to be clean.[39]

In 1990, 12 years after the original health emergency, 200 homes in the Love Canal neighborhood were put up for sale. About two-thirds of the ten-square-block area around the dump site was ruled to be habitable.[40] Within a year, however, two major hotspots of contaminated soil were found in and around streets where homes were for sale. It was estimated that it could cost another $10 million to remove 65,000 cubic yards of soil from these hotspots.[41]

Ironically, a federal trial to determine liability for the Love Canal disaster began in 1990 at the same time as the resettlement. The federal government sought $250 million in punitive damages from Occidental Chemical Corporation, the parent company to Hooker Chemical. Occidental has denied wrongdoing.[42] After two years' deliberation, the federal court in 1994 found no cause to hold Occidental liable for these damages.

Case Study Questions

1. With which white-collar offenses could Hooker Chemical Company have been charged?

2. What is the likelihood of detection in a case like this?
3. How does Hooker's defense differ from prosecution claims of responsibility?
4. What has been done to prevent this sort of problem in the future? Are these measures likely to be effective?

Endnotes

1. Edwin H. Sutherland, *White-Collar Crime* (New York: The Dryden Press, 1949).
2. Colin Goff and Charles Reasons, *Corporate Crime in Canada* (Scarborough, Ontario: Prentice Hall, 1978).
3. Marshall B. Clinard et al., *Illegal Corporate Behavior* (Washington, D.C.: U.S. Government Printing Office, 1979).
4. Timothy Flanagan and Kathleen Maguire, eds., *Sourcebook of Criminal Justice Statistics—1991* (Washington, D.C.: U.S. Government Printing Office, 1992), p. 577.
5. Georgette Bennett, *Crime-Warps: The Future of Crime in America* (Garden City, NY: Anchor Press, 1987).
6. Flanagan and Maguire, *Sourcebook of Criminal Justice Statistics—1991*, p. 407.
7. Ibid., p. 487.
8. Ibid., p. 563.
9. U.S. Department of Justice, *Forgery and Fraud-Related Offenses in 6 States, 1983–88* (Washington, D.C.: Bureau of Justice Statistics, 1992).
10. Flanagan and Maguire, *Sourcebook of Criminal Justice Statistics—1991*, p. 562.
11. Harold E. Pepinsky and Paul Jesilow, *Myths That Cause Crime*, 2nd ed. (Cabin John, MD: Seven Locks Press, 1985), p. 34.
12. Marshall B. Clinard and Peter Yeager, *Corporate Crime* (New York: The Free Press, 1980), p. 8.
13. Ronald C. Kramer, "Corporate Criminality: The Development of an Idea," *Corporations as Criminals*, ed. by Ellen Hochstedler (Beverly Hills, CA: Sage Publications, 1984), p. 19.
14. James W. Messerschmidt, *Capitalism, Patriarchy, and Crime: Toward a Socialist Feminist Criminology* (Totowa, NJ: Rowman and Littlefield, 1986), p. 100.
15. Laura S. Schraeger and James F. Short, "Toward a Sociology of Organizational Crime," *Social Problems*, 25 (April 1978), p. 413.
16. Victor E. Kappeler, Mark Blumberg, and Gary W. Potter, *The Mythology of Crime and Justice* (Prospect Heights, IL: Waveland Press, 1993), p. 103.
17. Marilyn E. Walsh and Donna D. Schram, "The Victim of White-Collar Crime: Accuser or Accused?" in *White-Collar Crime: Theory and*

Research, ed. by Gilbert Geis and Ezra Stotland (Beverly Hills, CA: Sage Publications, 1980), pp. 32–51.

18. Gilbert Geis, "Victimization Patterns in White-Collar Crime," *Victimology: A New Focus*, Vol. 5, ed. by I. Drapkin and E. Viano (Lexington, MA: Lexington Books, 1975), pp. 89–105; Gilbert Geis, "Defrauding the Elderly," *Crime and the Elderly*, ed. by J. Goldsmith and S. Goldsmith (Lexington, MA: Lexington Books, 1976), pp. 7–19; and Eric H. Steele, "Fraud, Dispute and the Consumer: Responding to Consumer Complaints," *University of Pennsylvania Law Review*, 123 (1975), 1107–1186.

19. Robert Elias, *The Politics of Victimization* (New York: Oxford University Press, 1986), p. 115.

20. Elizabeth Moore and Michael Mills, "The Neglected Victims and Unexamined Costs of White-Collar Crime," *Crime & Delinquency*, 36 (July 1990), pp. 408–418.

21. Colin Goff and Nancy Nason-Clark, "The Seriousness of Crime in Frederickton, New Brunswick: Perceptions Toward White-Collar Crime," *Canadian Journal of Criminology*, 31 (January 1989), pp. 19–34; Francis T. Cullen, B. G. Link, and C. W. Polanzi, "The Seriousness of Crime Revisited: Have Attitudes Towards White-Collar Crime Changed?" *Criminology*, 20 (1982), pp. 83–102; Peter H. Rossi, E. Waite, C. E. Bose, and R. E. Berk, "The Seriousness of Crimes: Normative Structure and Individual Differences," *American Sociological Review*, 39 (1974), pp. 224–237.

22. Irene Kiefer, *Poisoned Land: The Problem of Hazardous Waste* (New York: Atheneum, 1981), pp. 30–31.

23. New York State Assembly Task Force on Toxic Substances, *Inquiry into the Love Canal and Related Matters* (Albany: Special Majority Task Force of the New York State Assembly, 1980).

24. Eric Zuesse, "Love Canal: The Truth Seeps Out," *Reason*, February 1981, p. 19.

25. Ansley Wilcox, "Letter to Dr. Charles M. Brent, President, Board of Education, Re: 99th Street Property" (Niagara Falls, NY: Hooker Electrochemical Company, November 21, 1957).

26. Zuesse, "Love Canal: The Truth Seeps Out," p.22.

27. Wilcox, "Letter to Dr. Charles M. Brent," 1957.

28. Zuesse, "Love Canal: The Truth Seeps Out," p. 26.

29. For a review, see Gina B. Kolata, "Love Canal: False Alarm Caused by Botched Study," *Science*, 208 (June 1980); Adeline G. Levine, *Love Canal: Science, Politics, and People* (Lexington, MA: Lexington Books, 1980), p. 153; and Margery W. Shaw, "Love Canal Chromosome Study," *Science*, 209 (August 1980).

30. E. J. Dionne, "Ultrahigh Level of Poison Cited at Love Canal," *The New York Times*, July 13, 1982, p. B1.

31. Rae Tyson and Louis Peck, "Canal Report Controversy Continues," *Niagara Gazette*, July 17, 1982, p. 1.

32. U.S. Senate Committee on Governmental Affairs, Subcommittee on Oversight of Government Management, *Report on Hazardous Waste Management and the Implementation of the Resource Conservation and Recovery Act* (Washington, D.C.: U.S. Government Printing Office, 1980).
33. U.S. Comptroller General, *Hazardous Waste Sites Pose Investigation, Evaluation, Scientific, and Legal Problems* (Washington, D.C.: U.S. General Accounting Office, 1981), p. 33.
34. Ibid.
35. Ibid., pp. 42–43.
36. Philip Shabecoff, "Senate Votes, 78-9, A $16 Billion Fund on Chemical Wastes," *The New York Times*, November 25, 1980, p. 1.
37. U.S. Comptroller General, *Hazardous Waste Sites Pose Investigation, Evaluation, Scientific, and Legal Problems*, p. 47.
38. "Most of Love Canal Declared Safe Area," *USA Today*, September 28, 1988, p. 3.
39. "More Love Canal Problems," *USA Today*, March 7, 1989, p. 3; "Love Canal," *USA Today*, March 7, 1989, p. 3; and Paul MacClennan, "New Hot Spot Renews Old Questions About Love Canal," *The Buffalo News*, March 19, 1989, p. E5.
40. Paul MacClennan, "EPA Chief's Decision Clears Way for Resettlement of Love Canal," *The Buffalo News*, May 15, 1990, p.1; and Paul MacClennan, "More of Love Canal Area May Be Livable," *The Buffalo News*, November 10, 1990, p. C1.
41. Paul MacClennan, "Love Canal Cleanup May Take 2 More Years, Another $10 Million," *The Buffalo News*, March 6, 1991, p. B1.
42. Dan Herbeck, "Love Canal Trial Starts in U.S. Court," *The Buffalo News*, October 24, 1990, p. 1.

The Causes of White-Collar Crime

If the camel once gets his nose in the tent,
his body will soon follow.
— Arabic Proverb

When a crime occurs, or a suspect is arrested, for fraud, illegal toxic dumping, or other serious offense, people want to know, "How could somebody do that?" Why do individuals find it necessary to engage in crime to enrich themselves, their company, or to gain some other advantage? Most people respond by saying, "Greed!" But greed, of course, explains nothing. There are many greedy people who do not break the law, and what makes a person greedy anyway? Such "explanations" do nothing more than provide a rationalization to the observer without giving the problem more serious thought.

Classical and Positivistic Approaches

Serious efforts to explain crime, historically, are of two types. One type of explanation emphasizes rational decision making. According to this view, people freely choose to violate the law, because it brings them pleasure (usually financial gain or advantage) and the prospect of pain (i.e., apprehension) is low. This "pain–pleasure" principle runs through much of the criminological literature and is known as the "classical" school of thought.[1]

The other type of explanation places more emphasis on factors that influence the offender to act in a certain way. Whether illicit behavior is learned from others, or is promoted by social or economic social conditions, these explanations generally look outside the individual for the causes of crime.[2] According to these theories, crime will be reduced only through mitigating the influences that promote criminal behavior. This is known as "positivism" in criminology. Neither of these explanations has proven entirely satisfactory in explaining white-collar crime, and an alternative approach is proposed here.

Differential Association

The person who invented the term "white-collar crime" was sociologist Edwin Sutherland, who wrote a book of the same name in 1949. He claimed that these crimes are learned in the same way as one learns anything else: by association with those who approve of such illicit behavior and by isolation from those who perceive it unfavorably. Sutherland argued that white-collar crimes occur "if and only if, the weight of favorable definitions [to crime] exceeds the weight of the unfavorable definitions."[3]

An example provided by Sutherland of this theory called "differential association" was an interview with a shoe salesman who recounted a lecture given him by the shoe store manager.

> My job is to move out shoes, and I hire you to assist in this. I am perfectly glad to fit a person with a pair of shoes if we have his size, but I am willing to misfit him if it is necessary in order to sell him a pair of shoes. I expect you to do the same. If you do not like this, someone else can have your job. While you are working for me, I expect you to have no scruples about how you sell shoes.[4]

Through this example, Sutherland hoped to illustrate how otherwise conforming individuals "learned" to bend or break the rules. Sutherland also demonstrated how illicit practices flourish when *isolated* from definitions unfavorable to crime.

> The accounting firm for which I work is respected, and there is none better in the city. On my first assignment I discovered some irregularities in the books of the firm, and these would lead anyone to question the financial policies of that firm. When I showed my report to the manager of our accounting firm, he said that it was not part of my assignment, and I should leave it out. Although I was confident that the business firm was dishonest, I had to conceal this information. Again and again I have been compelled to do the same thing in other assignments. I get so disgusted with things of this sort that I wish I could leave the profession. I guess I must stick to it, for it is the only occupation for which I have training.[5]

When confined to the level just described, it can be argued that the illicit behavior in question is still the misbehavior of an individual, and not corporate criminality. A distinction must be made, however, between those goals pursued by the individual and those goals supported or encouraged by the organization.

As organization theorist James Thompson explains, "Organizational goals are established by individuals—but interdependent individuals who collectively have sufficient control of organizational resources to commit them in certain areas and to withhold them from others."[6] This group of interdependent individuals is called by Thompson the *dominant coalition* of the organization, and this coalition remains dominant only for as long as it has the power to force the organization to function in accord with its goals. Such a concept is very important because it distinguishes the actions of an individual against an organization from those actions taken in accord with organizational goals.

As Lawrence Sherman pointed out in a study of police corruption, "where deviant acts by organizational members are condoned and even expected by the dominant coalition, the deviance is organizational; the organization is deviant."[7]

Such a distinction between the acts of individuals and the acts of organizations helps to clarify the boundary between individual deviance and corporate deviance.[8] In both of Sutherland's examples, therefore, the deviance, although committed by an individual, is actually corporate deviance, because it is committed in support of organizational goals.

A third component of Sutherland's concept of differential association is that illicit practices are learned by *competitors*, in the same way they are learned by organization members. False advertising in the food industry is used as an example.

> When I got members of the firm off in a corner, and we were talking confidentially, they frankly deplored the misrepresentations in their advertisements. At the same time they said it was necessary to advertise in this manner to attract the attention of customers and sell their products. Since other firms are making extravagant claims regarding their products, we must make extravagant claims regarding our products. A mere statement of fact regarding our products would make no impression on customers in the face of the ads of other firms.[9]

The "snowball" effect of differential association becomes apparent as new organizational members learn illicit practices that are, in turn, learned by competitors.

While Sutherland admitted his theory was not a comprehensive explanation of white-collar crime, it is one of the few theories to have been subsequently retested on numerous occasions. Differential association has been employed in attempts to explain violations of price and rent regulations during World War II,[10] violations of labor relations and fair trade laws in the shoe industry,[11] price-fixing among electrical equipment manufacturers,[12] and the foreign payments of American multinational corporations in pursuit of sales overseas.[13] None of these studies found conclusive support for the differential association hypothesis, but all found at least partial support for it.

The consensus among the studies was that differential association appears to explain the propagation of illegal practices in a particular business within a market much more satisfactorily than it explains its origin. That is to say, each study found evidence of both the learning and diffusion of illegal practices, but as Clinard notes, "There appears to be ample evidence that rather complex evasive violations of rent regulations have appeared in relatively isolated areas, and they appear to have been independently devised, since there is ordinarily little association among landlords."[14] Similar problems in the ability of differential association to account for the genesis of corporate criminality were also noted in other examinations of Sutherland's hypothesis.[15] As James Coleman has observed, "we must still explain the origins of the deviant attitudes, values, and definitions that are passed from person to person."[16] This pressure toward deviance has also been manifested in several notable cases, such as B. F. Goodrich's cover-up of a defective aircraft brake it had designed and a price-fixing conspiracy among electrical equipment manufacturers.[17]

There are clear reasons why Sutherland's theory of differential association has not garnered more clear-cut support in empirical tests. While it is true that association with those who view illicit behavior as "O.K." can *influence* a person's behavior, it clearly does not *determine* it. In the same way, a person's isolation from others who might frown on a questionable activity may lead him or her in a certain direction, but it does not *cause* that behavior. What Sutherland's theory shortchanges is individual volition. Even in the face of pressure, a person must *decide* to go along the easiest route or to make his or her own path. Sutherland's explanation offers an example, therefore, of how learning principles can *influence* someone's behavior to violate the law, but it does not follow that learning is either *necessary or sufficient* to explain an individual instance of white-collar crime. As Diane Vaughn has observed, "although such normative constraints do influence individual choice, the fact that they exist does not lead to the invariable conclusion that people will abide by them." Furthermore, membership in numerous organizations (e.g., community, work, family) often subjects individuals to conflicting norms, resulting in deviance in one setting but conforming behavior in another.[18]

Organization Theory and White-Collar Crime

Another explanation of white-collar and organized crimes is offered by Dwight Smith in his book *The Mafia Mystique*.[19] He argues that organized crimes result from "the same fundamental considerations that govern [legitimate] entrepreneurship."[20] Smith suggests that the only difference between a legitimate banker and a loan shark, for example, is the (often arbitrary) interest rate charged. All organizations, legal and illegal, strive to survive and to make a profit. The "task environment" of these organizations puts pressure on them through inevitable problems with suppliers, customers, regulators, or competitors. Uncertainties posed by these influences can result in criminal activities, if these challenges cannot be met legally (while also ensuring survival and profit).

Like Sutherland, Smith cites *influences* that can result in *pressure* toward illegal activities. Growth and competition in the futures trading market, for example, has resulted in "dramatic changes in volume and activity," creating new opportunities to make money, as well as new opportunities for abuse and illegal profiteering.[21] These same market pressures, however, can cause businesses to redouble their efforts, change markets or products, or to engage in other noncriminal alternatives. Therefore, Smith's theory of enterprise offers *possible* factors that could influence the decision to commit a crime, but these factors *do not make the decision* to violate the law.

Neutralizing Harm in the Mind of the Offender

Another attempt to explain criminal behavior in the positive tradition is "neutralization" theory, originally posited by Sykes and Matza.[22] According to this view, the harm caused by criminal acts is neutralized in the minds of perpetrators *prior* to their commission. Denial of the extent of injury caused, responsibility for the harm, and higher justification for the act are examples of techniques of neutralization. There is empirical evidence that demonstrates that white-collar criminals use these techniques to "justify" illegal acts to themselves in many cases.[23] In a study of tax evasion, Doreen McBarnet found that neutralizing techniques "are not used to neutralize one's own self-image of criminality but to neutralize the public label itself."[24] Nevertheless, such a theory explains *how* these crimes are committed, rather than *why* they exist. Techniques of neutralization, like differential association, Smith's "task environment," and other positivistic theories are useful in explaining the *process* of criminal activity, but they do not explain its *origin* satisfactorily.

Coleman has organized these kinds of positivistic explanations of white-collar crime in a useful way: those that focus on problems in reaching organization *goals* (opportunity theory), a market *environment* that encourages or rewards illegal behavior (as Dwight Smith proposes), or an organization *structure* that promotes or inhibits criminal behavior.[25] In fact, Diane Vaughn has incorporated all three of these elements into a single theory of white-collar crime.[26]

Although examples can be found where problems with an organization's goals, environment, or structure influence the commission of a white-collar crime, these features of an organization do not explain the criminal decision that must be made at some point. Organizational problems may help us to *understand* how an individual or corporation was put in a position that lead to an illegal act, but they do not *explain* why that route was chosen over other possible alternatives, such as a redoubling of one's legal efforts to change organization goals, environment, or structure in a lawful fashion.

A Classical Explanation

A recent attempt to explain white-collar crime in the classical tradition was proposed by Hirschi and Gottfredson. They argue, as Sutherland did, that white-collar crime can be explained in the same manner as conventional crimes. Their theory of criminality finds crime to result from "the tendency of individuals to pursue short-term gratification in the most direct way with little consideration for the long-term consequences of their acts."[27] Indicators of this tendency, they argue, "include impulsivity, aggression, activity level, and lack of concern for the opinion of others." As a result, "people high on this tendency are relatively unable or unwilling to delay gratification."[28]

Unlike other explanations of crime, which emphasize to the affect of various external influences on behavior, Hirschi and Gottfredson argue that the tendencies they identify "do not lead ineluctably to crime." Instead, crimes require "physical opportunity and immunity from immediate punishment" in addition to the tendencies they identify. This explanation of crime is based on the "assumption that human behavior is motivated by the self-interested pursuit of pleasure and avoidance of pain."[29]

Hirschi and Gottfredson's explanation of crime is a classical, or "free-will," explanation, unlike those of Sutherland, Smith, and Sykes and Matza based in the positivist tradition. Unfortunately, Hirschi and Gottfredson's enumerated "tendencies" characterize not only criminals but many noncriminals as well, including most juveniles and professional athletes (i.e., they are also trained to be impulsive, active, and aggressive).

Most problematic is their notion of a criminal "tendency" toward short-term gratification with little regard for consequences. There exist many examples of white-collar offenders who acted in what they believed to be the long-term interests of their company or the public,[30] and the fact that most individuals do not violate the law, when given the opportunity, indicates that a remarkable number of people choose to exercise their free will in a noncriminal direction. This occurs despite the fact that the object desired has value and that the odds of apprehension are low. Furthermore, it is not clear where these "tendencies," identified by Hirschi and Gottfredson, come from and, if they do exist, why they are not manifested by most people who face criminal opportunities.

A test of Hirschi and Gottfredson's theory by Benson and Moore involved 2,462 individuals sentenced in federal court for one of a small group of white-collar crimes (bank embezzlement, bribery, income tax violations, false claims, and mail fraud). They were compared to 1,986 offenders sentenced for three "common" crimes (narcotics, postal forgery, and bank robbery). Hirschi and Gottfredson's theory predicts that distinguishing offenders on the basis of the conviction offense is meaningless because all offenders are similar in their criminal tendencies. Contrary to this theory, Benson and Moore found the white-collar offenders to have different criminal careers and less likely to have "deviance" problems (i.e., problems drinking, drug use, poor grades, or poor social adjustment). The researchers concluded that "self-control and opportunity are related more complexly than is envisioned in this theory as currently formulated and that motives cannot be ignored as important causal forces."[31] Other empirical comparisons of white-collar and traditional offenders have also found significant differences discounted by Hirschi and Gottfredson.[32]

The Structural Approach

A third approach to white-collar crime focuses less on individual behavior and more on the behavior of law. That is to say, social, political, and economic expectations and conditions in general cause certain behaviors to be defined as criminal. These conditions cause the law to be applied in certain ways, and they ultimately cause individuals to act in ways congruent with these structural considerations. According to this view, there are deeper roots to the crime problem than the immediate environment or pain–pleasure distinctions. Instead, there exists a system of beliefs in capitalistic economies that Coleman calls "the ideology of competitive individualism." This ideology supports individual responsibility for one's own destiny, which is defined "principally in terms of economic self-interest to surpass one's fellows in the accumulation of wealth and status."[33] This competitive individualism in capitalist economies has been traced to the industrial revolution and to the economic relationships that preceded it in agricultural economies.[34]

If one accepts the existence of an economically based competitive individualism that contributes directly to white-collar crime, one should expect communist and socialist economies to have significantly lower levels of white-collar crime.

Unfortunately, there appears to be substantial levels of white-collar crime in these nations.[35] This is not conclusive evidence, however, because measurement of the extent of white-collar crime across cultures is at a rudimentary stage. Nevertheless, a study of economic crime in Poland found, for example, that "not only does white-collar crime exist in socialism, but it displays some truly remarkable similarities with its Western counterpart."[36] It appears, therefore, that the desire of individuals toward personal gain, despite official ideology of socialist nations, is as strong a motivator for crime there, as it is in capitalist nations.[37]

Structural explanations of white-collar crime have had much more success explaining the selective formation and application of the law than in explaining the behavior of individuals or corporations.[38] Nevertheless, the reasons for the formation and application of laws may have little pragmatic importance. As Kitty Calavita has observed, the Occupational Safety and Health Administration was created as a symbolic gesture to appease workers. This initial symbolism created an agency, however, that has produced substantial improvements in the workplace.[39] On the other hand, interviews with 103 "immigrant-dependent" employers in southern California found numerous employer violations. Furthermore, the employers felt "protected" from government sanctions, due to the practices of the Immigration and Naturalization Service that emphasize "voluntary compliance" and "self-imposed restrictions." This result is seen by Calavita as the government's solution to the inherent problems of immigration policy: the economic siphoning caused by immigrant labor versus political consequences by employers who rely on this labor supply.

> The resulting dilemma for immigration policymakers in the early 1980s was that they were pressed on the one hand by a public demand for employer sanctions and on the other by the impossibility of passing such a law over the objections of employers. An employer sanctions law that satisfied employers by making it easy for them to "comply" was the solution to this dilemma.[40]

Concern about the causes of white-collar crime at the individual level has reduced interest in the structural approach. In its place, there has been renewed interest in the criminal choice from either the positive or classical perspectives. For example, Bob Roshier's "postclassical" criminology sees "perceived incentives and disincentives" as being much more significant than individual differences in explaining crime.[41] In a similar way, Edward Sieh places perceptions personal "equity" and fair treatment as fundamental causes of workplace crime.[42]

An Ethical Explanation

Whether one chooses to place most emphasis on learning, on pressures in the business environment, on criminal tendencies, or on competitive individualism, there remains the failure of an individual to *choose* the proper course of conduct. An alternative to the positive, classical, and structural approaches lies in the recognition of three facts:

1. External factors play a role in influencing some people to engage in crime, although these factors obviously do not *cause* the crime by themselves.
2. A freely willed decision lies at the base of virtually all criminal behavior, although there is no "tendency" to engage in crime, controlled only through the possibility of apprehension.
3. The explanation of crime lies in reducing contributory external factors to the extent possible *and* by altering the perceived "pleasure" achieved from law violation.

As shown, most attempts to explain crime lay the blame at bad influences, a bad environment, or criminal tendencies. Clearly, these factors are static attributes of an individual or his or her environment. Biographical attributes cannot cause crime. They may help one to justify (or blame) a bad decision, but they do not make the decision for the actor.

Making Noncriminal Decisions

The answer to understanding crime causation lies in discovering *how* people make noncriminal choices. Asked another way, "Where do people learn to make decisions in accord with legal and ethical principles?"

Studies have found that ethical behavior is often learned by imitating the example of others. In interviews with corporate auditors, Donald Cressey found that "every one of these financial executives said that the ethical behavior of company personnel is determined by the example set by top management."[43] The same situation was discovered by Marshall Clinard in interviews with middle managers in corporations.[44]

One does not have to look very far, however, for examples of suspect decision making in the white-collar world. Interviews with the former president of Lockheed Corporation, A. Carl Kotchian, revealed that significant business decisions were made only in economic terms. He agreed to make questionable, but legal, payments to Japanese officials to sell large civilian airplanes there. In justifying his actions, Kotchian argued, accurately, that competitors were making similar payments, Lockheed was "asked" to make the payments as a criterion for consideration, and the ultimate sale (totaling more than $430 million for 21 future aircraft) "would provide Lockheed workers with jobs, and thus redound to the benefit of their dependents, and local communities and stockholders of the corporation."[45] In this case, it is clear that any ordering of ethical principles, which should include an assessment of *ought* to be done given a number of contradictory particulars, was overwhelmed by economic considerations.

In the infamous case at Love Canal, it will be remembered that tons of toxic waste was buried, only to become the site of homes and schools years later, where many residents became ill and some died. Here, it appears that the corporate disposer, Hooker Chemical, informed the Niagara Falls School Board in writing and through on-site inspections of the danger of the area. Nevertheless, the board obtained the property, later selling it to developers and putting storm sewers directly through the sealed canal bed where the chemicals were buried.[46] This case provides a remarkable example of how Hooker Chemical attempted to carry out its ethical duties in light of pressure from the school board. In both the Lockheed and Love Canal cases, however, expediency overcame ethics, and there are victims still paying the price as a result. In neither case did any official ever claim to be motivated by what *should* happen. Instead, there was usually an a priori economic determination made, and the path of least resistance followed. Clearly, the example of others is not an appropriate way to inculcate ethical principles, given the existing business and political climate.

In the arena of white-collar crime, there exists a growing number of examples of business and professional decisions made by well-educated people who violate the law.[47] The principles of ethical decision making are rarely made explicit, as the educational process implicitly assumes that knowledge of facts implies knowledge of what to do with them. Given the pressures of the marketplace, "pro-criminal" definitions within industry, and the wide availability of techniques of neutralization, how is it that many choose to conduct business honestly and fairly, then, while others are not able to resist the pressures to "succeed" at all costs?

What is the process by which people choose to deny themselves an immediate gain for an ethical principle? Given the fact that most people have no education or experience in *prioritizing* values when they are placed in difficult situations, they often do what becomes second-nature in the business community: operate quickly, efficiently, and always in the best interests of the company. Therefore, shortcuts are chosen, safety is secondary, and the law is ignored, when it comes between profit and self-interest.

The method by which ethical principles are taught and internalized can vary, but it is not an overstatement to say that most people are incapable, generally, of thinking through a business or governmental decision in ethical terms. As James Coleman has observed, "any effort to deal with the problem of white-collar crime on this level must be aimed at changing the 'ethical climate' within the corporations and the government."[48] Ethics courses are now in vogue in many schools, but this approach, by itself, fails to integrate ethical considerations in all decision making. Management, personnel, public administration, financial, and political decisions all involve ethical questions with ethical solutions. These principles are simply omitted in most education in these subjects today.

If positivists lay too much blame for crime on the doorstep of social and economic conditions, classicists give too much credence to the impact of threatened penalties, and structuralists too much emphasis on economic inequality, an ethical approach would redirect the focus on external conditions and penalties to individual responsibility for decisions to commit crimes. When ethical principles are internalized, criminal conduct is prevented when *pleasure* is no longer derived from crime, due to the understanding and value placed on the crime's wrongfulness and impact.

A commitment to ethical decision making would mean that people could be held liable for their bad decisions without the continual recriminations and debate over "who" or "what" was responsible for their behavior. Individuals would be held responsible for their own poor decisions with the knowledge that they did *in fact* know better. This approach is distinguished from the positivist approach in its focus on individual responsibility for personal or corporate decisions, rather than on external influences. It is distinct from classical approaches in that it focuses not on the certainty of apprehension or on punishment, but rather on the "pleasure" portion of the pain–pleasure principle. That is to say, crime would be avoided more often due to its failure to bring pleasure (by applying the principles of ethics) rather than due to the fear of pain through apprehension and punishment.

White-collar crimes are especially amenable to this approach because they involve planning, rationality, and status. Unlike street crimes, which are more random, more often committed in an emotional or drug-influenced state, and more often committed by uneducated people, white-collar criminals are easier for the law to reach. Attempts to inculcate ethical principles find a more receptive audience among those who contemplate their actions, consider the consequences, and have a degree of social status by nature of their employment.

Summary

Table 7.1 summarizes the major aspects of the four perspectives regarding the causes of criminal behavior. The logic between the identified causes and prescribed remedy for each approach should be noted. A reliance on external factors, as in the positivistic and structural approaches, argues for changes in these social and economic influences in the hope they will alter individual behavior. On the other hand, a reliance on individual decision making, as in the classical and ethical approaches, demands changes in what is seen as the primary determinants of these decisions. In the case of the classical approach, apprehension and penalties are needed to deter unlawful behavior by increasing the possibility of pain over the gain of law violation. In the ethical approach, inculcation of ethical principles is seen as a way to reduce the perceived pleasure of illegal behavior, due to a greater appreciation of its wrongfulness and impact on others.

If evaluations of past and current policies can be trusted, prevention approaches based on positivistic, classical, and structural explanations have had little impact on white-collar crime. The ethical approach has yet to be attempted in any serious way, and it would require a national commitment toward teaching ethical decision making throughout the educational process and enforced in the public arena. As Gary Green has suggested, "Moral education that discourages illegal behavior must be continuous. Inculcation must start early in life and be reiterated constantly, because early moral socialization can be mitigated by subsequent pro-criminal associations."[49] Marshall Clinard interviewed 64 retired middle managers from *Fortune* 500 companies and found that top management in a company also is critical because it "sets the corporate ethical tone."[50]

An example of the existing indifferent attitude toward unethical behavior is provided by an investigation of alleged ethical misconduct on the part of federal employees. Federal agencies must refer such cases to the Department of Justice

Table 7.1 Four Approaches to Criminal Behavior

Approach to Crime Causation	Primary Cause of Crime	Prescribed Remedy
Positive	External factors (usually social and economic)	Rehabilitation or reform by changing social and economic conditions or changing someone's reaction to them
Classical	Free-will decision (guided by hedonistic tendency to maximize pleasure and minimize pain)	Deterrence through threat of apprehension and punishment
Structural	Political and economic conditions that promote a culture of competitive individualism in which individual gain becomes more important than the social good.	More equitable distribution of power and wealth in society, so that all individuals have a greater stake in a better society
Ethical	Free-will decision guided by ethical principles unknown to most people (that involve prioritizing of values in unclear situations based on the failure of illegal conduct to bring pleasure)	Education in ethical decision-making from an early age; reduction to the extent possible the external factors that promote unethical decisions

when their Offices of Inspector General find that violations of criminal law may have occurred. In a sample of ten agencies over two years, the U.S. General Accounting Office found that 124 allegations of criminal ethical violations were referred to the Department of Justice. Only 2 of the 124 cases were prosecuted.[51] Clearly, a more sincere effort is needed to promote ethical decision making, if white-collar crime is to be more effectively controlled.

CASE STUDY

This is a case study that summarizes the background of a tragic incident resulting from faulty organizational interactions and defective decision making. Read the case carefully, and answer the questions that follow it, applying principles from this chapter and earlier ones.

The Explosion of the Challenger Space Shuttle

The *Challenger* space shuttle exploded in midair, minutes after it was launched in 1986. All those on board, six astronauts and a school teacher, were killed. The school teacher, Christa McAuliffe, was the first private citizen on a space mission. The question that came to be the focus of a presidential investigation was,

"How could such an expensive and carefully constructed device fail so miserably?" As it turned out, this assumption was not entirely accurate.

The choice to develop the space shuttle took place during the Nixon administration for budgetary reasons.[52] The use of nonreusable rockets during the *Apollo* program's trips to the moon was very expensive, with each trip to space requiring a completely new rocket. The notion of a reusable space shuttle was seen as an economical option, certainly cheaper than a proposed Mars expedition or space station that were offered as alternatives to the shuttle program.

The development of the shuttle program, however, was not without problems. NASA's (National Aeronautics and Space Administration) original design was altered several times, always in response to continued budget pressures. In a book-length analysis of the *Challenger* disaster, Richard Lewis claims it was "the end product of budget compromises."[53] Another book about the incident concluded that budget constraints led NASA to embrace solid-fuel boosters, rather than more expensive liquid-fuel engines, because of their lower cost. A significant problem with the solid-fuel boosters, however, was that they could not be aborted if something went wrong.[54] This is precisely what occurred during the ill-fated *Challenger* launch in 1986.

Political pressure compounded the budgetary pressures on NASA during the Reagan administration in the 1980s. First, it was proposed that the shuttle carry both military and commercial payloads to help pay for its scientific expeditions. Second, the shuttle would have to fly much more often to keep income ahead of expenditures. Third, during President Reagan's first major speech on space in 1982, he announced the shuttle was "fully operational" when, in fact, it was not. These factors combined to place "relentless pressure" on NASA to accelerate the shuttle's readiness and increase its anticipated flight schedule.[55]

Still another pressure, competition from Europe, led NASA to hurry its development and crowd its launch schedule with 24 proposed flights per year. The European Space Agency's satellite launcher would compete directly with the shuttle's proposed deployment of commercial and military payloads, so time and scheduling became paramount, if paying customers were to be attracted. The announcement of President Reagan's "Star Wars" space military defense plan "clearly put additional demands on an already overburdened and underfunded space agency."[56]

The budgetary, political, and competitive pressures were exacerbated by two factors NASA was unable to overcome: (1) not enough time to develop the shuttle as originally planned and (2) insufficient resources to meet a tight deadline and high expectations. This failure to devote adequate resources to the shuttle program continued even after the system became operational. As Ronald Kramer observed, the lack of spare parts forced NASA to "cannibalize" each shuttle upon its return to ready another shuttle for launch.[57]

Given this background, it is not surprising that space shuttles were pushed to the launch pad earlier than planned, much like a new model car is introduced before all the bugs are worked out. In space, however, the room for survivable error is much smaller than it is for flawed automobiles.

Spectators view the explosion of the space shuttle *Challenger.* The contrail of the *Challenger* can be seen over the apparent explosion of the orbiter. A subsequent investigation found budgetary, political, and competitive pressures at NASA resulted in the launch of the space shuttle with unsolved technical problems. *(Bill Mitchell, UPI/Bettmann)*

As it turned out, the immediate cause of the *Challenger* explosion was a poorly designed O-ring seal on one of the solid rocket boosters. The presidential commission that investigated the shuttle disaster blamed both NASA and the contractor, Thiokol, which had an $800 million contract to manufacture the rocket boosters that contained the O-ring. The commission concluded that "neither Thiokol nor NASA responded adequately to internal warnings about the faulty seal design."[58] This is an understatement.

In early tests it was discovered that there was leakage from a pressure seal that would erode the O-rings. Further erosion could result in "an actual flame path," bursting the booster at the joint, destroying it and the space shuttle.[59] These test results were not reported by Thiokol to NASA. Also, the O-rings had never been tested below 50 degrees, due to the rush to keep the shuttle program moving on schedule. After a test flight in 1981, hot gas had leaked and damaged an O-ring, but this was not reported by NASA engineers to higher management. Further tests in 1982 led the NASA engineers to conclude that the O-rings were a potential "single failure point" that could result in "loss of mission, vehicle and crew."[60]

The space shuttle program continued, however, while NASA asked Thiokol to investigate the problem. A "launch constraint" was put on all future flights when the primary O-ring failed, and the secondary ring was scorched in a 1985 *Challenger* flight. Nevertheless, this launch constraint was waived for the next flight (and each subsequent flight) up through the *Challenger* disaster. As one writer argued, there was "irrefutable evidence that both [NASA] and Thiokol realized that they were risking disaster by allowing shuttle flights to continue despite the chronic O-ring erosion."[61]

A briefing took place among NASA headquarters, its engineers, and Thiokol engineers in August 1985, prompting Thiokol to form an "O-Ring Task Force" to investigate and report on the problem. There appears to have been sluggishness in the activity of this task force, apparently because Thiokol was renegotiating its contract with NASA at the time and did not want to feature problems with its products.[62] Inexplicably, Thiokol requested that the O-ring matter be closed before it had arrived at any solution to the problem. In January 1986, five days before the *Challenger* explosion, a NASA report reads, "the problem is considered closed."[63]

Case Study Questions

1. What do you see as the most significant factors in attempting to trace the causes of the *Challenger* disaster?
2. Do these factors appear to support a positive, classical, structural, or ethical explanation of the disaster?
3. If you were forced to explain the *Challenger* disaster using all four types of explanation (listed in question 2), how would you do it?

Endnotes

1. Cesare Beccaria, *On Crimes and Punishments* (1764), trans. Henry Paolucci (Indianapolis: Bobbs-Merrill, 1963).
2. Edwin H. Sutherland, *White-Collar Crime* (New York: The Dryden Press, 1949); and Robert K. Merton, "Social Structure and Anomie," *American Sociological Review*, 3 (October 1938), pp. 672–682.
3. Sutherland, *White-Collar Crime*, p. 234.
4. at 238.
5. at 239.
6. James D. Thompson, *Organizations in Action: Social Bases of Administrative Theory* (New York: McGraw-Hill, 1970), p. 128.
7. Lawrence W. Sherman, *Scandal and Reform: Controlling Police Corruption* (Berkeley: University of California Press, 1978), p. 18.
8. See Edward Gross, "Organization Structure and Organizational Crime," in *White-Collar Crime: Theory and Research*, ed. by Gilbert Geis and Ezra Stotland (Beverly Hills, CA: Sage Publications, 1980).
9. Ibid., pp. 241–242.

10. Marshall B. Clinard, "Criminological Theories of Violations of Wartime Regulations," *American Sociological Review*, 11 (1946).
11. Robert E. Lane, "Why Businessmen Violate the Law," *Journal of Criminal law, Criminology, and Police Science*, 42 (1953).
12. Gilbert Geis, "The Heavy Electrical Equipment Anti-Trust Cases of 1961," in *Criminal Behavior Systems*, ed. by Marshall Clinard and Richard Quinney (New York: Holt, Rinehart and Winston, 1967).
13. Jay S. Albanese, *Organizational Offenders* (Niagara Falls, NY: Apocalypse, 1982).
14. Ibid. p. 269.
15. James W. Coleman, *The Criminal Elite: The Sociology of White-Collar Crime*, 2nd ed. (New York: St. Martin's Press, 1989).
16. James W. Coleman, "The Theory of White-Collar Crime: From Sutherland to the 1990s," in *White-Collar Crime Reconsidered*, ed. by Kip Schlegel and David Weisburd (Boston: Northeastern University Press, 1992), p. 56.
17. Kermit Vandivier, "Why Should My Conscience Bother Me?"; and Gilbert Geis, "The Heavy Electrical Equipment Antitrust Cases of 1961," in *Corporate and Governmental Deviance*, 3rd ed., ed. M. David Ermann and Richard J. Lundman (New York: Oxford University Press, 1987), pp. 103–144.
18. Diane Vaughn, "The Macro-Micro Connection in White-Collar Crime Theory," *White-Collar Crime Reconsidered*, ed. by Kip Schlegel and David Weisburd (Boston: Northeastern University Press, 1992), p. 129.
19. Dwight C. Smith, Jr., *The Mafia Mystique*, rev. ed. (Lanham, MD: University Press of America, 1990).
20. Dwight C. Smith, "Organized Crime and Entrepreneurship," *International Journal of Criminology and Penology*, 6 (1978), p. 164. See also Dwight C. Smith, "Paragons, Pariahs, and Pirates: A Spectrum-Based Theory of Enterprise," *Crime & Delinquency*, 26 (July 1980).
21. Kip Schlegel, "Crime in the Pits: The Regulation of Futures Trading," *The Annals*, 525 (January 1993), p. 67.
22. Gresham Sykes and David Matza, "Techniques of Neutralization: A Theory of Delinquency," *American Sociological Review*, 22 (1957), pp. 667–670.
23. For a review, see Gary S. Green, *Occupational Crime* (Chicago: Nelson-Hall, 1990), pp. 81–82.
24. Doreen McBarnet, "Whiter than White-Collar Crime: Tax, Fraud Insurance and the Management of Stigma," *British Journal of Sociology*, 42 (September 1991), 323–344.
25. Coleman, "The Theory of White-Collar Crime," pp. 64–70.
26. Diane Vaughn, *Controlling Unlawful Organizational Behavior* (Chicago: University of Chicago Press, 1985); and Vaughn, "The Macro-Micro Connection in White-Collar Crime Theory," pp. 124–145.
27. Travis Hirschi and Michael Gottfredson, "Causes of White-Collar Crime," *Criminology*, 25, no. 4 (November 1989), pp. 959.

28. Ibid.
29. Ibid.; and Michael R. Gottfredson and Travis Hirschi, *A General Theory of Crime* (Stanford, CA: Stanford University Press, 1990).
30. For examples, see Albanese, *Organizational Offenders*, 2nd ed.
31. Michael L. Benson and Elizabeth Moore, "Are White-Collar and Common Offenders the Same? An Empirical and Theoretical Critique of a Recently Proposed General Theory of Crime," *Journal of Research in Crime and Delinquency*, 29 (August 1992), pp. 251–272.
32. David Weisburd, Ellen F. Chayet, and Elin J. Waring, "White-Collar Crime and Criminal Careers: Some Preliminary Findings," *Crime & Delinquency*, 36 (1990), pp. 342–355; and Stanton Wheeler, David Weisburd, Nancy Bode, and Elin Waring, "White-Collar Crime and Criminals," *American Criminal Law Review*, 25 (1988), pp. 331–357.
33. Coleman, "The Theory of White–Collar Crime," p. 61.
34. James W. Coleman, "Toward an Integrated Theory of White–Collar Crime," *American Journal of Sociology*, 93 (1987), pp. 406–439.
35. John Braithwaite, "White-Collar Crime, Competition, and Capitalism: Comment on Coleman," *American Journal of Sociology*, 94 (1988), pp. 627–632; Gilbert Geis, *On White-Collar Crime* (Lexington, MA: Lexington Books, 1982); and Maria Los, "Economic Crimes in Communist Countries," in *Comparative Criminology*, ed. by Israel L. Barak-Glantz and Elmer H. Johnson (Beverly Hills, CA: Sage Publications, 1983).
36. Wojciech Cebulak, "White-Collar Crime in Socialism: Myth or Reality?" *International Journal of Comparative and Applied Criminal Justice*, 15 (Spring 1991), pp. 109–120.
37. James W. Coleman, "Competition and the Structure of Industrial Society: Reply to Braithwaite," *American Journal of Sociology*, 94 (1988), pp. 632–636.
38. See D. L. Donnelly, "Origins of the Occupational Safety and Health Act of 1970," *Social Problems*, 30 (1982), pp. 13–25; and A. E. McCormick, "Rule Enforcement and Moral Indignation: Some Observations on the Effects of Criminal Anti-Trust Convictions upon Societal Reaction Processes," *Social Problems*, 25 (1977), pp. 30–39.
39. Kitty Calavita, "The Demise of the Occupational Safety and Health Administration: A Case Study in Symbolic Interaction," *Social Problems*, 30 (1983), pp. 437–448.
40. Kitty Calavita, "Employer Sanctions Violations: Toward a Dialectical Model of White-Collar Crime," *Law & Society Review*, 24 (1990), pp. 1041–1069.
41. Bob Roshier, *Controlling Crime: The Classical Perspective in Criminology* (Chicago: Lyceum, 1989), p. 74.
42. Edward W. Sieh, "Employee Theft: An Examination of Gerald Mars and an Explanation Based on Equity Theory," *Advances in Criminological Theory*, Vol. 4 (New Brunswick, NJ: Transaction, 1993).
43. Donald R. Cressey, "Employee Theft: The Reasons Why," *Security World*, October 1980, pp. 31–36.

44. Marshall B. Clinard, *Corporate Ethics and Crime* (Beverly Hills, CA: Sage Publications, 1983).
45. Albanese, *Organizational Offenders*, pp. 104–105; and A. Carl Kotchian, *Rikkiedo Jiken* [Lockheed Incident] (published in Japan, 1976).
46. Jay Albanese, "Love Canal Six Years Later: The Legal Legacy," *Federal Probation Quarterly*, 48, no. 2 (June 1984), pp. 53–58; and Albanese, *Organizational Offenders*, pp. 117–137.
47. See Coleman, *The Criminal Elite;* and Nancy Frank and Michael Lombness, *Controlling Corporate Illegality: The Regulatory Justice System* (Cincinnati: Anderson, 1988).
48. Coleman, *The Criminal Elite*, p. 249.
49. Green, *Occupational Crime*, p. 230.
50. Clinard, *Corporate Ethics and Crime: The Role of Middle Management*, p. 145.
51. U.S. Comptroller General, *Ethics Enforcement: Results of Conflict of Interest Investigations* (Washington, D.C.: U.S. General Accounting Office, 1988).
52. Ronald C. Kramer, "The Space Shuttle *Challenger* Explosion: A Case Study of State-Corporate Crime," in *White-Collar Crime Reconsidered*, ed. by Kip Schlegel and David Weisburd (Boston: Northeastern University Press, 1992), pp. 214–243.
53. Richard S. Lewis, *Challenger: The Final Voyage* (New York: Columbia University Press, 1988).
54. James J. Trento, *Prescription for Disaster: From the Glory Days of Apollo to the Betrayal of the Shuttle* (New York: Crown, 1987).
55. President's Commission on the Space Shuttle *Challenger* Accident, *Report of the Presidential Commission on the Space Shuttle Challenger Accident* (Washington, D.C.: U.S. Government Printing Office, 1986), p. 201; and Kramer, "The Space Shuttle *Challenger* Explosion," p. 221.
56. Kramer, "The Space Shuttle *Challenger* Explosion," p. 223.
57. Ibid., p. 224.
58. President's Commission on the Space Shuttle *Challenger* Accident, *Report of the Presidential Commission on the Space Shuttle Challenger Accident*, p. 148
59. Michael McConnell, *Challenger: A Major Malfunction* (Garden City, NY: Doubleday, 1987), p. 118.
60. President's Commission on the Space Shuttle *Challenger* Accident, *Report of the Presidential Commission on the Space Shuttle Challenger Accident*, p. 125; and Lewis, *Challenger: The Final Voyage*, p. 74.
61. McConnell, *Challenger: A Major Malfunction*, p. 121.
62. Kramer, "The Space Shuttle *Challenger* Explosion," p. 228; and McConnell, *Challenger: A Major Malfunction*, p. 181; President's Commission on the Space Shuttle *Challenger* Accident, *Report of the Presidential Commission on the Space Shuttle Challenger Accident*, p. 210; and Lewis, *Challenger: The Final Voyage*, p. 88.
63. Lewis, *Challenger: The Final Voyage*, p. 88.

Enforcement, Prosecution, and Defense Alternatives

There is no den in the wide world to hide a rogue.
Commit a crime and the earth is made of glass.
— Ralph Waldo Emerson (1841)

Thus far, we have come to know the definition, types, extent, and causes of white-collar crime. Much of the remainder of this book addresses how white-collar crimes are enforced, prosecuted, defended, and sentenced. This chapter is divided into three major parts: the enforcement, the prosecution, and the defense of white-collar crime cases. It will be seen that the conceptual difficulties surrounding the nature of white-collar crime, discussed earlier, have a profound impact on the adjudication of white-collar crime in the criminal justice system.

Investigators of White-Collar Crime

There are two major types of government investigators of white-collar crime: legislative branch investigators and executive branch investigators. They each work to enforce laws in one of these two branches of government. In state government, these investigators enforce state laws for the governor and state legislature. At the federal level, these investigators work for Congress (in the legislative branch) or for an agency in the executive branch (such as the Justice or Treasury departments). This discussion will focus on federal investigators, as their organization and approach to the enforcement of federal law is often used as a model by the states in their approach to white-collar crime.

Congressional investigators usually work for a committee of the U.S. House of Representatives or Senate that holds investigative hearings. There exist a large number of congressional committees, each of which is responsible for oversight in a specific area, such as government affairs, the judiciary, foreign affairs, and many others. Witnesses can be invited or subpoenaed to testify before these committees, and the committees have the authority to grant immunity from prosecution to reluctant witnesses. Immunity allows witnesses to testify without fear that their statements will be used against them in a subsequent prosecution. Prosecution is always the prerogative of the executive branch, however, and cannot be undertaken by the legislative branch of government.

Executive branch investigators work for a department or agency of the executive branch of government. There are two types of executive branch enforcement agencies: nonindependent agencies and independent regulatory agencies (IRAs).

Nonindependent Investigative Agencies

Nonindependent agencies are usually located within one of the departments of the president's cabinet. For example, the Department of Agriculture has an Office of Investigations, and the Department of Treasury encompasses the Bureau of Alcohol, Tobacco, and Firearms, the Internal Revenue Service, Customs Service, and the Secret Service. The Department of Justice houses the Drug Enforcement Administration and Federal Bureau of Investigation. Each of these agencies is responsible for enforcement of the laws delegated to it. The Treasury Department is responsible for control of U.S. currency, and therefore, it is responsible for enforcement of federal laws prohibiting forgery and counterfeiting. This enforcement responsibility is assigned specifically to the U.S. Secret Service. Likewise, the Treasury Department has the responsibility to collect taxes and enforce the tax laws, and this is carried out by the Internal Revenue Service. The Federal Bureau of Investigation enforces all federal laws not specifically designated to other agencies.

These nonindependent agencies rely on the Department of Justice for both civil and criminal prosecution, although they have full authority to conduct investigations of suspected law violations. These agencies usually have no subpoena power of their own.[1] The Department of Justice established Organized Crime Strike Forces in 14 cities in the United States and suboffices in 12 others, although these strike forces have now been subsumed within U.S. attorney's offices. It has been found that 83 percent of the organized crime cases they prosecute come from four agencies: the Bureau of Alcohol, Tobacco, and Firearms; the Drug Enforcement Administration; the Federal Bureau of Investigation; and the Internal Revenue Service.[2]

Independent Regulatory Agencies

The second type of executive branch investigative agency is the independent regulatory agencies (IRAs). Each of these agencies is headed by a *commission* that holds executive, legislative, and prosecution powers. Examples include the Securities and Exchange Commission, which is responsible for regulating publicly held corporations; the Environmental Protection Agency, which enforces all federal laws and establishes regulations dealing with the environment; and the Consumer Product Safety Commission, which regulates the manufacture of safe consumer products. There are many other IRAs, and each is headed by a commissioner, who is appointed by the president for a five-year term. The five-year term is designed to keep the regulatory agency objective in its enforcement duties and above the political machinations of the day.

Each independent regulatory agency has a division of enforcement that monitors and investigates compliance with the regulations it issues. That division files a memorandum of recommendation in each case that summarizes the facts of the investigation, details suspected violations of law, and provides the recommendations of the investigators. This memorandum is forwarded to the commission for a prosecution decision.

Prosecution Avenues

A nonindependent regulatory agency must refer any suspected law violation to the Department of Justice for either criminal or civil prosecution. An IRA, however, has several options.

An IRA has three prosecution alternatives: administrative action, criminal referral, and civil prosecution. An administrative action involves a hearing within the agency by a hearing examiner or administrative law judge (who works for the IRA), and the case is prosecuted by the IRA's own attorneys. The findings of this administrative hearing are appealable to the U.S. Court of Appeals.

A second option is a criminal referral. This involves a memorandum of recommendation to the Justice Department. The decision to prosecute rests solely with the Justice Department, as no IRA or any other investigative agency has criminal jurisdiction of its own.

The third alternative is a civil prosecution. The IRA's own attorneys would prosecute the case in court. The agency can ask for a "cease and desist" order in court and for monetary damages and civil fines. A "consent decree" is usually chosen over civil prosecution, however. The consent decree indicates that the corporation agrees to a permanent injunction (to refrain from the alleged activity) without admitting that it ever engaged in the prohibited conduct. This option saves court time and costs, and allows the IRA to regulate the industry without having to sue corporations in court to ensure compliance.

Problems of Regulatory Enforcement

It can be seen that independent regulatory agencies have broad authority to prosecute and also have a degree of insulation from political influences. Many enforcement agencies devoted to the investigation of white-collar crimes have been criticized, however, for failure to be effective for several reasons. As Nancy Frank has noted, many of these agencies have resources "inadequate to their tasks," exhibit a "lack of expertise" to investigate complex technological industries, and place "excessive reliance on voluntary compliance" by businesses to legal standards, as well as exhibiting a tendency "to become captives of the industries they regulate" and share the ideology and perspective of the businesses rather than the role of the enforcer.[3] Laureen Snider has recognized similar shortcomings of the regulatory system, noting especially the "disparity in resources" between the regulators and the regulated.[4] This results in an unwitting marriage of convenience, where the less powerful party finds it less problematic to rely on the voluntary cooperation of the more powerful (rather than fighting a battle that is difficult to win) to maintain the relationship.[5] As Frank Hagan has remarked, "most agencies are 'outgunned' by the industries they are supposed to control, and, in fact, they are sometimes controlled by these industries."[6]

Other criticisms of enforcement by regulatory agencies include the fact that there exist many "loopholes and omissions" in the regulations that allow businesses to avoid compliance, and corporations can "thwart the process of justice" through the veil of complex corporate transactions, seeking delays in enforcement actions and attempting to alter public opinion through "their influence on the media."[7] These criticisms will continue to have validity as long as political influence is permitted to affect the operations of agencies of enforcement.

Investigative Techniques: Proactive and Reactive

Investigations of white-collar crime are more difficult to accomplish than are investigations of conventional crimes due to the complexity of the conduct being regulated. The investigation of robbery, for example, is made easy because it does not take long to determine if, in fact, a crime has occurred. For white-collar crimes, there can be months of investigation just to determine if a violation has occurred, and additional investigation is often required to prove responsibility.

The investigation of white-collar crime relies on *proactive* investigations, because victims do not often realize they have been victimized until much later, and harm often appears later as well. Unlike conventional "street" crimes, there is rarely a complainant that appears that can identify a specific criminal incident or offender. Therefore, the largely reactive enforcement strategies of traditional police agencies are not adequate for the investigation of white-collar misconduct. Unfortunately, proactive law enforcement is time consuming, and it often results in dead-ends. But the results can be significant. In a California insider trading case, a computer surveillance program at the National Association of Securities Dealers noticed heavy selling of a particular stock and a quadrupled increase in volume in a single day. This resulted in several SEC investigations and prosecutions.[8] Proactive market surveillance is widely used to screen for possible insider trading cases, but its success rate is low.[9] An assessment by the U.S. General Accounting Office found less than 1 percent of questionable cases uncovered by such industry screening programs were referred to the Securities and Exchange Commission for investigation. Once referred, however, 10 percent resulted in SEC enforcement actions being taken.[10]

Overt and Covert Methods of Investigation

To gather information for a proactive investigation, both overt and covert methods are used by investigative agencies. *Overt methods* include examination of bank and credit records, tax records, and civil and criminal records available at a county clerk's office, for example. Other information sources include Dun & Bradstreet reports, which provide information about a business's ownership and net worth, and "mail covers," which are used to record the addresses from which a suspect is receiving mail. These overt methods can be conducted with or without the knowledge of the target. These methods can be considered to be overt because most of this information is either generally available to the public or else it can be obtained without a search warrant. Hence, there is no burden of proof prior to obtaining this kind of information. Independent regulatory agencies are also able to conduct administrative searches without a warrant and issue administrative subpoenas to force the appearance of reluctant witnesses (or documents) under the authority granted to the IRA.

Covert methods involve obtaining information without the knowledge of the suspect, and they generally require a search warrant, or other burden of proof, to justify the intrusion. Physical and electronic surveillance, use of informants, and undercover investigations are examples of covert methods of investigation. The primary drawback of covert methods "is the expense these investigations often involve" and the invasions of privacy they engender.[11]

Tracing Financial Transactions

Much white-collar crime, as noted earlier, involves an attempt to secure financial gain through theft, through offenses against public administration, or regulatory offenses. Tracing financial transactions, therefore, is one of the most common techniques in the investigation of white-collar crime.

There are two primary methods of investigating financial transactions: directly through bank and credit records or indirectly through the net worth or bank deposits method. A direct method is to analyze bank records, such as signature cards (to verify identification), negotiated checks (to determine creditors), and credit records (to assess indebtedness and payment records). Such an investigation becomes complex when lawyers or accountants have helped to obscure the paper trail. In the savings and loan crisis, for example, it was found that of the 450 thrifts seized by mid-1990, malfeasance was involved in 55 percent of the bank failures. A problem for law enforcement arose when it was found that 40 percent of these cases involved questionable or illegal activities of accountants or lawyers.[12] If the fraud is large enough, as in the case of the savings and loan crisis, one case can result in hundreds of criminal and civil investigations. In 1990, there were nearly 1,300 savings and loan cases in the Department of Justice that were *inactive*, due to the inability to keep up with the investigative load created by this scandal.[13]

White-collar offenders are often clever, and detection of illegally obtained finances can require indirect methods of investigation. The net worth method is "based on the theory that increases or decreases in a person's net worth during a period, adjusted for living expenses, result in a determination of income."[14] Establishing the difference between an individual's or corporation's assets and liabilities at a given time determines his or her net worth. The courts have approved the use of the net worth method in numerous cases.[15] This investigative method is usually employed when the suspect maintains no financial records, or such records are not available for examination. Once liabilities and living expenses are subtracted from someone's assets, the remainder is funds from unknown (and possibly illegal) sources. Large amounts of cash in this category have formed the basis for many prosecutions of white-collar crime.

A third method of financial investigation is the bank deposits method. This method is "based on the theory that if a subject receives money, only two things can be done with the money—it can be deposited or it can be spent in the form of cash."[16] Total bank deposits, transfers, and cash expenditures are examined to establish all available funds; any funds remaining must come from unknown (and possibly illegal) sources. Similar to the net worth method, the bank deposits method is used when financial records of the target are poor, unavailable, or nonexistent.

These three methods of financial analysis form the basis for many investigations of white-collar crime. The use of electronic surveillance, and the other methods just noted, have continued to grow in use, although they are more expensive in terms of cost and personnel requirements.

CASE STUDY

What follows is a summary of an actual case. Read the scenario carefully, and answer the questions that follow, applying the principles in this chapter.

The ZZZZ Scam

Barry Minkow started a carpet cleaning service out of his garage at age 16. His company, ZZZZ Best Carpet, was doing well, but Minkow was not ready for the hard work of cleaning carpets and running a company. He began to lose money and designed a series of schemes to conceal it.

First, he concocted false financial statements, using them to obtain bank loans. When his credit ran out, he borrowed from loan sharks. When he needed still more money, he decided to sell stock in his company.

He bought a bankrupt corporation that was once listed on the stock exchange and had the auditors of a public accounting firm clear his company for a stock offering by supplying them with fake documentation. Although the company was insolvent, the auditors did not discover Minkow's manipulations.

The stock sale seemed to work. The value of the stock grew steadily. In fact, ZZZZ Best Carpet sold $15 million in shares in one week.

Ironically, Minkow's house of cards began to fall when a customer complained to the *Los Angeles Times* that she was overcharged by Minkow in having her carpet cleaned. An investigation by a reporter uncovered that Minkow had cheated hundreds of customers. A published exposé of Minkow's business practices resulted in his stock value falling precipitously.

Barry Minkow, known as the "carpet cleaning king," started a carpet cleaning service out of his garage at age 16. Using false financial information, he obtained bank loans, a stock offering, and assets on paper of $200 million. Later, it was found that more than 80 percent of his assets never existed. Minkow was later bankrupted and sentenced to 25 year in prison.
(UPI/Bettmann)

Later, it was found that more than 80 percent of Minkow's listed assets never existed. His $200 million company on paper was eventually sold for less than $50,000. By 1990, Barry Minkow was bankrupted and serving 25 years in prison.*

Case Study Questions

1. Minkow's scheme could have been interrupted at several points. What measures could have been taken to prevent a scheme of this size from developing?
2. What kinds of investigative tools would have been useful in detecting Minkow's scheme? How would they be employed?
3. Should the bank or auditing firm share liability with Minkow for their failure to detect the fraud? Explain why or why not.

---

* For more details and analysis of this case, see Joe Domanick, *Faking It in America: Barry Minkow and the Great ZZZZ Scam* (Chicago: Contemporary Books, 1989); and Joseph T. Wells, "Accountancy and White-Collar Crime," *The Annals*, 525 (January 1993), pp. 83–94.

Who Is Prosecuted?

The prosecution of white-collar crime can result in many different types of outcomes. As noted earlier in this chapter, criminal prosecution is only one of a number of prosecution alternatives.

The decision to prosecute a case is arguably the most important decision in the justice system, although there has been relatively little systematic attention given this decision in white-collar crime cases. A national survey of more than 1,000 district attorneys in the United States revealed that they "generally do not regard corporate crime as a serious problem and most do not anticipate doing more prosecutions in the future."[17] Nevertheless, this survey found that there are significantly more jurisdictions with specialized economic crime units than was the case 20 years earlier. Interestingly, approximately two-third of the local prosecutors "never cooperate" in joint ventures with federal agencies.[18] This lack of coordination among agencies has been a long-standing problem of law enforcement that continues to detract from its effectiveness.

A number of attempts have been made to assess the results of white-collar crime prosecutions that do occur. An examination of prosecutions by a large-county economic crime unit found that one-third of its cases resulted in criminal prosecution and two-thirds were closed without prosecution.[19] An analysis of a sample of these cases discovered that cases involving individual defendants and corporate or multiple victims were the most likely to be prosecuted. It was found that "pressure to win cases" was coupled with "a rather limited set of investigative and prosecutorial resources." Cases involving multiple or organizational victims were prosecuted due to the "increased likelihood of securing a conviction," inasmuch as multiple victims strengthened testimony and a victimized bank, for example, often had the accountants or auditors who discovered an embezzlement and did much of the preparation necessary for prosecution. Finally, the prosecution of individual, versus corporate, defendants appeared to result from the difficulty people have "to think of organizations as criminal actors" and the political liability for an elected prosecutor "to alienate the business interests of the community" through prosecution of businesses.[20]

In a study of prosecutions of corporations by the Securities and Exchange Commission (SEC), Susan Shapiro found that cases chosen for prosecution more often involved multiple offenders, multiple victims, and large amounts of money. The nature of the offense and offender, and whether the violation was continuing, were also important factors.[21] Although additional analyses are obviously needed, it appears that the local prosecutor preferred smaller, less complex, cases for prosecution, whereas the SEC went after large cases. As Joan Neff Gurney has pointed out, this difference may be related to the relative level of investigative resources enjoyed by prosecutors and perhaps the degree of insularity from political considerations, such as might cause the reluctance to go after corporations in favor of individual defendants. As she concluded, a campaign to fight white-collar crime "can easily become a campaign against small-time con artists, embezzlers, and welfare cheaters unless more emphasis is placed on the quality of cases as opposed to producing good 'stats.'"[22]

Indeed, what has been termed the dichotomy between "seriousness and convictability" is more pronounced in white-collar crime cases than in other types of criminal cases. The maintenance of public confidence in the ability of the government to react appropriately to incidents of white-collar crime is clearly necessary. At the same time, as Michael Levi observes in Britain as well, "it is hard to resist demands that [an agency] should actively investigate a major case, even if that case is not as likely to yield a result as other less politically significant cases or if it consumes resources that might lead to convictions in many cases that are more convictable."[23]

To Regulate or Punish?

In the case of regulatory offenses, the situation is further muddied. Regulatory agencies exist to *ensure compliance*, whereas prosecution agencies exist to *assess responsibility and punish* violations. These separate mandates often lead to conflict, when regulatory agencies are criticized for not pursuing cases of wrongdoing more aggressively, and they respond by saying their mandate is not to pursue wrongdoers but to correct business practices at variance with law. It certainly can be argued that the criminal justice process is an inefficient way to ensure compliance with business regulations, due to the small number of prosecutions that occur, the selectivity in choosing targets, the incredible sluggishness of the process, and the often inconsequential penalties exacted.

One way out of this quagmire has been suggested by Nancy Frank.[24] She argues that occupational health, for example, must be protected through "overlapping systems of standard-setting and enforcement." In addition to the regulatory system and the criminal justice system, Frank believes that the tort system (civil suits) and expanded workers' compensation coverage provide a system of checks and balances, especially when regulatory agencies "fail to fulfill their mandate."[25] As she concludes,

> Concerned persons will continue to disagree about the precise levels of risk at which the costs of a regulatory standard outweigh the benefits. Whatever the level finally adopted, some residual risk will remain that is judged too expensive to eliminate. The workers' compensation system must be reinvigorated and expanded to compensate for the harms that ensue. The tort system must be readily available to workers who suffer illness due to exposures beyond legal limits. Criminal prosecution should be used judiciously to punish for reckless conduct that results in injury.[26]

Therefore, the enforcement of regulations in business and industry can be carried out at several levels: by the government through regulatory agencies, by the individual worker through compensation claims, by classes of employees or victims through civil suits, and by the community through criminal prosecution. Unfortunately, these alternatives are all available only for regulatory offenses, and not for other white-collar crimes, where the corrective force of the criminal law must be relied upon more heavily.

The Racketeering Law and White-Collar Crime

One controversial use of the criminal law against white-collar crime are the "Racketeer Influenced and Corrupt Organizations" (RICO) provisions.[27] This law was enacted as part of the Organized Crime Control Act of 1970, but was little used until the 1980s. It makes it unlawful to acquire, operate, or receive income from an *enterprise* through a *pattern* of *racketeering activity*. This means that any individual or group that commits two or more felonies within a 10-year period is subject to 20 years imprisonment, fines up to $25,000, forfeiture of any interest in the enterprise, as well as civil damages and dissolution of the enterprise itself. RICO's application against white-collar crime, as opposed to its original target group, was promoted by two U.S. Supreme Court cases that expanded RICO's scope. In *United States v. Turkette*,[28] the Court made it clear that the provisions of RICO encompass *both* the crimes of illegitimate enterprises, as well as crimes committed by otherwise legitimate business or government agencies. In *Sedima v. Imrex*,[29] the U.S. Supreme Court intervened in a case that arose from a civil suit between two corporations engaged in a joint venture. Sedima believed it had been cheated by Imrex in an overbilling scheme. It sued Imrex for mail and wire fraud (as the two predicate acts needed to establish a "pattern" of racketeering activity under RICO). Sedima claimed injury of at least $175,000 from the overbilling scheme and sought treble damages and attorney's fees. The U.S. Supreme Curt ruled that prior criminal convictions are *not* required for a RICO suit, as long as two predicate acts can be established in the current complaint. The Court also held that mere monetary loss is a sufficient "racketeering injury" to qualify for prosecution under RICO. As the Court concluded, "RICO is to be read broadly," which the Court believed was Congress's intent that RICO "be liberally construed to effectuate its remedial purposes."[30]

A four-justice dissent in the *Sedima* case reflects the current controversy surrounding the use of RICO in white-collar cases. The dissent argued that Congress did not intend RICO to apply to "garden variety frauds" and that RICO's organized crime connotation and severe penalties will encourage spurious suits in white-collar cases.

> Litigants, lured by the prospect of treble damages and attorney's fees, have strong incentive to invoke RICO's provisions whenever they can allege in good faith two instances of mail or wire fraud. Then the defendant, facing tremendous financial exposure in addition to the threat of being labeled a "racketeer," will have a strong interest in settling the dispute."[31]

Despite this liberal application of RICO, the controversy continues. The U.S. Court of Appeals, in reversing a tax conviction on other grounds, has suggested that RICO may be inappropriate for tax cases.[32]

The use of RICO's forfeiture provisions have come to play a significant role in white-collar crime prosecutions. In *Russello v. United States*, the U.S. Supreme Court held that the forfeiture of "any interest" in an enterprise, as required by RICO, includes all assets, profits, and proceeds from illegal activity.[33] There is, of course, fear that a defendant facing forfeiture under RICO will sell, transfer,

Table 8.1 Prosecution Outcomes of Felony Arrests

Status	White-Collar Crimes	Violent Crimes	Property Crimes	Public Order Offenses
Arrest prosecuted?	88%	82%	86%	81%
Conviction resulted?	74	66	76	67
Incarceration?	60	67	65	55
More than 1 year in prison?	18	39	26	18

Source: Compiled from Don Manson, *Tracking Offenders: White-Collar Crime* (Washington, D.C.: Bureau of Justice Statistics, 1986).

or give away his or her assets before a trial is concluded. As a result, prosecutors often ask for a pretrial "freezing" of assets, so they will not vanish during court proceedings. This procedure has raised constitutional questions of due process (by imposing restrictions before proof of a crime is demonstrated). The courts have, thus far, upheld pretrial freezing of assets.[34]

Prosecution Outcomes of White-Collar Cases Versus Conventional Crimes

Only during the last two decades has there emerged comparative information to assess the relative impact of white-collar crime prosecutions to those of conventional street crimes. The U.S. Bureau of Justice Statistics has published the prosecution outcomes for the three white-collar crimes it counts: forgery/counterfeiting, fraud, and embezzlement. Data were collected from eight states (California, Minnesota, Nebraska, New York, Ohio, Pennsylvania, Utah, and Virginia) and the Virgin Islands. These jurisdictions account for more than a third of the nation's population and an equal proportion of serious crime.

Of the nearly 459,000 felony arrests examined, 6 percent involved forgery, fraud, or embezzlement. This was the smallest category of crime in all but one of the states. This 6 percent constituted primarily forgery cases (54 percent), followed by fraud (38 percent), and embezzlement (8 percent). It is perhaps most instructive to *compare* the prosecution outcomes of these white-collar crimes to that for violent crimes (e.g., homicide, kidnapping, rape, robbery, assault), property crimes (e.g., burglary, larceny, arson, and stolen property), and public order offenses (e.g., commercialized vice, drug offenses, disorderly conduct, and weapons offenses). The findings are summarized in Table 8.1.

Table 8.1 illustrates that white-collar offenders are prosecuted and convicted at least as often as those charged with violent, property, or public order felonies. White-collar offenders were incarcerated somewhat less often than violent and property offenders, but more often than were public order offenders. Likewise, forgery, fraud, and embezzlement offenders received prison sentences of more than a year at the same rate (18 percent) as did public order offenders but less often than violent or property offenders.

It should be noted that these offenses, taken from the Uniform Crime Report, contain a high proportion of low-level forgery, fraud, and embezzlement arrests. More serious white-collar cases, such as insider trading and price-fixing, often do not result in arrests or escape criminal prosecution due to administrative or civil regulatory enforcement. Therefore, the white-collar prosecution and conviction percentages may actually be lower than that reported here, to the extent that low-level cases are overrepresented, something impossible to determine with accuracy given existing data sources.

Offender Backgrounds

The demographic characteristics of white-collar offenders provide interesting comparisons with offenders for other offenses. Table 8.2 illustrates the similarities and differences. For all felony arrests combined, most suspects were male (85 percent), white (60 percent), and under 30 years old (63 percent). Those arrested for white-collar crimes had a very similar racial background, but they were older and more were females than were those arrested for violent, property, and public order crimes. More than one-third of all forgery, fraud, and embezzlement arrestees were female, which is nearly three times the proportion found among property and public order offenders and nearly four times greater than for arrestees for violent crimes. This higher rate of female participation in white-collar crimes is examined more closely in Chapter 11.

In a similar way, white-collar crime arrestees were more likely to be at least 30 years old, and less likely to be under 20 years old, than were suspects for any other category of crime. The demographic patterns found when comparing *convicted* offenders were "quite similar to the patterns for those arrested."[35] This indicates that white-collar offenders contain a greater proportion of females and older offenders, and about the same racial background as offenders convicted of violent, property, or public order crimes. Because crime is strongly associated with opportunity, it is not surprising that offenses like forgery, fraud, and embezzlement, which require greater planning and access (and less physical force) than conventional crimes, are more often committed by females and older persons.

There have been other analyses of white-collar offenders, but most focus on the sentences received of those prosecuted and convicted for certain specific types of offenses. These are summarized in Chapter 9.

Prosecution Problems and Solutions

Like most solutions, the prosecution solution yields temporary results. The impact of prosecution is diluted by the comparatively low ratio of offenses

Table 8.2 Offender Characteristics by Type of Crime

Persons Arrested	White-Collar Crimes	Violent Crimes	Property Crimes	Public Order Offenses
Male	61%	89%	86%	86%
Female	34	9	13	13
White	61	47	61	67
African-American	30	49	35	30
Under 20 years	6	11	16	7
20–29 years	49	54	54	50
30–39 years	30	22	20	25
40 or older	15	12	10	18

Source: Compiled from Don Manson, *Tracking Offenders: White-Collar Crime* (Washington, D.C.: Bureau of Justice Statistics, 1986).

detected per prosecution, by the selectivity in choosing among prosecution targets, and by the extent to which offenders are not deterred by prosecution outcomes. An added problem is that corporations, like individuals, are resourceful, and can be clever in their response to increased prosecutions.

The Environmental Protection Agency, for example, has become more aggressively "enforcement oriented" in recent years and less "compliance oriented" in forcing companies to undertake clean-up efforts in toxic spills and dumps. As Harold Barnett has found, "major corporations are not pleased with the EPA's new strategy."[36] The corporations see themselves as victims, by having to pay for entire clean-ups at sites where others have dumped. This has resulted in increased use of third-party suits. For example, Du Pont, and others, have sued 50 New Jersey municipalities for clean-up costs at a landfill. B. F. Goodrich has done the same in Connecticut, as have General Electric and Polaroid in Massachusetts.[37] The down side of this trend is that it further complicates and delays the proper assessment of responsibility and clean-up. The up side, however, is that companies issued orders by EPA for cleanups are now conducting investigations of their own to establish shared responsibility for clean-ups. For example, Monsanto reduced its liability by 40 percent in a $40 million clean-up by identifying 20 additional responsible parties.[38] As Barnett concluded, "potentially liable minor contributors, faced with the threat of third-party suits, have found settlement to be less expensive than litigation."[39] This may ultimately be a fruitful prosecution avenue, for it relieves some of the time-consuming government burden of establishing shared responsibility for multi-party corporate violations, replacing it with negotiations among the corporate actors themselves.

The Defense of White-Collar Cases

The burden on the defendant in a white-collar civil or criminal prosecution bears many similarities to a typical trial. The judge or jury sees an injured victim, harmed public, or defrauded victim, and it wants to assess blame. The person in the defendant's chair may be seen as culpable simply due to the fact that he or she has been accused and there are no other suspects around.

The defenses available to white-collar defendants are the same as those available to defendants in cases of traditional crimes. In practice, the choice of defenses are much more limited because self-defense, defense of property, or insanity defenses have few conceivable applications in white-collar crime cases.

Entrapment

Perhaps the most commonly used defense in white-collar crime cases is entrapment. Entrapment arises when the government entices a defendant to commit a crime in an unfair way. Under current U.S. law, there are two legal formulations of the defense: objective and subjective.

The objective formulation defines entrapment when government agents induce or encourage a person to commit a crime by making false representations or by employing methods that create a substantial risk an offense will be committed by an innocent (i.e., unpredisposed) person. As the U.S. Supreme Court held in 1932, government officials may not "implant in the mind of an innocent person the disposition to commit the alleged offense and induce its commission in order that they may prosecute."[40] This was the finding of the trial court in the case of John Delorean who was accused of trafficking in drugs to keep his car company afloat. The court decided in his case that his involvement was the product of the "creative" activity of law enforcement, the result of inducements made to him.[41]

The subjective formulation looks to the defendant's predisposition to commit a crime. If the defendant's actions indicate he or she was predisposed to commit a crime, the government's actions are not controlling. The convictions of members of the U.S. Congress in the Abscam bribery scandal of the late 1970s were based on the subjective formulation of the entrapment defense.[42] This was the first major federal investigation to rely on videotaped transactions to allow jurors to assess the illegality of transactions. On appeal from his Abscam conviction, Senator Harrison Williams argued that he had initially rejected the offer to violate the law and, therefore, was not predisposed (and, hence, entrapped). The U.S. Court of Appeals found that he had indeed rejected an initial offer, but the totality of evidence permitted a finding that he was "ready and willing" to commit the crimes "as soon as the opportunity was first presented."[43] In such a case, the prosecution must prove predisposition to commit the crime *prior* to contact by government agents. Once this is proven, the tactics of the government, whether they involve the use of known criminals, incredible incentives, or misrepresentation of the facts, are not controlling. In states where the objective formulation is used, questionable police tactics would be examined carefully, for their ability to entrap innocent persons would determine the case outcome.

The subjective formulation of the entrapment defense is in force in the majority of states and also is used in the federal courts.[44]

Covert Facilitation: Balancing Privacy and Justice

The use of "covert facilitation" tactics by police has always been on the border of acceptable police policy. This is because it threatens privacy, can be abused by manufacturing excessive temptations, and can undermine public confidence in the system, if not used with extreme care.

Whether or not these tactics should be abandoned can be considered a moot point for two reasons: first, they are well established in law and policy so their abolition is unlikely, and second, there are often not any other alternatives in investigating suspected cases of white-collar crime. As Braithwaite, Fisse, and Geis point out, these crimes "are generally incapable of stirring complainants." Therefore, "a choice must be made between proactive enforcement and neglect of crimes of the powerful."[45]

To maintain a "balanced policy position," Braithwaite, Fisse, and Geis argue that methods of covert facilitation may only be used as evidence in criminal cases when

1. Probable cause is established,
2. The operation is reviewed by a judge,
3. The targeted behavior is not a victimless crime and is regarded as serious by the community, and
4. There are severe penalties for covert facilitation without judicial approval.

Interestingly, these conditions are remarkably similar to those now in place in the United States for electronic surveillance. Restrictions on electronic surveillance include probable cause, a warrant signed by a judge, a suspected felony, and civil and criminal penalties for warrantless electronic surveillance. Braithwaite, Fisse, and Geis add as a caveat, however, that probable cause should not be required in cases against public corporations, "which do not have the same claim on a right to privacy as private citizens."[46] The debate regarding the appropriate limits of the state in attempting to intervene in criminal activity at its earliest stages continues.[47]

Defense Attorneys for White-Collar Defendants

Kenneth Mann surveyed all defense attorneys who handled white-collar cases in federal court in Manhattan over a five-year period and also observed some of the lawyers working on their cases. He found that these attorneys "rarely try cases" and work very hard using both substantive argument and information control "before an official charge is made." Their objective is to prevent the government "from discovering the guilt of the client or from coming to the conclusion that it can prove the guilt of the client."[48]

This raises an ethical issue regarding the proper role of the defense attorney. Is the proper role to protect a client's legal rights, or is it to win acquittal at any cost? It appears that, in practice, the latter is what occurs, despite its ethical ambiguities. As Mann found, it is considered "a significant failure for the defense attorney" if a criminal charge is issued.[49]

Unlike attorneys in cases of conventional crimes, the defense attorney specializing in white-collar cases devotes more time per case to a much smaller caseload. When charges are brought, the common plea-bargain works somewhat differently from pleas in conventional crimes. Because the defense attorney is involved in the case very early (usually before a charge is even filed), he or she enhances the bargaining position "by attempting to limit the government's access to facts inculpatory of his client."[50] This includes protecting documents from discovery and influencing the statements of witnesses.

Strategy in negotiating a plea is complex because the defense attorney must (1) keep it from looking like the defendant is guilty and (2) keep the government from believing it can prove the case in court. In conventional cases, guilt is the starting point of plea-negotiations, a more logical sequence. It can be seen that the defense of white-collar cases is more a cat-and-mouse game involving access to information and legal arguments that begin before an arrest or indictment is issued. Given the power, position, and status of many white-collar defendants, the goal of the defense is to avoid the stigma of a criminal charge at all costs. Defendants in conventional cases, however, do not have so far to fall. For them, mitigating the punishment to the extent possible is the focus of the defense in most cases. For white-collar defendants, the focus is avoidance of the process entirely.

Summary

The investigation, prosecution, and defense of white-collar crime are more complex than for conventional crimes. The complexity derives largely from the nature of the behavior and the status of the suspects under investigation. The ability of white-collar suspects and defendants to manipulate the adjudication process to some extent is enhanced by their access to outstanding legal talent, close relationship with regulators, and ability to face protracted legal battles. The ability of economically powerful defendants to take on a government prosecution more aggressively and successfully than less advantaged defendants is an issue of grave concern that affects public confidence in the adjudication process and, ultimately, in the government itself.

Endnotes

1. August Bequai, *White-Collar Crime: A 20th Century Crisis* (Lexington, MA: Lexington Books, 1978).
2. U.S. Comptroller General, *Stronger Effort Needed in Fight Against Organized Crime* (Washington, D.C.: U.S. General Accounting Office, 1981).

3. Nancy Frank, *Crimes Against Health and Safety* (Albany, NY: Harrow and Heston, 1985), pp. 69–71; see also Andrew Szaz, "Corporations, Organized Crime, and the Disposal of Hazardous Waste: An Examination of the Making of a Criminogenic Regulatory Structure," *Criminology*, 24 (February 1986).
4. Laureen Snider, "Cooperative Models and Corporate Crime: Panacea or Cop-Out?" *Crime & Delinquency*, 36 (July 1990), pp. 373–390.
5. See, also, Nancy Reichman, "Moving Backstage: Uncovering the Role of Compliance Practices in Shaping Regulatory Policy," *White-Collar Crime Reconsidered*, ed. by Kip Schlegel and David Weisburd (Boston: Northeastern University Press, 1992), pp. 244–268.
6. Frank E. Hagan, *Introduction to Criminology*, 2nd ed. (Chicago: Nelson-Hall, 1990), p. 415.
7. James W. Coleman, *The Criminal Elite: The Sociology of White-Collar Crime*, 2nd ed. (New York: St. Martin's Press, 1989), pp. 187–192.
8. Elizabeth Szockyj, "Insider Trading: The SEC Meets Carl Karcher," *The Annal*, 525 (January 1993), pp. 46–58.
9. Susan P. Shapiro, *Wayward Capitalists: Target of the Securities and Exchange Commission* (New Haven, CT: Yale University Press, 1984).
10. U.S. Comptroller General, *Securities Regulation: Efforts to Detect, Investigate and Deter Insider Trading* (Washington, D.C.: U.S. General Accounting Office, 1988).
11. Leigh Edward Somers, *Economic Crimes: Investigative Principles and Techniques* (New York: Clark Boardman, 1984), p. 49.
12. Cited in Henry N. Pontell and Kitty Calavita, "White-Collar Crime in the Savings and Loan Scandal," *The Annals*, 525 (January 1993), p. 41.
13. Ibid., p. 43.
14. Ibid., p. 98.
15. See *Holland v. United States*, 348 U.S. 121 (1954).
16. Somers, *Economic Crimes*, p. 102.
17. Michael L. Benson, Francis T. Cullen, and William J. Maakestad, *Local Prosecutors and Corporate Crime* (Washington, D.C.: National Institute of Justice, 1993); and Michael L. Benson, Francis T. Cullen, and William J. Maakestad, "Local Prosecutors and Corporate Crime," *Crime & Delinquency*, 36 (July 1990), pp. 356–372.
18. Benson, Cullen, and Maakestad, "Local Prosecutors and Corporate Crime," p. 368.
19. Joan Neff Gurney, "Factors Influencing the Decision to Prosecute Economic Crime," *Criminology*, 23 (November 1985), p. 611.
20. Ibid., pp. 618–621.
21. Shapiro, *Wayward Capitalists*.
22. Gurney, "Factors Influencing the Decision to Prosecute Economic Crime," p. 623.
23. Michael Levi, "White-Collar Crime: The British Scene," *The Annals*, 525 (January 1993), p. 81.

24. Nancy Frank, "Maiming and Killing: Occupational Health Crimes," *The Annals*, 525 (January 1993), pp. 107–118.
25. Ibid., p. 118.
26. Ibid.
27. 18 U.S.C. Sec. 1961–1968.
28. 101 S.Ct. 2524 (1980).
29. 105 S.Ct. 3275 (1985).
30. at 3286.
31. at 3294.
32. *United States v. Regan*, 937 F.2d 823 (2d Cir. 1991).
33. 464 U.S. 16 (1983).
34. P. Shaw, "Fifth Amendment Failures and RICO Forfeitures," *American Business Law Journal*, 28 (1990), p. 169.
35. Don Manson, *Tracking Offenders: White-Collar Crime* (Washington, D.C.: Bureau of Justice Statistics, 1986), p. 4.
36. Harold C. Barnett, "Crimes Against the Environment: Superfund Enforcement at Last," *The Annals*, 525 (January 1993), p. 130.
37. Robert Tomsho, "Pollution Ploy: Big Corporations Hit by Superfund Cases Find Way to Share Bill," *The Wall Street Journal*, April 2, 1991.
38. Robert Tomsho, "Gumshoes Help Companies Cut Dump Cleanup Bills," *The Wall Street Journal*, November 5, 1991.
39. Barnett, "Crimes Against the Environment," p. 131.
40. *Sorrells v. United States*, 53 S.Ct. 210 (1932).
41. Thomas J. Gardner and Terry M. Anderson, *Criminal Law: Principles and Cases*, 5th ed. (St. Paul, MN: West, 1992), p. 185.
42. Robert W. Greene, *The Sting Man: Inside Abscam* (New York: Ballantine Books, 1982).
43. *United States v. Williams*, 705 F.2d 603 (2d Cir 1983), cert. denied, 104 S.Ct. 524 (1983).
44. Ellen S. Podgor, *White-Collar Crime* (St. Paul, MN: West, 1993), p. 10.
45. John Braithwaite, Brent Fisse, and Gilbert Geis, "Covert Facilitation and Crime: Restoring the Balance to the Entrapment Debate," *Journal of Social Issues*, 43 (1987), pp. 5–41.
46. Ibid., p. 36.
47. See Gary T. Marx, "Restoring Realism and Logic to the Covert Facilitation Debate," *Journal of Social Issues*, 43 (1987), pp. 43–55; and Jerome H. Skolnick, "The Risks of Covert Solicitation," *Journal of Social Issues*, 43 (1987), pp. 79–85.
48. Kenneth Mann, *Defending White-Collar Crime: A Portrait of Attorneys at Work* (New Haven, CT: Yale University Press, 1985), p. 9.
49. Ibid.
50. Ibid., p. 14.

CHAPTER 9

Criminal Sentences and Other Remedies

*I am surprised, in visiting jails, to find
so few respectable looking convicts.*
— *Charles Dudley Warner (1873)*

Concern About Sentencing

The sentences imposed on white-collar criminals have drawn concern on at least four distinct grounds:

1. Are the sentences *proportionate* to the harm caused?
2. What should be the *purpose* or goal of the sentence?
3. Is there an appropriate way to sanction an *organization*, as opposed to an *individual* white-collar offender?
4. Which sentencing alternatives have the *most impact* on white-collar crime: civil remedies, new types of fines, corporate rehabilitation, whistle-blowing incentives, or other strategies?

Proportionality

The concern over proportionality is fundamental. There is truth in the fact that one is more likely to go to prison for a longer period for a candy store robbery than for toxic waste dumping into drinking water. Is this just?

An examination of the sentences imposed for 31 white-collar offenses in ten different federal courts found that white-collar offenders of high social status (as measured by college education and income level) received more severe sentences than did persons committing nonwhite-collar offenses.[1] In another study of sentences for eight categories of federal white-collar crimes, it was found that defendants with higher social status *were not* sentenced more leniently than were those of lower social status.[2] These results seem to contradict popular wisdom that white-collar offenders are handled more leniently than other offenders, due to their comparatively high social status or positions of power.

Subsequent studies by some of the same investigators came to different conclusions that *support* the popular wisdom. For example, Kathleen Daly reanalyzed the data of the study of eight categories of federal offenses just cited and found that, for the women in the sample, "occupational marginality" best explained the results. That is to say, most of the women in the sample were either clerical workers or unemployed persons who happened to commit white-collar offenses.[3] For the men in the study, it was found that a significant portion were unemployed at the time of their offenses.[4] In a subsequent study by Hagan and Parker, the authors examined securities violations over a 17-year period in Ontario, Canada. Unlike earlier work, the authors used "relational indicators" (such as ownership and authority) to assess the power of those accused. The authors found that employers were more likely to escape adjudication than were managers.[5] Tillman and Pontell compared the sentences imposed for frauds by California Medicaid providers with those imposed on those charged with simple grand theft. They found that the fraud offenders "were much less likely" to be incarcerated than were nonwhite-collar offenders charged with grand theft. This result was despite the fact that the monetary losses from the Medicaid frauds, "on average, were much greater."[6]

An interesting analysis was conducted by Hagan and Palloni of sentences received by federal white-collar offenders before and after the Watergate affair. They found that "white-collar offenders were more likely to be imprisoned after Watergate than before, but for shorter periods."[7] This was seen as a way in which the judiciary responded "to calls for stiffer sentencing" by imposing more jails sentences, but for shorter periods. An earlier statistical study, just noted, of federal white-collar offenders found defendants with high socioeconomic status to receive more severe sentences than others. The authors suggested that the time period of their study (cases from 1975 to 1978) may have influenced the findings in the aftermath of Watergate and heightened concern about white-collar crime in general.[8] In a subsequent analysis of the same data, it was concluded that "common-crime offenders have committed less serious crimes than white-collar offenders, but their backgrounds, particularly their criminal records, are much more damaging.[9] Perhaps like the Watergate scandal of the 1970s, the savings and loan crisis of the 1980s and 1990s may have provoked a trend toward punitive responses to white-collar crime. Between 1988 and 1991, a total of 764 defendants were charged in savings and loan cases, and 550 defendants (93 percent of those tried) were convicted. Of the 412 defendants who had been sentenced, 79 percent received prison terms, together with fines of more than $8 million and restitution of more than $270 million.[10]

What one is to make of these conflicting studies is not clear. The conclusion reached by many is that those holding positions of power and, hence, higher-class positions, more successfully escape punishment, due to the influence their position brings. This is speculative, however, and alternative conclusions are just as tenable. Could it be that those with positions of power are more often targeted as public examples, and hence weaker cases are brought against them that would not be pursued as far with lower-profile defendants? Could it be that superior legal talent available to those of higher-class positions bring better results for their clients? Could it be that fewer successful cases are brought against those holding positions of power due to the comparative complexity of the schemes required and the difficulty in making successful cases? Could it be that many of their offenses are handled within the regulatory system and avoid the criminal justice system? If the answer to any of these questions is "yes," then the problem does not necessarily mean one of official deference to those holding positions of power. Instead, the problems lie in inequalities in selecting cases for prosecution in a manner that contradicts current assumptions, the availability of effective legal counsel, the competence of law enforcement in investigating complex cases, and the effectiveness of the regulatory adjudication process. These alternative explanations must be kept in mind, because a finding that those with power receive lighter sanctions does not necessarily mean that one *causes* the other. Other plausible explanations must be tested to rule out competing conclusions.

The Philosophy of Sentencing

The debate over the proper goals of sentencing continues for white-collar crime, as it has for centuries for traditional crimes. The debate centers on four familiar themes:

1. *Retribution*: Punish the offender simply in proportion to the harm caused.
2. *Deterrence*: Impose penalties that will serve to prevent the offender, and inhibit others, from engaging in unlawful behavior.
3. *Incapacitation*: Make it impossible for the offender, through physical or legal means, to cause future harm.
4. *Rehabilitation*: Change the offender, or the offender's environment, to reform subsequent behavior.

Both deterrence and incapacitation are evaluated largely in their effort to prevent repeat criminality. Obviously, it is difficult, if not impossible, to assess the impact of penalties on crimes that never occurred. The next best thing is to examine the impact of penalties on subsequent offending. In one of the only studies of this type for white-collar offenders, Weisburd, Chayet, and Waring found that white-collar offenders are often repeat offenders. In addition, they found that their crimes "begin later and evidence lower frequency of offending than do those of street criminals."[11] These findings raise yet unanswered questions about the deterrent effect of different kinds of first-time penalties, or whether incapacitation strategies, such as delicensing or disbarment, may be appropriate in the same way that some have argued for longer-term incarceration of predicted high-rate street crime offenders.[12]

Selective incapacitation of white-collar offenders would be even more problematic than if applied to traditional criminals. There exists the same serious constitutional issue of imposing long sentences for crimes not yet committed, but that are *predicted* to occur. In addition, our ability to predict crimes, even among first- or second-time offenders, is still quite poor. Severe penalties imposed on those wrongly predicted to commit future crimes (false-positives) also carry a high price in human, legal, and financial terms. Finally, in the case of white-collar crime, there may well be a secondary deleterious impact on employees, the community, and consumers, if businesses are forced to close due to the misconduct of their owners or managers. These arguments make incapacitation an unworkable, and perhaps undesirable, policy.

The deterrent effect of sanctions has been shown to be low in several studies. Recall that each of the surveys of corporate violations reported in Chapter 6 found a significant recidivism rate among offending companies. Either this demonstrates the law's poor deterrent effect, or else the nature, frequency, or seriousness of the penalties imposed is suspect. As numerous studies have suggested, for deterrence to be achieved, there must be a high certainty of apprehension, and the time elapsed between offense and sanction must be as short as possible. Clearly, neither of these conditions is met in the case of white-collar crime. What Donald Scott has observed in antitrust prosecutions holds true for other forms of white-collar crime: "Given the limited resources available for enforcement, the reliance on reactive sources of intelligence, and the tremendous breadth of the modern economy, the probability of detection must be incredibly low."[13] Due to the low visibility, high probability of concealment, lack of a complainant, and likelihood of a protracted legal battle, it is unlikely that the certainty or celerity of sanctions can ever be increased to the extent necessary to deter white-collar crime.

That leaves retribution and rehabilitation. Retribution as a purpose of punishment dates from biblical times. The "eye for an eye" argument is an early statement of retribution as a goal of punishment. In contemporary criminology, Andrew von Hirsch brought new legitimacy to retribution, arguing that "the central principle of a desert rationale for sentencing is commensurability. Sentences should be proportionate in their severity to the gravity of offenders' criminal conduct." In addition, "prospective considerations—the effect of the penalty on the future behavior of the defendant or other potential offenders—should not determine the comparative severity of penalties."[14] It is this second aspect of the retribution or "desert" philosophy of punishment that distinguishes it from deterrence, incapacitation, or rehabilitation. These other rationales for sentencing all are pragmatic in their focus on the prevention of *future* behavior. Von Hirsch argues that such considerations are inaccurate, unfair judgments are made based on wrong predictions of future behavior, and they overlook that the purpose of punishment is reprobation. To use a person to prevent other crimes is inconsistent with "the idea that each person (even an offender) have value in himself—and should not be used just as a means to benefit others."[15]

Rehabilitation "requires the assumption that even the most recalcitrant seeming individuals can be made to change their characters, values, and habits through state-sponsored treatment efforts."[16] Efforts to accomplish this lofty objective have experienced mixed results at best. Given the environment in which most white-collar offenders commit their crimes (as shown in Chapter 7), there appears to be a large number of market, organizational, individual, and governmental factors that must be changed to achieve rehabilitation. Nevertheless, the ability of a corporation to alter and mold its environment, unlike the comparative powerlessness of an individual, has given rise to interest in corporate rehabilitation. This is discussed later in this chapter.

Braithwaite and Pettit have offered what they term "a republican theory of criminal justice" that attempts to find common ground in answering questions about punishment, law, enforcement, and adjudication. This theory promotes "dominion" (i.e., equal liberty) ruled by four assumptions: "parsimony, the checking of power, reprobation, and the reintegration of victim and offender."[17] The authors argue that even retributivists must consider the consequences of penalties. Otherwise, no answers are provided to the fundamental questions of who to punish, how, and why.[18] As a result, we are drawn, by necessity, to be "consequentialists," who are backward thinking in punishing for past acts, but also forward thinking in answering the questions of why punish, whom to punish, and in what way. Therefore, some combination of retribution (backward looking) and deterrence, incapacitation, and/or rehabilitation (forward looking) are considered in most proposals for sentencing both white-collar and traditional offenders, although federal sentencing guidelines adopt no philosophy of sentencing. The problems this poses are discussed in Chapter 12.

Sanctioning the Organization Versus the Individual

Donald Cressey has argued that organizational, or corporate, crime does not actually exist. Instead, corporate crimes are committed by corporate officials, making corporate liability a mask covering the liability of individual corporate officials.[19] This position is not held by many others, including Braithwaite and Fisse, who argue that the actions and outcomes of organizations "are more than the sum of the products of individual actions."[20] In addition, the decision-making process of organizations can be observed, whereas the decision-making process of individuals is usually not observable.

In a book-length study of corporate crime in the pharmaceutical industry, and a follow-up article ten years later, John Braithwaite documented the extent of the white-collar crime problem and new ways to respond to it.[21] In his book, he reported that 19 of the 20 largest U.S. pharmaceutical companies had been involved in recent bribery scandals. Widespread problems of ineffective, impure, unsterile, or otherwise unsafe products added to the larger problem of fudged drug tests on animals and on humans as well. The pharmaceutical market has since become more international in scope, causing severe problems in knowing the nature, extent, and seriousness of violations.

Given the immense scope of the problem, how can it be addressed in an effective way? Braithwaite argues the criminal law is "too clumsy and costly a device to be the front-line assault weapon." Instead, he sees the role of the criminal law as important as "heavy artillery that provides the backing to push the front-line troops forward" that do most of the fighting against the problem.[22] So who are the front-line troops?

Braithwaite argues that these heretofore "underrated" sources for industry regulation are international organizations, consumer and professional groups, and self-regulation within and among firms. He anticipates criticism of what appears to be a weak set of "front-line troops," but Braithwaite believes their strength derives from their web of relations. The apparent weakness of consumer and professional groups is offset, according to Braithwaite, by their ability to change attitudes. These groups can "mobilize media assaults, sow seeds of professional distrust of the industry, foment consumer cynicism about the products the industry sells, heighten the threat of government regulation, nurture industry self-regulation to fend off the latter threat, and initiate mass tort litigation."[23] Such an assault on many fronts can change the conduct of the industry through pressure and by bringing out whistle-blowers within the industry who see a supportive external environment for doing so.

When we compare the use of the criminal law in addressing pharmaceutical industry offenses, the United States is a leader in its use of the criminal sanction. Nevertheless, criminal adjudication is still relatively rare in the United States.[24] Braithwaite uses the examples of Guatemala and Sweden, two countries that do not use the criminal law to regulate or punish pharmaceutical companies. Despite this fact, there exists a huge difference among the countries in the relative safety of their drugs in terms of morbidity and mortality. This difference, he argues, is due to the "total fabric of the web of controls" just outlined.[25]

The sentencing guidelines set forth by the U.S. Sentencing Commission include a provision for "organizational probation" that permits corporations to be placed under court-ordered supervision, make restitution, reorganize, or perform other tasks. This new form of corporate sanctioning is described in more detail in the next section.

Creative Approaches

Many alternatives exist to the use of criminal sanctions, which can be highly effective in correcting wrongs and in promoting lawful behavior. These include civil sanctions, corporate rehabilitation, informant incentives, and enforced codes of ethics.

Alternative Sentences and Their Impact

Civil sanctions are less time consuming and costly than criminal sanctions. Civil procedure is simpler, and the burden of proof lower. Also, the threat of civil penalties "typically evokes a less defensive response" from the accused, increasing the chances for a faster, negotiated solution, rather than a slower, litigated verdict.[26] The monetary penalties imposed under civil law can be formidable, creating the desired deterrent effect.

Monetary fines are the most common penalty imposed in both criminal and civil cases. This is especially true in the case of white-collar crimes. Innovative methods have been proposed to structure fines in a manner that maximizes their fairness to all concerned. For example, equity fines have been proposed, where a company would be required to issue additional stock in the amount of its fine. The shares would be deposited and used as part of a crime victim compensation fund. This would devalue a company's stock, arguably something more feared by corporations and their officers than a temporary loss of profit. The equity fine also would not take away working capital that would hurt a company's operations.[27]

In a similar way, a pass-through fine could achieve fairness in the assessment of corporate sanctions. In this case, the fine is forfeiture of a certain number of a company's shares. The shares' value would remain the same, but they would no longer be owned by the company's shareholders. This would combat indifference among shareholders of the company's business activities.[28]

Corporate rehabilitation is used to connote mandatory changes in corporate structure, policy, or operations imposed as a condition of sentencing for a civil or criminal violation. These changes would be designed to alter the corporation's method of doing business, making it more difficult to repeat violations. Corporate rehabilitation is similar in intent to what has been tried in the corrections systems for many years with individuals. It can be argued, however, that it may be easier to change the conduct of corporations, due to their more observable decision-making processes. John Braithwaite has argued, for example, that corporations be forced to restructure their internal notification procedures, so that employees would notify directly (and anonymously) the head of the company about any abuses, avoiding the oftentimes oppressive management structure that can kill negative messages. This would make it impossible for the head of the company to claim ignorance about violations.[29] It has also been suggested that "impartial and informed outsiders" be placed within offending corporations, "a process analogous to detective squad surveillance of an identified trouble spot."[30]

Other innovative sentencing ideas, based on the notion of corporate rehabilitation, include community service orders for corporations that benefit the community. These orders, according to Brent Fisse, should make use of the company's "skills and resources to develop or apply new and improved methods of resolving the problems caused."[31] Publicity regarding nonoffending firms that manage to comply with legal standards, as well as negative publicity for firms that violate standards, has also been suggested.[32] In a Los Angeles case, a plating firm was found to have discharged wastes illegally through multiple sewer connections. As part of its sentence, the company was forced to place a notice in *The Wall Street Journal* admitting it had violated the law.[33] Donald Scott in a study of criminal prosecutions of collusive trade agreements found that "public exposure of trade conspiracies" serves as a deterrent, despite the weak penalties imposed.[34]

The U.S. Sentencing Commission has considered some of these ideas regarding corporate rehabilitation in its sentencing guidelines, and it has embraced the concept of "organizational probation" in its guidelines enacted in late 1991.[35]

These guidelines incorporate some of the innovative ideas just discussed. For example, organizational probation can be ordered by the court "if necessary to ensure that changes are made within the organization to reduce the likelihood of future criminal conduct." Likewise, payment of a fine, restitution, or community service is a mandatory condition of the probation. In addition, discretionary conditions include "Publicity paid for by the defendant in media specified by the court detailing the crime, conviction, sentence, and remedial steps taken"; development of a court-approved prevention program, periodic reports to the court, employees, and shareholders regarding compliance; as well as periodic inspections of facilities, records, and employee interviews by the court or a "special probation officer" to monitor compliance.[36] These sentencing provisions reflect some of the innovations suggested by the criminological community, but also pose some problems discussed in Chapter 12. It will be interesting to see how often these conditions are imposed and what their impact will be in practice. As William Lofquist has observed, it is likely that organizational probation will receive regular use by the federal courts, because it is mandatory in many cases, detailed and remedial conditions are often required, and the "nonadversarial" regulations imposed on corporations may all work to promote its acceptance.[37]

An important prerequisite for any form of corporate rehabilitation should be an external investigation of an offending company by "outside persons of unquestioned integrity" to prepare a public report of the wrongdoing.[38] Such a report could be considered similar to a presentence report in criminal cases, or it can be mandated as part of a settlement. The findings of such a report would serve as an accurate record of the incident, maintain public confidence in sanctioning procedures (that are often not visible), and offer an *objective* view of how best to avoid future incidents (rather than the usual negotiated compromise by adversaries). Such an external investigation was commissioned by Gulf Oil in the 1970s, after it had been accused of improper payments. The report ultimately led to significant reforms within the company, as well as the resignation of senior executives.[39]

Controlling the Spread of Illicit Practices

Intermediate white-collar crime control strategies focus on the *spread* of illicit practices in business, industry, or government. Many of these are based on Sutherland's concept of differential association discussed in Chapter 7. Such strategies might involve providing incentives for whistle-blowers to reduce the fear of being fired and increase the likelihood that employees will resist learning criminal definitions. This has been attempted recently in several states that have passed laws to encourage citizen reporting of illegal hazardous waste disposal. Due to continuing problems of detection, and the fact that most prosecutions in hazardous waste cases have resulted from tips from citizens, New Jersey passed a law in 1985 allowing for payment of one-half the penalty collected for an illegal disposal.[40] Boss and George have argued along similar lines by proposing "a statutory duty be imposed upon employers to put in place a system that clearly indicates to employees that they are fully protected if they blow the whistle."[41] Likewise, the U.S. General Accounting Office, the investigative arm of Congress, established a 24-hour hotline in 1979 to allow citizens to report anonymously suspicions of frauds against the government. In its first seven years, more than 74,000 calls were received. Nearly 12,000 were referred to inspectors general of the agencies involved, and approximately 1,300 allegations were substantiated.[42] These allegations involved many types of white-collar crime. Consider the three incidents that follow:

An informant alleged postal carriers were accepting payments for providing special mail service to certain firms within a particular building. Because of the payments, the firms allegedly received their mail before anyone else. An investigation by the Inspection Service confirmed that some carriers were accepting payments from customers. As a result, three arrests were made.

An anonymous informant alleged an Interior Department employee working in Virginia was using a government charge account with a local auto dealer to purchase automobile parts for his personal vehicle. A Departmental Inspector General investigation disclosed that during a ten-month period the employee made 20 fraudulent automobile replacement part purchases, totaling $3,994, and had submitted the invoices to the Department of Interior for payment. The employee resigned after receiving notice of proposed removal. In addition, he entered a guilty plea to three counts of embezzlement and agreed to $3,994 being withheld from his retirement funds. He received a one-year suspended sentence on each count and two years' probation, and was required to do 300 hours community service and pay a $1,000 fine.

In another case, the caller alleged the owners of two San Francisco stores were involved in food stamp trafficking, possibly including stamps stolen from the Redwood City, California, food stamp office. After a nationwide investigation, both owners were indicted, convicted, and fined a total of $50,000 plus restitution, and sentenced to seven years in prison.[43]

It can be seen that informant incentive programs can be an effective means to uncover both large and small cases of white-collar crime. For these programs to be effective, however, they must be well publicized, and the incentives must be great enough to counteract possible repercussions to the informant.[44] A survey of federal workers by the GAO found that "fear of reprisal was a concern to many employees" in reporting misconduct.[45] The "hotline" approach, allowing for anonymous tips, and the "percentage" approach, providing for a portion of the fine to the informant, are two methods now being employed to stop the spread of illicit practices. Several important hazardous waste cases in Los Angeles were discovered from informants' tips.[46]

Another strategy, based both on Sutherland's assumptions and the ethical approach, would be the adoption of enforced codes of ethics so that loyalty to one's profession would outweigh the loyalty to any particular job. The purpose, of course, would be to increase the definitions unfavorable to crime. In a similar way, it has been suggested that *incentives*, rather than *penalties*, be used to promote conforming behavior, rather than punish deviance. Like ethics, this approach would be directed at preventing violations by emphasizing their harmfulness and their failure to bring pleasure under the pain–pleasure principle. One way to do this is to establish performance standards for a particular industry. Companies that meet these standards would be rewarded through tax breaks or other incentives.[47] Stephen Rackmill, chief U.S. probation officer for the Eastern District of New York, has concluded, "the prognosis for a positive change is ultimately contingent upon a sincere commitment to a higher standard of business ethics and reevaluation of our value systems."[48]

Summary

Historically, there has been too much attention given to the "more of" strategy in the control of white-collar crime. If white-collar criminals appear too successful, the crime control "strategy" has been a cry for "more" law enforcement officers or "more" laws to increase the chances for successful prosecution. The equivocal results of this strategy in the past clearly indicates the need for alternative approaches.[49] As Mary McIntosh suggests, increasing sophistication of law enforcement techniques may produce only more sophisticated forms of organizational crime.[50] What is needed, therefore, is a more informed approach based on a rational search for the causes of white-collar criminality. Theoretical efforts to clarify causal circumstances have, so far, been relatively few (as shown in Chapter 7). Given the clues provided by existing explanations, however, and the accumulation of case studies to apply and reformulate them, prevention strategies for white-collar crime can be based on an understanding of its causes rather than the reinvention of ineffective "solutions."

Better explanations are also required for the behavior of the law. The peculiarities of detection and selection for prosecution have not yet been adequately explained. As Michael Levi has expressed, "Is it acceptable that such judicial reflection about the value of punishment tends to be restricted to the small elite of white-collar offenders who are not selected out of the prosecution process and is so seldom extended to those who have no grace from which to fall?"[51]

CASE STUDY

Read the following case summary carefully, and answer the questions that follow, employing the concepts from this chapter.

Ford Pinto Deaths

During the 1970s Ford Motor Company manufactured a subcompact car called the "Pinto." Lee Iacocca, president of Ford, wanted to design and produce this car in only two years, much faster than the usual time frame for a new model. Also, Iacocca wanted the car to weigh no more than 2,000 pounds and cost no

The Ford Pinto was introduced as the smallest U.S.-made subcompact. Questions arose when the car would catch fire and explode after low-speed rear-end collisions. Ford Motor Company was indicted for reckless homicide in a Pinto explosion that resulted in three deaths. It was the first time a major American corporation was tried for homicide. *(UPI/Bettmann)*

more than $2,000. The timetable was met, and the first Pintos hit the road in 1971, only to be discontinued by 1980.

There seemed to be a problem with the location of the gas tank. At relatively low-speed rear-end collisions, a Pinto's gas tank would rupture, gas would leak out, and the car would burn. In one case, a Pinto suddenly stalled on a California highway and was struck from behind by a van traveling between 30 and 50 mph. The Pinto's gas tank ruptured, gas spilled out, the car caught fire and was enveloped in smoke. The driver was burned to death, and the passenger suffered burns over 80 percent of his body.

At the trial for a civil suit in this case, the star witness was a former Ford engineer. His testimony was devastating:

Q: In your opinion, how many of the survivable, of the 700 to 2,500 people who died from fire would have lived if the fuel tank had been located over the axle?

A: Ninety-five percent . . .

Q: Of your own knowledge, did Ford Motor Company know in 1970 that an over-the-axle location would prevent the death of the survivable people who would otherwise have lived?

A: Yes.

Q: Do you know of your own knowledge why the industry and Ford Motor Company have not placed—did not place the gas tank over the axle in 1970?

A: Yes.

Q: Why is that?

A: Cost . . .

Q: What was the cost of mounting a fuel tank over the axle to the Ford Motor Company?

A: For a fully protected tank with a metal barrier around it so it is completely between the wheel houses with metal coming up and forming an enclosure, the cost of that design was $9.95.

This testimony, supporting documentation, and Pinto test films that showed a Pinto bursting into flames when rear-ended at speeds as low as 20 mph, led the jury to conclude that Ford had wrongfully injured the passenger and awarded him $2.8 million. The family of the driver who was killed was awarded nearly $660,000. The jury also imposed $125 million in punitive damages against Ford, which the judge reduced to $3.5 million.

Cases like this one led Ford to recall in 1978 all the 1.5 million Pintos it had manufactured. Unfortunately, before recall notices were sent, a Pinto with three teenage girls inside was rear-ended in Indiana. The car exploded, and all three girls were burned to death. The case was similar in many respects to the Pinto cases preceding it, but this case was to make history.

Instead of just a civil suit against Ford, the prosecutor in Indiana brought homicide charges against the company. A grand jury indicted Ford Motor Company on three counts of reckless homicide for manufacturing an unsafe automobile. The case drew national attention, because it was the first time a major American corporation would be tried for murder. Rules of evidence in criminal cases are more stringent than in civil cases, so some documentation available in civil cases was not permitted in the murder trial. Ford also received outstanding defense representation and was ultimately acquitted. Nevertheless, Ford paid millions of dollars in settling civil suits arising from this and many other cases involving Pinto fires and explosions.

Case Study Questions

1. It has been said that monetary penalties, common in product liability cases, have only a short-term effect. Can you design a remedy for the Pinto case that might have a longer-term impact?
2. If Ford had been convicted of reckless homicide, what do you think would be an appropriate penalty, and why?
3. It can be argued that no monetary penalty or prison sentence is adequate in corporate liability cases that result in death or permanent injury. This is especially true when a corporate decision is involved and liability is spread over many corporate decision makers. Who should be held liable in a case like this one: Ford Motor Company, its executives, those who worked on the Pinto? How would you propose to distinguish between the liability of individual executives and responsibility of the corporation as a whole?

For more detailed information regarding liability in the Ford Pinto case, see Francis T. Cullen, William J. Maakestad, and Gray Cavender, *Corporate Crime Under Attack: The Ford Pinto Case and Beyond* (Cincinnati: Anderson, 1987); Stuart M. Speiser, *Lawsuit* (New York: Horizon Press, 1980); and Mark Dowie, "Pinto Madness," *Mother Jones*, September–October 1977.

Endnotes

1. John Hagan, Ilene Nagel, and Celesta Albonetti, "The Differential Sentencing of White-Collar Offenders in 10 Federal District Courts," *American Sociological Review*, 45 (1980), pp. 802–820.
2. Stanton Wheeler, David Weisburd, and Nancy Bode, "Sentencing and the White-Collar Offender: Rhetoric and Reality," *American Sociological Review*, 47 (1982), pp. 641–659.
3. Kathleen Daly, "Gender and Varieties of White-Collar Crime," *Criminology*, 27 (1989), pp. 769–793.
4. Stanton Wheeler, David Weisburd, Ellen Waring, and Nancy Bode, "White-Collar Crimes and Criminals," *American Criminal Law Review*, 25 (1988), p. 346.
5. John Hagan and Patricia Parker, "White-Collar Offenses and Punishment: The Class Structure and Legal Sanctioning of Securities Violations," *American Sociological Review*, 50 (1985), pp. 302–316.
6. Robert Tillman and Henry Pontell, "Is Justice 'Collar-Blind'?: Punishing Medicaid Provider Fraud," *Criminology*, 30 (November 1992), pp. 547–574.
7. John Hagan and Alberto Palloni, "'Club Fed' and the Sentencing of White-Collar Offenders Before and After Watergate," *Criminology*, 24 (November 1986).
8. Stanton D. Wheeler, David Weisburd, and Nancy Bode, "Sentencing and the White-Collar Offender: Rhetoric and Reality," *American Sociological Review*, 47 (October 1982).
9. David Weisburd, Stanton Wheeler, Elin Waring, and Nancy Bode, *Crimes of the Middle Classes: White-Collar Offenders in the Federal Courts* (New Haven, CT: Yale University Press, 1991), p. 163.
10. Office of the Attorney General, *Attacking Financial Fraud: A Report to Congress* (Washington, D.C.: U.S. Department of Justice, 1991).
11. David Weisburd, Ellen F. Chayet, and Elin J. Waring, "White-Collar Crime and Criminal Careers: Some Preliminary Findings," *Crime & Delinquency*, 36 (July 1990), pp. 342–355.
12. Peter Greenwood and Allan Abrahamse, *Selective Incapacitation* (Santa Monica, CA: Rand Corporation, 1982).
13. Donald W. Scott, "Policing Corporate Collusion," *Criminology*, 27 (August 1989), p. 582.
14. Andrew von Hirsch, *Past or Future Crimes: Deservedness and Dangerousness in the Sentencing of Criminals* (New Brunswick, NJ: Rutgers University Press, 1985), p. 31.
15. Ibid., p. 54.
16. Ibid., p. 4.
17. John Braithwaite and Philip Pettit, *Not Just Deserts: A Republican Theory of Justice* (New York: Oxford University Press, 1990), p. 133.

18. Ibid., p. 181; see also W. Byron Groves and Nancy Frank, "Punishment, Privilege and Structured Choice," in *Punishment and Privilege*, ed. by W. Byron Groves and Graeme Newman (Albany, NY: Harrow and Heston, 1986).

19. Donald R. Cressey, "The Poverty of Theory in Corporate Crime Research," *Advances in Criminological Theory*, Vol. 1, ed. by William Laufer and Freda Adler (New Brunswick, NJ: Transaction Books, 1989), pp. 31–56.

20. John Braithwaite and Brent Fisse, "On the Plausibility of Corporate Crime Theory," *Advances in Criminological Theory*, Vol. 2, ed. by William Laufer and Freda Adler (New Brunswick, NJ: Transaction Books, 1990), pp. 15–38.

21. John Braithwaite, *Corporate Crime in the Pharmaceutical Industry* (London: Routledge & Kegan Paul, 1984); and John Braithwaite, "Transnational Regulation of the Pharmaceutical Industry," *The Annals*, 525 (January 1993).

22. Braithwaite, "Transnational Regulation of the Pharmaceutical Industry," p. 27.

23. Ibid.

24. Braithwaite, *Corporate Crime in the Pharmaceutical Industry*, pp. 290ff.

25. Braithwaite, "Transnational Regulation of the Pharmaceutical Industry," p. 27.

26. Joseph F. DiMento, "Criminal Enforcement of Environmental Law," *The Annals*, 525 (January 1993), p. 142; see, also, Michael Levy, *Regulating Fraud: White-Collar Crime and the Criminal Process* (New York: Tavistock, 1987).

27. John C. Coffee, "'No Soul to Damn, No Body to Kick': An Unscandalized Inquiry into the Problem of Corporate Punishment," *Michigan Law Review*, 79 (1981), pp. 386–459.

28. C. Kennedy, "Criminal Sentences for Corporations: Alternative Fining Mechanisms," *California Law Review*, 73 (March 1985), pp. 443–482.

29. John Braithwaite, "Enforced Self-regulation: A New Strategy for Corporate Crime Control," *Michigan Law Review*, 80 (1982), pp. 1466–1507.

30. DiMento, "Criminal Enforcement," p. 143.

31. Brent Fisse, "Community Service as a Sanction Against Corporations," *Wisconsin Law Review*, (1981), pp. 970–1017.

32. John Scholz, "Voluntary Compliance and Regulatory Enforcement," *Law and Policy*, 6 (1984), pp. 385–404; and Marshall B. Clinard, *Corporate Corruption: The Abuse of Power* (New York: Praeger, 1990).

33. Theodore M. Hammett and Joel Epstein, *Prosecuting Environmental Crime: Los Angeles County* (Washington, D.C.: National Institute of Justice, 1993).

34. Donald W. Scott, "Policing Corporate Collusion," *Criminology*, 27 (August 1989), pp. 559–587.

35. Amitai Etzioni, "The U.S. Sentencing Commission on Corporate Crime: A Critique," *The Annals*, 525 (January 1993), pp. 147–156.
36. William S. Lofquist, "Organizational Probation and the U.S. Sentencing Commission," *The Annals*, 525 (January 1993), pp. 157–169.
37. Ibid., p. 168.
38. DiMento, "Criminal Enforcement," p. 145.
39. John McCloy, *The Great Oil Spill: The Inside Report* (New York: Chelsea House, 1976).
40. U.S. Comptroller General, *Illegal Disposal of Hazardous Waste: Difficult to Detect or Deter* (Washington, D.C.: U.S. General Accounting Office, 1985).
41. Maria S. Boss and Barbara Crutchfield George, "Challenging Conventional Views of White-Collar Crime," *Criminal Law Bulletin*, 28 (January–February 1992), pp. 32–58.
42. U.S. Comptroller General, *7-Year GAO Fraud Hotline Summary* (Washington, D.C: U.S. General Accounting Office, 1986).
43. U.S. Comptroller General, *5-Year Summary of Results of GAO Fraud Hotline* (Washington, D.C.: U.S. General Accounting Office, 1984).
44. Jay S. Albanese, "Victim Compensation in Hazardous Waste Cases: Current Options and Needed Reforms," *Victimology: An International Journal*, 11 (1986).
45. U.S. Comptroller General, *Whistleblower Protection* (Washington, D.C.: U.S. General Accounting Office, 1992).
46. Theodore M. Hammett and Joel Epstein, *Prosecuting Environmental Crime: Los Angeles County* (Washington, D.C.: National Institute of Justice, 1993).
47. DiMento, "Criminal Enforcement," p. 144.
48. Stephen Rackmill, "Understanding and Sanctioning the White-Collar Offender," *Federal Probation Quarterly*, 56 (June 1992), pp. 26–33.
49. See Charles E. Reasons and Colin H. Goff, "Corporate Crime: A Cross-national Analysis," and Neal Shover, "The Criminalization of Corporate Behavior: Federal Surface Coal Mining," in *White-Collar Crime: Theory and Research*, ed. by Gilbert Geis and Ezra Stotland (Beverly Hills, CA: Sage Publications, 1980).
50. Mary McIntosh, *The Organisation of Crime* (London: Macmillan, 1975).
51. Michael Levi, "White-Collar Crime: The British Scene," *The Annals*, 525 (January 1993), p. 82.

Women in White-Collar Crime

> *Women are not men's equals in anything*
> *except responsibility. We are not their*
> *inferiors, either, or even their superiors.*
> *We are quite simply different races.*
> — *Phyllis Ginley (1959)*

In the case of traditional crimes of violence, male offenders outnumber females at a rate of almost 10 to 1. There is reason to believe, however, that white-collar crimes, relying on variations of conspiracy and fraud, may be more evenly distributed by gender. This chapter employs data from both the United States and Canada to examine trends in white-collar crimes committed by females. Economic, technological, and demographic changes have resulted in a dramatic increase in the proportion of females in the white-collar work force. This may have increased both the access and opportunities for female involvement in white-collar crime. Similarities and differences between the seriousness of male versus female white-collar crimes and what level of "equity" may be expected in the future will be assessed. The potential impact of changes in economic conditions, the importance of sex differences, and the glass ceiling phenomenon are each considered.

Women and the Newest Profession

The invention of the term "white-collar crime" is now more than 50 years old. As such, it is one of the "newest" forms of crime, compared to more traditional forms of criminal behavior. The term's progenitor, sociologist Edwin Sutherland, focused primarily on a survey of crimes committed by corporations in his pioneering book, *White-Collar Crime*. The issue of the offender's sex, therefore, did not figure in his writing. In recent years, however, white-collar crimes committed by individuals have received a great deal of attention, due to a number of large and highly publicized frauds. Changes in the economy, technology, and demographics have resulted in a dramatic escalation of female involvement in this form of criminal behavior, compared to males, during the last two decades in both the United States and Canada.

Opportunity Factors: Economy, Technology, Demography

The best predictor of crime, especially white-collar crime, is opportunity. One cannot engage in certain criminal behaviors, if denied the opportunity to do so. Although a trash collector can engage in income tax fraud, he or she generally lacks the opportunity to engage in securities fraud. It can be expected, therefore, that white-collar crime will increase as the opportunities for it expand.

Opportunities for white-collar crime enlarge primarily as the result of three influences: changes in the economy, technology, and demographics. As both the economy and technology have become more advanced over the years, opportunities for fraud have increased.[1] Computerized transactions of all sorts, 24-hour stock trading, and purchases on credit are examples of this trend. Demographics play a role, inasmuch as young people are generally denied the opportunity to commit white-collar crime. Embezzlement, forgery, and fraud generally require bank accounts, credit ratings, and oftentimes, occupational access. This is supported by the fact that most offenders arrested for crimes of fraud are older (over 25 years old) and better educated than are the "typical" criminal. Therefore, an aging population will likely affect the opportunities for white-collar crime, and clearly, this is now occurring. In 1970, the median age in both the United States and Canada was approximately 27. Now, the median age is 33 in both countries, and it is expected to continue rising past the age of 40 by the year 2020, as life expectancy increases and birth and immigration rates remain low.[2]

Another demographic factor that contributes to the incidence of white-collar crime is gender. If the proportion of female white-collar workers is increasing (compared to males), we can expect as a matter of probability that they will engage in white-collar crime at an increasing rate (as compared to males). Although, as James Messerschmidt argues, stereotypes might prevail, will the growing presence of women in the white-collar work force actually produce a change in "the sexual division of labor, reproduced within the corporation today, [that] places men in the positions of *power* where corporate crimes originate?"[3]

These potential influences suggest four possible scenarios:

1. Female white-collar workers are increasing at a faster rate than are males, resulting in proportionally increasing new opportunities for white-collar crime by females.
2. The rate at which females engage in white-collar crime is increasing faster than it is for males, due to the higher rate of female infiltration into the white-collar work force.
3. The types of white-collar crimes committed by women are generally less serious than are those committed by men, because men still occupy a higher proportion of higher-level positions of financial trust and control.

Table 10.1 Women in Managerial Positions, 1970–1988
(As a Percentage of All Managerial Positions)

Year	United States	Canada
1970	31.7	15.4
1980	36.8	37.1*
1988	44.7	42.5

Source: A 1978 statistic (37.1%) is substituted for a 1980 figure not available for Canada. Compiled from M. Patricia Connelly and Martha MacDonald, *Women and the Labour Force* (Ottawa: Canadian Government Publishing Centre, 1990); Statistics Canada, *Women in Canada: A Statistical Report,* 2nd ed. (Ottawa: Canadian Government Publishing Centre, 1990); U.S. Department of Labor, *Handbook of Labor Statistics* (Washington, D.C.: U.S. Government Printing Office, 1989); and U.S. Bureau of Census, *Statistical Abstracts of the United States* (Washington, D.C.: U.S. Government Printing Office, 1975 and 1980).

4. The comparative seriousness of male versus female white-collar crime will equalize, as female infiltration of the white-collar work force slows, and women are promoted to positions of financial trust and control in similar proportions to men.

Females in the White-Collar Work Force

Census data, and data gathered from the Departments of Labor in both the United States and Canada, indicate that the infiltration of female workers into the white-collar work force is increasing at a dramatic pace.

As Table 10.1 illustrates, nearly 45 percent of all managerial positions in the United States, and 43 percent in Canada, are held by women. This contrasts with 32 percent and 15 percent, respectively, 20 years earlier. These employment gains are significant and include positions such as public officials, public administrators, business managers, accountants, architects, engineers, natural scientists, health professionals, teachers, counselors, social scientists, lawyers, writers, artists, and designers. Therefore, scenario 1 appears to be hold, inasmuch as female infiltration into the white-collar work force has grown by 176 percent in Canada and 41 percent in the United States during the last two decades. This also implies, of course, that the number of males holding managerial positions has declined proportionally during this period.

The Female White-Collar Crime Rate

Men still hold the majority of management and professional positions, although Table 10.1 makes it clear that they now hold approximately 55 to 57 percent of these positions, versus 68 percent (in the United States) and 85 percent (in Canada) in 1970, a huge decline in only 20 years. A consequence of this trend is many new female employees in the white-collar work force in North America.

Table 10.2   Female participation in White-Collar Crime, United States, 1970–1990
(Total Arrests/Percentage Female)

Offense	1970	1980	1990	Percentage Change
Fraud	66,465 27%	259,330 41%	279,776 44%	+63%
Forgery and counterfeiting	39,811 24%	71,496 31%	74,393 35%	+46
Embezzlement	7,531 25%	7,790 28%	12,055 41%	+64

Source: Compiled from Federal Bureau of Investigation, *Crime in the United States* (Washington, D.C.: U.S. Government Printing Office, published annually).

The rapidly rising rate of female employment gains would suggest that the rate at which females are committing white-collar crimes might be increasing faster than the male rate. This assumes, of course, that increased opportunities are a reliable predictor of increased crimes.

Table 10.2 presents the female rate of participation in white-collar crimes in the United States as measured by arrests. It can be seen that the total number of arrests for the crimes of fraud, forgery and counterfeiting, and embezzlement have increased significantly over a 20-year period. The rate at which females are arrested for these crimes has increased significantly as well. In 1970, females accounted for approximately 25 percent of all these white-collar arrests overall, but two decades later the proportion has increased by 63 percent for fraud, 46 percent for forgery and counterfeiting, and 64 percent for embezzlement. Although males still comprise the majority of arrests for these white-collar crimes, their arrest rate has dropped as the female rate has climbed.

The situation in Canada is similar. As Table 10.3 indicates, the rate at which females are arrested for frauds has increased 38 percent since 1974.

The only significant exceptions to the rise in the proportion of female arrests are large declines for the offenses of counterfeiting Canadian currency and bankruptcy and securities act violations. These will be discussed later.

It should be noted that arrests are not the most reliable indicator of crime, as arrest rates can change independent of crime rates, due to changes in police practices, personnel, and the reporting behavior of victims. Also, arrests for these offenses may contain a disproportionate number of less serious frauds, because more serious corporate frauds are often handled civilly through the regulatory enforcement system and therefore do not result in arrests. As Kathleen Daly has observed, many occupational positions held by females, such as bank tellers, may have higher levels of surveillance than higher management positions more often held by men. This may increase the likelihood that females will be apprehended for crimes such as embezzlement.[4] There also exist many

Table 10.3   Female Participation in White-Collar Crime, Canada, 1970–1990
(Total Adult Arrests/Percentage Female)

Offense	1970*	1980	1990	Change in Proportion Female Arrests
Fraud (total)	18,452 21%	30,681 24%	37,800 29%	+38%
Bank cheque	11,834 22%	18,420 26%	20,957 31%	+41
Credit card	1,163 22%	2,252 23%	3,965 21%	−5
Other frauds	5,415 18%	10,009 21%	12,878 27%	+50
Counterfeiting	333 18%	112 21%	216 12%	−28
Bankruptcy act	246 15%	107 14%	76 11%	−27
Securities act	251 24%	108 6%	174 6%	−75

* The year 1974 was the first year fraud arrest breakdowns by type were tabulated.

Source: Centre for Justice Statistics, *Canadian Crime Statistics* (Ottawa: Statistics Canada, published annually).

more white-collar crimes than are included in these short lists, but the American and Canadian governments have not seen these as frequent or serious enough to count. Examples of omitted offenses include conspiracy, extortion, bribery, perjury, obstruction of justice, official misconduct, and regulatory offenses (see Chapters 2 through 4 of this book). Nevertheless, these data on national arrest trends are the most comprehensive available.

Given the information presented in Tables 10.2 and 10.3, and the caveats just noted, it appears that scenario 2 is supported. The rate at which females participate in white-collar crime (as measured by arrests) appears to be increasing significantly in the United States during the last 20 years, matched by a substantial increase in female arrests for fraud in Canada. The extent to which women are scrutinized differently from men in the workplace, and its effect on apprehension for crimes, remains to be investigated. In either case, these trends may ultimately "dismantle the longstanding dichotomy of the devilish and daring man and the unappealing and inert conforming woman," as Ngaire Naffine predicted in her critique of women in the study of criminology.[5]

It is not clear whether these results are generalizable around the world. An examination of arrest trends for females in the Netherlands between 1958 and 1977 showed inconsistent results in the male–female proportions for both fraud and embezzlement arrests.[6] More recent data from a larger number of industrialized countries may shed more light on the emerging relationship between male and female white-collar crimes and their comparative proportions and positions in the white-collar work force.

Gender and White-Collar Delinquency

An interesting study by Hagan and Kay examined what they call "white-collar delinquency." They investigated the characteristics of patent and copyright violations by juveniles in copying audiotape, videos, and computer software as manifestations of this type of unlawful behavior. They administered mailed questionnaires to several hundred adolescents living in the wealthiest section of Toronto. Their responses were compared to a heterogeneous group of students from three different schools. They found that "sons were less likely than daughters to be instrumentally controlled (i.e., supervised) by their parents, more likely to prefer risks, less likely to perceive risks of getting caught for delinquency, and more likely to violate patents and copyrights."[7] After examining the impact of social class, parental communication, role modeling, and supervision, as well as risk preferences and perceived risk, it was found that gender had the strongest influence on patent and copyright violations. The male adolescents averaged in excess of five more violations of patents and copyrights than did females.[8] Hagan uses a "power-control theory" in an attempt to link parental control of juveniles within the family to the behaviors of men and women in the workplace.[9] Hagan and Kay argue, for example, that power-control theory ties speculation about women possibly being more closely scrutinized at work than men to "earlier experiences of family socialization, in which daughters are more instrumentally controlled than sons."[10]

The Seriousness of Female White-Collar Crime

The precipitous rise of females in the white-collar work force is a relatively recent phenomenon, due to a host of economic, social, technological, and political influences.[11] Although it is difficult to measure precisely, it is probably true that many more females than males hold lower management and professional positions, due to their shorter tenure in these jobs. As a result, it might be expected as a consequence that men would commit more serious white-collar crimes than females, due to their greater access to higher positions of financial trust and control.

Neither Canada or the United States distinguishes among the relative severity within the types of white-collar crimes they count in national arrest statistics. Unlike the United States, however, Canada includes violations of the Bankruptcy Act and Securities Act in its arrest figures. These are offenses that, presumably, require a greater degree of occupational access than would a credit card or check fraud. Although arrests for these offenses are few (less than 153 for each offense each year), the proportion of females arrested for these offenses has dropped by approximately 100 arrests per offense since 1974 (see Table 10.3). Daly's study of convicted white-collar offenders in a sample of federal court cases found only 1 percent of women's cases, versus 14 percent of men's, involved indictments against businesses or corporations.[12] These data may offer an indirect indication that the seriousness of white-collar crimes by females is lower than that for males, perhaps due to their more limited access to higher management positions. More information is needed, however, about more types and larger numbers of white-collar crimes and their characteristics before firm conclusions can be drawn about the relative seriousness of male versus female white-collar crime.

An Equitable Future?

The rationalizations provided by female white-collar criminals in certain limited studies appear to differ somewhat from those of males. Perhaps the best of these were separate studies conducted by Cressey, Zietz, and Daly. Both Cressey and Zietz examined the motives of imprisoned male and female bank embezzlers, respectively, whereas Daly analyzed white-collar convictions for several different offenses involving both males and females. Cressey found males to justify their embezzling as "borrowing" resulting largely from personal financial problems, such as business debts, gambling, and overspending in general.[13] On the other hand, Zietz found female offenders more often to rationalize their embezzlement as a means to preserve family integrity.[14] Daly found both men and women to employ the same justifications, although women cited family financial need versus personal problems twice as often as did men.[15] Regardless of the rationalization, however, there appear to be no inherent biological differences that make one sex more susceptible to the temptations of white-collar crime than the other.

Empirical evidence suggests that there are interesting differences in the treatment of males and females once they are caught. Bickle and Peterson examined the sentences imposed on more than 500 individuals convicted of forgery. They found that those holding familial positions as economic providers or support did not influence sentencing decisions. On the other hand, marital status, presence of dependents, caretaking support, and living arrangements made a difference. Therefore, these "family role variables cannot be described or interpreted in terms of either race or sex alone."[16] Unfortunately, familial roles did not appear to control sentences either. It was found, for example, that married males and white females were more likely to be sentenced to prison, but married black females were less likely. Also, the source and degree of economic support for dependents had "little influence on sentence outcomes regardless of gender."[17] These findings display both similarities and differences from prior work on the role of race, gender, and family roles in court decision making.[18] It is clear that more analysis of differing groups of offenders is required before firm conclusions can be drawn regarding the role of gender in sentencing decisions, especially as it relates to family roles.

The infiltration of females into the work force undoubtedly will slow as they achieve greater "parity" with male white-collar workers (however "parity" may be defined). It would be reasonable to expect that the rate at which females commit white-collar crimes will slow correspondingly.

Nevertheless, it should also be expected that women will continue to commit white-collar crimes in proportion to their opportunity, as men do. Whether or not the rate at which males and females white-collar workers commit crimes will equalize cannot be determined until females hit their "saturation" point in the white-collar work force. This is impossible to know in advance, although the data presented in Tables 10.1, 10.2, and 10.3 are suggestive. For all three white-collar crimes counted in the United States, women account for approximately 40 percent of all arrests. They also constitute 45 percent of the white-collar work force. Two decades earlier, women accounted for approximately 25 percent of all arrests and 32 percent of the white-collar work force. There appears to be a remarkable correspondence between female white-collar crime arrests and the presence of women in white-collar positions of employment.

In Canada, the results are similar, although not as dramatic. In 1974, females constituted approximately 20 percent of white-collar arrests and 15 percent of the work force. Now, they comprise 27 percent of white-collar arrests and 42 percent of the work force. The direction of these results follow those in the United States. The slight "lag" in arrest rates behind white-collar work force participation may be attributable to a greater proportion of lower-level positions held by females. Darrell Steffensmeier suggests another reason: work "may lessen temptations toward crime by assuring a steady income," and because work is "indicative of upward mobility," these upwardly mobile women may be more conforming, as "upwardly mobile persons tend to be."[19] Other, yet unmeasured, factors may also account for this difference. The proportion of women in closely monitored "pink-collar" positions, those who commit white-collar crimes that are not occupationally related, and knowledge of the arrest preferences of employers and police would also help to explain the inexact association between arrests and work force participation.[20]

Summary

The implications of these scenarios and data are significant. The proportion of female white-collar workers in North America has increased dramatically during the last two decades. This has been matched by an increase in the proportion of females arrested for white-collar crimes during this period, suggesting an association between opportunity (white-collar work force participation) and arrests of women for white-collar crimes, a relationship that has held for men for many years.

Whether or not females ultimately will reach "parity" with men in both white-collar work force infiltration and in crime commission will depend on three factors: the economy, sex differences, and the "glass ceiling" phenomenon. If the economies of the United States or Canada experience a significant recession in the coming years, female participation in the white-collar work force could drop substantially, due to their lack of seniority in many management and professional positions. If the opportunity–white-collar crime relation holds up, female white-collar arrests also could be expected to drop.

Second, female white-collar arrests tend to lag behind their relative numbers in the white-collar work force (i.e., men commit more crimes than their relative presence in the work force would suggest). It remains to be seen whether this is due to differential opportunity of females in the white-collar occupations, employer complaints and their relation to police arrest practices, female participation in nonoccupational white-collar crimes, or to sex differences, such as in the case of violent crime where men consistently commit nearly ten times more homicides, rapes, robberies, and serious assaults than do women.[21]

Finally, it has been reported that a number of female management workers experience a "glass ceiling," where employers promote women to supervisory positions that never quite reach the levels of their male counterparts.[22] As Richard Sparks has observed, the nonparticipation of women in sophisticated white-collar crimes may be "a clear indication of the continued exclusion of women from the social and economic roles that would make that participation possible."[23] If this phenomenon continues, opportunities for women to commit white-collar crimes on the scale that men do will never be reached.

CASE STUDY

Read carefully the following summary of an actual case. Answer the questions that accompany it, employing ideas from this chapter.

The Dalkon Shield

As is the case for conventional crime, women historically have participated in crimes more often as victims than as offenders. This is especially true for violent crime, and less so for white-collar crime. The case of the Dalkon Shield raises several gender-related issues, beyond the obvious victimization of women.

The intrauterine device, or IUD, became a popular birth control device during the 1960s, when the birth control pill was discovered to cause some dangerous side effects. The IUD is a penny-size plastic or metal device that is inserted into the uterus to prevent conception. The IUD remains in the uterus, and is not inserted or removed before or after intercourse, as the diaphragm is.

The Dalkon Shield was the product name for the IUD manufactured by A. H. Robins Company in Richmond, Virginia, although IUDs were made by other companies as well. A. H. Robins was one of the largest manufacturers of IUDs and distributed 4.5 million Dalkon Shields in 80 countries. Problems arose in a significant number of women, however, resulting in investigations into the testing and medical complications of this product.

In one case, a woman had a Dalkon Shield inserted by her doctor, but she became pregnant. The IUD was not removed during the pregnancy, according

Women protesting outside a court hearing to determine the amount of compensation to be established for women injured by the Dalkon Shield intrauterine birth control device. The illustrations on the women's blouses and poster represent an enlarged view of the device. *(Joe Mahoney, UPI/Bettmann)*

to standard medical practice at the time. It was believed it would come out by itself at child birth. All went well until the 17th week of the pregnancy showed massive problems. The woman showed signs of infection, lost the baby, and went into shock, becoming critically ill. After massive blood transfusions to restore her blood pressure, exploratory surgery was performed. A quart of blood from no clear source was found and an emergency hysterectomy was performed.[24] This tragic scenario was not unique. It occurred thousands of times.

The women suffered from what came to be known as pelvic inflammatory disease (PID), which impairs or prevents the ability to bear children. An estimated 110,000 women became pregnant using the Dalkon Shield, and 66,000 miscarried, usually from spontaneous abortions. A total of 18 woman died in the United States from this condition, and hundreds gave birth prematurely to stillborn children or children with birth defects.[25]

A. H. Robins started to receive complaints from doctors about pain, bleeding, high pregnancy rates, and spontaneous abortions, less than two years after the Dalkon Shield was marketed in 1971. It was not until a pending research report about the spontaneous abortions that Robins acted. The company called a conference of 12 doctors, not inviting those who had been critical of the IUD. A vote among the doctors, as to whether or not the Dalkon Shield was a factor in second trimester spontaneous abortions, ended in a tie.[26] And the complaints continued.

An important feature of the Dalkon Shield was a string, encased in nylon, that hung down from the IUD out of the uterus. This permitted a woman to check to make sure the IUD was in place. Reports from physicians revealed that the string had a "wicking" effect in facilitating the movement of bacteria up the string and into the uterus, causing internal infections.[27] In addition, the Dalkon Shield had barbed spurs to hold it in place. It was found that these spurs would cause infections by hooking into the uterine lining.

A quality control supervisor for A. H. Robins warned his supervisor about the wicking problem, "I told him that I couldn't, in good conscience, not say something I felt could cause infections. And he said that my conscience did not pay my salary . . . and that if I valued my job I would do as I was told."[28] It was not until May 1974, almost two years after A. H. Robins received warnings from its own consultant about the dangers of the IUD, that the company sent a letter to physicians about the device. The letter advised doctors of the risk of leaving the Dalkon Shield in place in women who became pregnant and recommended that women who became pregnant while wearing the IUD be administered therapeutic abortions.[29]

Soon thereafter, Planned Parenthood advised its member clinics to cease prescribing the Dalkon Shield, finding that more than 25 percent of its patients with the Shield experienced severe cramps and bleeding. The Food and Drug Administration asked A. H. Robins to suspend commercial distribution of the Dalkon Shield in June 1974 "pending the accumulation of definitive data."

Lawsuits began to mount, and A. H. Robins asked physicians to remove the Dalkon Shield from women still wearing it in 1980.[30] Approximately 15,000 users of the Dalkon Shield have sued Robins, and the company has settled about half the cases for more than $200 million. In the cases that went to trial, Robins' attorneys attempted to shift blame away from their device and inquired into the sexual practices, frequency, and number of partners of the female litigants. As one plaintiff's attorney complained, "they made her look like a whore."[31] Robins also took great pains to avoid the discovery of relevant documents, using the attorney–client privilege.[32] Nevertheless, in August 1985, facing a growing number of civil suits, A. H. Robins asked a federal judge to let it reorganize under Chapter 11 of the bankruptcy law.

Case Study Questions

1. Legal changes since the invention of the Dalkon Shield require the manufacturer to submit test results to the government regarding safety and effectiveness of the product *before* it is marketed. What are reasons for and against this idea as an effective consumer protection tool?

2. Do you believe the fact that women are the sole users of IUDs, had any effect on how the product's risks were made known? Provide evidence to support your position.
3. Given the nature of the injuries suffered in this case, what do you believe would be a just way to resolve these cases?
4. If monetary settlements continue to be the most common method of settlement in cases like this, how do you think amounts should be determined?

Endnotes

1. Jay Albanese, "Tomorrow's Thieves," *The Futurist*, 22 (1988), pp. 25–28; and Mary McIntosh, *The Organisation of Crime* (London: Macmillan, 1975).
2. Jean Dumas, "Report on the Current Demographic Situation in Canada," *Current Demographic Analysis*, 2 (1987); and Gregory Spencer, *Projections of the Population of the United States by Age, Sex, and Race: 1988 to 2080*, U.S. Bureau of Census Current Population Reports, Series P-25, No. 1018 (Washington, D.C.: U.S. Government Printing Office, 1989).
3. James W. Messerschmidt, *Capitalism, Patriarchy, and Crime: Toward a Socialist Feminist Criminology* (Totowa, NJ: Rowman and Littlefield, 1986), p. 117.
4. Kathleen Daly, "Gender and Varieties of White-Collar Crime," *Criminology*, 27 (November 1989), pp. 769–794.
5. Ngaire Naffine, *Female Crime: The Construction of Women in Criminology* (Boston: Allen and Unwin, 1987).
6. Ineke Haen Marshall, "The Women's Movement and Female Criminality in the Netherlands," in *Comparative Criminology*, ed. by Israel L. Barak-Glantz and Elmer H. Johnson (Beverly Hills, CA: Sage Publications, 1983), pp. 87–102.
7. John Hagan and Fiona Kay, "Gender and Delinquency in White-Collar Families: A Power-Control Perspective," *Crime & Delinquency*, 36 (July 1990), pp. 391–407.
8. Ibid., p. 401.
9. John Hagan, *Structural Criminology* (New Brunswick, NJ: Rutgers University Press, 1989), Ch. 6.
10. Hagan and Kay, "Gender and Delinquency in White-Collar Families," p. 405.
11. Freda Adler, *Sisters in Crime* (New York: McGraw-Hill, 1975); and Rita J. Simon, *Women and Crime* (Lexington, MA: Lexington Books, 1975).
12. Daly, "Gender and Varieties of White-Collar Crime," pp. 775, 788.

13. Donald R. Cressey, *Other People's Money: A Study in the Social Psychology of Embezzlement* (Montclair, NJ: Patterson Smith, 1953).
14. Dorothy Zeitz, *Women Who Embezzle or Defraud: A Study of Convicted Felons* (New York: Praeger, 1981).
15. Kathleen Daly, "Gender and Varieties of White-Collar Crime," *Criminology*, 27 (1989), pp. 769–794.
16. Gayle S. Bickle, "The Impact of Gender-Based Family Roles on Criminal Sentencing," *Social Problems*, 38 (August 1991), pp. 372–394.
17. Ibid., p. 390.
18. Kathleen Daly, "Neither Conflict nor Labeling nor Paternalism Will Suffice: Intersections of Race, Ethnicity, Gender, and Family in Criminal Court Decisions," *Crime & Delinquency*, 35 (1989), pp. 136–168.
19. Darrell J. Steffensmeier, "Trends in Female Crime: It's Still a Man's World," in *The Criminal Justice System and Women*, ed. by Barbara Raffel Price and Natalie J. Sokoloff (New York: Clark Boardman, 1982), p. 128.
20. Jane Roberts Chapman, *Economic Realities and the Female Offender* (Lexington, MA: Lexington Books, 1980); Kathleen Daly, "Gender and Varieties of White Collar Crime"; and Louis Kapp Howe, *Pink Collar Workers* (New York: Avon, 1977).
21. Federal Bureau of Investigation, *Crime in the United States* (Washington, D.C.: U.S. Government Printing Office, published annually); and Lisa D. Bastian, *Criminal Victimization in the United States, 1990* (Washington, D.C.: Bureau of Justice Statistics, 1992).
22. Susan B. Garland and L. Driscoll, "Can the Feds Bust Through the 'Glass Ceiling'?" *Business Week*, April 29, 1991.
23. Richard F. Sparks, "'Crime as Business' and the Female Offender," in *The Criminology of Deviant Women*, ed. by Freda Adler and Rita J. Simon (Boston: Houghton Mifflin, 1979), p. 178.
24. Russell Mokhiber, "Dalkon Shield," in *Corporate Crime and Violence* (San Francisco: Sierra Club Books, 1988), pp. 149–162.
25. Morton Mintz, *At Any Cost: Corporate Greed, Women, and the Dalkon Shield* (New York: Pantheon Books, 1985), p. 3.
26. Mokhiber, "Dalkon Shield," pp. 154–156.
27. Mintz, *At Any Cost*, p. 61.
28. Ibid., p. 141.
29. Mark Dowie and Tracy Johnson, "A Case of Corporate Malpractice," *Mother Jones*, November 1976, p. 48.
30. "Maker of Dalkon Shield Urges Removal of Devices from Women Having Them," *The Wall Street Journal*, September 26, 1980.
31. "Piercing the Dalkon Shield," *National Law Journal*, June 16, 1980, p. 13.
32. Mokhiber, "Dalkon Shield," p. 158.

CHAPTER 11

Organized Crime Infiltration of Legitimate Business

Crime in every possible form, like business, has progressed to the stage where the little unorganised participant hasn't much chance of success.
— *Emanuel H. Lavine (1930)*

The relationship between legitimate business and organized crime is not as distant as one might wish. In fact, there have been a growing number of instances where legitimate businesses have been established as fronts for organized crime activity, or have been infiltrated by force, threat, or co-optation by organized crime interests. Examples abound:

- The "Pizza Connection" case, where heroin was imported to the United States through "legitimate" pizza parlors
- Contractors in the New York City construction industry found to have been influenced by organized crime, causing a $20 million building to cost $40 million to erect
- Garbage collection and toxic waste transport and disposal firms controlled by organized crime groups in some areas
- The wholesale meat industry and garment industry infiltrated by organized crime in some cities
- Immigration into the United States exploited by organized crime interests

Similar cases have been discovered, where organized crime has infiltrated labor unions, bars, restaurants, and theaters, among many other businesses. Many of these cases will be discussed in this chapter.

Legitimate Business to Organized Crime: Where's the Connection?

Infiltration of legitimate business by organized crime can be defined as misuse of a lawfully existing enterprise for criminal purposes, either with the corrupt consent of the business's managers or through coercion. It will be shown that there are several distinct ways in which organized crime comes to infiltrate a business, and that businesses are not always the innocent victim of predatory gangsters. Finally, this chapter presents a prediction model that delineates *high-risk factors* that have been shown to be predictive of businesses ripe for organized crime infiltration. The utility of such a model for law enforcement and crime prevention will be discussed.

A Typology for the Infiltration of Legitimate Business

The infiltration of legitimate business by organized crime is not a one-dimensional phenomenon. It occurs in distinct manifestations. This section will present two different types of infiltration schemes and will provide actual case examples that illustrate their differences. The two types of schemes are

1. Using a legitimate business as a "front" for primarily illegal activity (*scam*), and
2. "Bleeding" a legitimate business of some of its profits through illegal means without the use of force and (hopefully) without causing it to fail (*corruption*).

Characteristics common to each of these types of infiltration are the crimes of conspiracy and bribery or extortion. Conspiracy is always present because both types of infiltration involve a planned effort to misuse a lawfully existing business for criminal purposes. Bribery exists when an offer is made to turn a failing business around in an unlawful manner, and the owners or management see that both they *and* the organized crime infiltrators can make money in the arrangement. Extortion may be present if the legitimate business owners or managers are threatened, or otherwise coerced, into a corrupt relationship with organized crime interests. The threats may consist of labor unrest, supply or product disruption, or physical harm. Some examples help to illustrate these characteristics.

The Scam

Edward DeFranco's analysis of a planned bankruptcy in the wholesale meat business may be the classic exposition of a scam.[1] First, a large bank deposit is made, to establish credit for a struggling business. This deposit is made by a "new" management that has either corrupted the existing ownership through bribery or has infiltrated the company by extortionate force or threat. No notice is given to the firm's suppliers, customers, or regulators that a "new" management is now in place operating under a "new" agenda. Next, large orders are placed, using the bank deposit as credit. Third, after the orders are received, the merchandise is converted into cash through a fence or surplus property dealer.

Finally, the company is then forced into bankruptcy by its creditors, when it becomes clear that no payment is forthcoming.

In a slight variation, Joseph Lombardo conducted what were called "bust-outs," where he allegedly set up entirely fictitious businesses and obtained a credit rating. Then, he proceeded, as De Franco warned, to order merchandise based on this credit, liquidate it, and leave town.[2]

The warning signals that should make businesses and banks wary of a scam in the works are four:

1. A large bank deposit used for a credit reference elsewhere,
2. An unusual number of credit inquiries,
3. New business management with only vague information about the principals, and
4. Requests for "rush" deliveries that do not correspond to normal patterns.[3]

Circumstances like these should cause banks or businesses to be suspicious of transactions, especially because they can result in uncollectible debts.

The Savings and Loan Scam

It can be argued that the savings and loan crisis of the 1980s represented a case study in the infiltration of legitimate business by criminal interests in perhaps the largest scam in U.S. history. A chronology of events in the savings and loan crisis illustrates how criminal interests were able to bankrupt a sizable portion of an entire industry.

Federally insured savings and loan banks were established during the 1930s to help the United States out of the Great Depression. The U.S. government encouraged banks to lend, and consumers to save, by making money available for lending and by guaranteeing deposits, if banks failed.

Banks lost a great deal of money during the 1970s, as the economy went into recession. Double-digit inflation made savings and loans unprofitable because they were limited by law to lending at a rate of 6 percent interest and paying depositors three percent. They also could deal only in home mortgages. During the Reagan years of the 1980s, the entire industry was deregulated, phasing out controls on interest rates, allowing for mortgage loans without any down payment from the borrower, allowing individuals to own banks (rather than a minimum of 400 stockholders), and making other lenient borrowing and lending provisions.[4] It was hoped that the deregulation would result in higher-yield investments and bale out the savings and loans.

Unfortunately, this new environment, combined with the knowledge that every deposit was federally insured up to $100,000, made speculative, high-risk, foolish, and fraudulent lending and borrowing possible. As Pontell and Calavita have observed, "some of the transactions were legitimate, if foolhardy, attempts to raise capital; others were outright scams involving insiders, borrowers, Wall

Charles Keating made large political contributions as head of Lincoln Savings and Loan. Five U.S. senators intervened on his behalf in regulatory matters, causing a delay that cost taxpayers an additional $2 billion when the bank failed. *(Lee Celano, Reuters/ Bettmann)*

Street brokers, and developers."[5] This observation has been supported by several subsequent investigations.

The U.S. General Accounting Office investigated 26 of the most costly bank failures in the savings and loan crisis. They found that *in every case* the bank was the victim of fraud and abuse. In one of these institutions, the chairman of the board was found to have been paid a $500,000 bonus in the same year the bank lost nearly $23 million. In another, a majority stockholder used $2 million of institutional funds to buy a beach house and spent an additional $500,000 for household expenses.[6]

Irresponsible and illegal behavior on such a large scale has been called "collective embezzlement."[7] This means siphoning off (or "looting") institutional funds for personal gain with at least the implied endorsement of the management. This method of bankrupting a legitimate business historically has been associated with force and extortionate threats. The case of the savings and loan industry in the 1980s illustrates that this is not necessarily the case. It is not necessary that thieves come from outside the institution, nor is it necessary that they threaten the institution's managers. Simply put, it is possible "to make an offer they can't refuse" by merely creating an environment where lax regulatory controls make stealing not only profitable, but an accepted business practice.

If we reserve the term "organized crime" for continuing conspiracies that include the corruption of government officials, as Pontell and Calavita suggest, "then much of the savings and loan scandal involved organized crime."[8] Their interviews with regulatory agencies, Federal Bureau of Investigation, and Secret Service investigators uncovered a "recurring theme" of conspiratorial arrangements between "insiders" (savings and loan officials) and "outsiders" (accountants, lawyers, real estate agents, and developers).[9] A comparison of these fraudulent arrangements in the savings and loan industry with more traditional organized crime infiltration of legitimate business, through no-show jobs at construction sites, or payoffs for "protection," show them to be more similar than different. For example, Charles Keating made large political contributions as head of Lincoln Savings and Loan that resulted in five U.S. senators intervening on his behalf in regulatory matters. This caused a delay that ultimately cost taxpayers an additional $2 billion when the bank failed.[10] How this differs from corruption of government officials by members of traditional organized crime groups is not a matter of kind or, in many cases, even a matter of degree. As the National Advisory Committee on Criminal Justice Standards and Goals has recognized, "the perpetrators of organized crime may include corrupt business executives, members of the professions, public officials, or members of any other occupation group, in addition to the conventional racketeer element."[11]

The Pizza Connection

The so-called "Pizza Connection" case involved an elaborate drug-smuggling operation that began in Turkey and ended with distribution of heroin through pizza parlors in the United States. It culminated in a case that ended in one of the longest and most complex trials in U.S. history, covering 18 months and 22 defendants.

The use of pizza parlors as a front for illegal activity was the end of an international drug conspiracy between organized crime groups in Sicily and New York. Tons of morphine were smuggled from Turkey to Sicily, where the drug was processed into heroin. Then, the heroin was smuggled through U.S. airports and distributed through pizza parlors in the Northeast and Midwest. Finally, illegal profits in excess of $40 million were funneled back to Sicily in a money laundering scheme that involved banks in the Bahamas, Bermuda, New York, and Switzerland.

Eighteen defendants ultimately were convicted, most notably Gaetano Badalamenti, a former leader of the Sicilian Mafia, and Salvatore Catalano, a New York City bakery owner with ties to organized crime. The pizza connection case was perhaps one of the most sophisticated drug importation and distribution conspiracies ever to be exposed. It clearly illustrates how linkage is established between legitimate businesses (i.e., pizza parlors and banks) and their knowing misuse to engage in illegal acts (i.e., distribute heroin and accept and transfer large sums of cash in small denominations with no questions asked).[12]

Business-Type Activities of Organized Crime

An important study of business activities engaged in by organized crime was conducted by Edelhertz and Overcast.[13] They analyzed 165 indictments and civil complaints occurring over a two-year period in a purposive sample taken from state and federal investigators and prosecutors of organized crime. The business-type activities they examined formed a continuum from strictly legal businesses, legal businesses that were conduits for illegal activity, illegal businesses that were a vehicle for legal activity, and entirely illegal businesses. Edelhertz and Overcast found "startlingly clear" evidence of the overlap between white-collar and organized crime in the cases they examined.

They found a large number of the 165 organized crime cases they studied to involve white-collar violations. This finding corresponds with that of the President's Commission on Organized Crime, which discovered a similarly high rate of white-collar offenses in its investigation of labor union-related crimes by organized crime.[14] A comparison of the President's Commission findings and those of Edelhertz and Overcast is presented in Table 11.1.

Table 11.1 illustrates the large numbers of white-collar violations engendered by organized crime investigations. Edelhertz and Overcast also found smaller numbers of cases that also involved the white-collar offenses of currency violations, money laundering, bid-rigging, and securities fraud.[15] They concluded from these, and other, analyses of actual cases that "there is a high likelihood that wherever organized crime figures are involved in apparently illegal enterprises, white-collar criminal violations (such as fraud, false statements, usury, embezzlement, and tax violations) may play a prominent role" as well.[16] They found "no consensus" regarding any preferred method by which organized crime either establishes new businesses or infiltrates existing ones. They found patterns to depend on local concerns regarding market, competition, and opportunity. Indeed, as they conclude, "there is no reason to think that organized criminal groups act differently than other businessmen when they acquire an interest in a business."[17] They follow accepted business procedures and respond to the demands of the marketplace.

It can be seen that scams that involve the use of a legitimate business as a front for illegal activity can range from the wholesale meat industry to the savings and loan industry. In both cases, offenders (be they organized crime figures or "legitimate" businesspersons) misuse a lawfully existing business for purposes of exploiting its assets for personal gain.

Corruption of a Legitimate Business

In many cases of infiltration, the purpose is not to steal from the business until it is bankrupt. Instead, it makes more sense to misuse the business in way that it can provide a steady source of illegal income without endangering its survival. This was clearly the objective in the savings and loan scandal, although the

Table 11.1 White-Collar Violations in Organized Crime Cases

White-Collar Violations Charged	President's Commission Study of Labor Union Cases	Edelhertz and Overcast Study of Business-Type Organized Crime Cases
Embezzlement	356	27
Fraud	101	89
Tax violations	81	43
Fiduciary violations/kickbacks	9	29
Fraud against the government	5	9

Sources: Herbert Edelhertz and Thomas D. Overcast, *Organized Crime Business-Type Activities and Their Implications for Law Enforcement* (Washington, D.C.: National Institute of Justice, 1990), and President's Commission on Organized Crime, *The Edge: Organized Crime, Business and Labor Unions* (Washington, D.C.: U.S. Government Printing Office, 1985).

extent of the abuse was so great, the banks failed. There exist several fascinating case studies of organized crime infiltration of legitimate business that works as intended: exploiting a business in illegal ways without bankrupting it.

The New York City Construction Industry

A massive investigation of corruption and racketeering in the New York City construction industry was carried out by the New York State Organized Crime Task Force. Their report found that control of construction unions was the "base of power and influence in the industry" by organized crime, together with direct interests in contracting and construction supply companies. This hidden interest in construction companies was accomplished by using "nominees" who "front" for the company on public records for purposes of certificates of incorporation, accounting, licensing, and permits.[18] For example, the report found that Anthony Salerno, later convicted as "boss" of the Genovese crime family in New York City, controlled Certified, one of the two major concrete suppliers in Manhattan.[19] Paul Castellano, boss of the Gambino crime family until his murder in 1985, controlled Scara-Mix Concrete Company, which was owned by his son.[20]

In other cases, it was discovered that known organized crime figures were openly listed as owners, managers, or principals of construction companies. Salvatore Gravano, counselor to John Gotti, was president of JJS Construction Company; John Gotti, Jr., was president of Sampson Trucking Company; and John Gotti, convicted boss of the Gambino crime family (and for the murder of Paul Castellano), held the position of salesman for ARC Plumbing Company.[21] Even though these individuals were sometimes found to have very little to do with the business that employed them, such an "on the books" profession "provides a legitimate position in the community and a reportable source of income."[22]

John Gotti raises his fist in victory after one of his three acquittals before he was ultimately convicted for orchestrating the killing of Paul Castellano. Gotti held the position of salesman for ARC Plumbing Company. *(Nina Berman, Reuters/Bettmann)*

The ability of organized crime interests to infiltrate the construction industry in New York City was promoted by several factors. Unlike most industries, the employment of a construction worker lies in the hands of the union rather than the employer. The unions have been "all too easy for racketeers to control and exploit," because there historically has been no oversight of union affairs, despite a number of criminal prosecutions. Dissidents within the unions have had little success because the unions have effective control over layoffs, blacklisting, and physical intimidation.[23] Added to union control is the construction marketplace itself, where there are "a large number" of contractors and subcontractors, with many "small firms" among them, all locked in intense competition. This makes legitimate businesses "vulnerable to extortion." Racketeers can coerce payoffs by threatening loss of labor, loss of supplies, delays, or property damage.[24] Likewise, businesses can be easily corrupted when given competitive advantages by powerful racketeering elements, such as sweetheart contracts (to avoid some union requirements) and cartels that allocate contracts among favored firms.[25]

The Business of Garbage Collection

Reuter, Rubinstein, and Wynn conducted a case study of the garbage (solid waste) collection business in New York City and also in an unnamed northeastern state. In both cases, they found the market to be dominated by small partnerships or family corporations. They found the garbage collection business

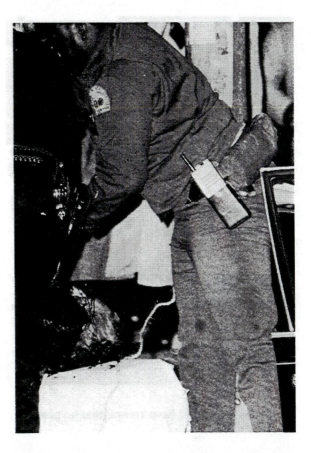

Police remove the blood-covered body of Paul Castellano, the reputed Boss of Bosses of the Gambino Crime Group in New York City. Castellano controlled Scara-Mix Concrete Company which was owned by his son. John Gotti was eventually convicted for arranging Castellano's murder to obtain control of the criminal organization. *(Rick Harbus, UPI/Bettmann)*

"has a longstanding reputation for anticompetitive practices and racketeer involvement."[26] The investigators discovered there are "mutual benefits derived by entrepreneurs and criminals in the operation of cartel arrangements" where independent businesses are organized into a "cartel" that prevents open and fair competition in the marketplace.[27] As a result, the role of the infiltrating racketeers centers on disputes about "customer allocation agreements" in dividing up the garbage collection market. Corruption characterizes the role of organized crime in this instance, more than does extortion. Indeed, as Reuter, Rubinstein, and Wynn observe, "policies which assume that the racketeers are parasites on unwilling hosts, and that the legitimate entrepreneurs would welcome a clean-up of the industry, are doomed to failure."[28]

As noted earlier, there often is not a clear distinction between the individual offender and the organizational "victim." An investigation in Los Angeles found a suspect who rented Ryder trucks, loaded them with hazardous waste from paint products, and then abandoned the trucks. The suspect was easily found because he rented the trucks in his own name. He was convicted and sentenced to nearly three years in prison, but the district attorney *also* sought indictments against the businesses that hired the suspect on the grounds that these compa-

Anthony "Fat Tony" Salerno controlled Certified, one of the two major concrete suppliers in Manhattan. He was later convicted as "boss" of the Genovese crime family in New York City. *(Ezio Petersen, UPI/Bettmann)*

nies knew, or should have known, that he planned to dispose of the hazardous waste illegally.[29]

A study by Donald Rebovich examined 71 cases of hazardous waste crime in four states found "little evidence," based on his case analysis and interviews with law enforcement officials, that syndicate (traditional organized) crime has established strong control of the hazardous waste transport and disposal industry.[30] Nevertheless, those cases connected to organized crime were found to be "among the most flagrant offenders," with many of these firms dumping hazardous waste illegally at the highest levels and for the longest periods.[31]

The Vending Machine Industry

Organized crime infiltration of the vending machine industry has been investigated in both New Jersey and New York. The investigators were unable to find "any evidence" of labor racketeering, violence, extortion, and price manipulation.[32] In fact, the entire industry was found to have changed in recent years, as large, publicly held corporations, have bought family vending businesses. Nevertheless, the industry is still affected by continued allegations of organized crime involvement. Ironically, the investigators were "told by legitimate people already established in the industry that they have found the negative image of the business a significant barrier to the obtaining of credit from banks and other finance institutions."[33] The investigators concluded that the vending machine industry has "outgrown the racketeers," as market forces "simply prevent old-time muscle tactics and coercion from being effective." The demand for certain games drives the market now, as new games are introduced and rise to popularity and decline rather quickly. The industry was found to make decisions "based on economic factors and shaped by market demand."[34]

It can be seen in all these cases that business considerations are used in the infiltration of legitimate business. Weaknesses in legal businesses themselves, or pressures in the marketplace, are exploited by criminal elements. This leads us to the question of whether common factors in known cases of infiltration can be isolated and used to anticipate such exploitation in the future.

Predicting the Infiltration of Legitimate Business by Organized Crime

If the conditions that give rise to the infiltration of organized crime into legitimate businesses could be predicted, lawful businesses, law enforcement agencies, and the general public could realize major benefits. Police resources would not be wasted on fruitless investigations, regulatory personnel could be allocated more rationally according to which industries are predicted to be especially vulnerable, and the long-range interests of the community would be better served through a concentration on truly serious organized misbehavior.

The good news is that criminological prediction models have proved to be fairly simple. Therefore, they are easily adopted in practice. A number of states and the federal government are using probation, parole, and sentencing guidelines that are based on prediction models. The models utilize the experience of past probation or parole candidates, or those awaiting sentences, and compare it with similar current cases to help make an informed judgment.

The predictive model described here is different from earlier work in criminological prediction that has primarily involved the prediction of the future behavior of *individuals* based on the performance of similar individuals in the past. This model attempts to predict *business conditions* that render a business vulnerable to organized crime infiltration, based on the experiences of similar businesses in the past. Therefore, this organized crime model is predicting an intermediate condition (i.e., high-risk businesses) rather than the ultimate behavior of concern (organized crime infiltration). The model, then, does not attempt to predict organized crime per se, but seeks to predict conditions within a business that are conducive to organized crime infiltration.

It is assumed that different types of businesses may well have different probabilities of organized crime infiltration, depending upon the nature of the business, its complexity, the manner in which it conducts business, and the history of the industry. As a result, this model deals solely with businesses in general. It will remain for subsequent investigations to gather empirical evidence to determine whether different models are required to predict high-risk conditions in various industries.

A prediction model merely summarizes the experience of the past to use as a guide in making decisions that affect the future. Given the case studies discussed earlier of the infiltration of legitimate business by organized crime, are there common elements that can be isolated? It appears that there are.

Joseph Albini found that an important factor in both business and personal relationships involving organized crime was "patronage." Obviously, in certain markets there are individuals who hold positions of power and influence ("patrons"), who can help others ("clients") requiring their assistance. A "patron–client" relationship forms as a natural consequence of these conditions. For example, in certain businesses it may be difficult to obtain a license or loan, or to attract customers. If a financially or politically influential "patron" can assist in overcoming these problems, a patron–client relationship is formed. Now, the client owes his patron money or favors, which may result in a wide variety of illicit activities such as loan sharking, political "favors," or extortion. This relationship can become extended throughout a business or market when the client later acts as a patron for someone with less power and influence. The result, according to Albini, is the emergence of "powerful syndicate figures who serve as patrons to their functionaries [and who] may also serve as clients to others more powerful than they."[35] It is reasonable to hypothesize, therefore, that poorly trained owners or managers, who are ill-equipped to deal with business problems, are more likely to become targets (potential "clients") for organized crime infiltration than are professional, well-trained, and well-equipped operators.

Borrowing from general organization theory, Dwight Smith hypothesized that organized crime develops in the same manner as does legitimate business. That is, it responds to the "task environment" of a market, consisting of customers, suppliers, regulators, and competitors. Like legitimate business, organized crime attempts to survive and make a profit, while dealing with the pressures of its task environment.[36]

Applying the Model in Practice

Extrapolating from Smith's and Albini's explanations, it would appear that certain types of business conditions (i.e., configurations of customers, suppliers, regulators, competitors, and patron-client relationships) would be more conducive to organized crime infiltration than others. Applying the principles of Smith's theory of enterprise to De Franco's study of a planned bankruptcy, for example, it can be seen that certain elements of the wholesale meat business's task environment were ripe for infiltration. Entry into the wholesale meat business was easy (little regulation), the demand for meat was fairly constant (guaranteed customers), the market in the area was favorable (customers and suppliers would not readily move to other competitors because product and costs are similar throughout the market), and there was a need for capital (supply). As Albini might suggest, a "new" management disseminating "vague" information about the principals may also indicate infiltration resulting from an illicit patron–client relationship. In this way, specific market conditions may help to predict the incidence of organized crime infiltration of legitimate business.

Table 11.2 Predicting Organized Crime Infiltration into Legitimate Business

Predictors	Low Risk	High Risk
Supply	Few available small, financially weak businesses	Readily available small, financially weak businesses
Customers	Elastic demand for product	Inelastic demand for product
Regulators	Difficult to enter market	Easy to enter market
Competitors	Monopoly/oligopoly controlled market	Open market with many small firms
Patronage	Entrepreneurs are professional, educated managers	Entrepreneurs are nonprofessionals ill-equipped to deal with business problems
Prior record	No prior history of organized crime involvement in market	Prior history of organized crime infiltration in industry

Reuter, Rubinstein, and Wynn's investigation of the garbage collection industry in New York City found conditions similar to those identified in the wholesale meat business: it was easy for individuals to enter the market (little regulation), the industry was populated by numerous "small, frequently family-based, enterprises," with little difference in service among vendors (open competition in a market of nonprofessional managers), there was inelastic demand for the service (customers always available), and many firms were identified with "minimal capital and no reserve equipment" (supply for illicit patrons). In fact, when one examines the circumstances of infiltration in the New York City construction industry, or even the massive savings and loan scandal, there appear to be common factors in each case.

Table 11.2 summarizes the prediction model. The first four predictors are taken from Smith's use of organization theory, the fifth from Albini's notion of "patron–client" relationships, while the sixth (prior history) is taken from previous research in criminological prediction that has found prior record to be predictive of criminal behavior.[37]

The model described in Table 11.2 is likely to require refinement in several important areas, most of which result from problems inherent in all prediction research. First, the model may be "overfitted" to the available empirical research. As shown, there have been comparatively few detailed, empirical investigations of organized crime infiltration into legitimate business. The case studies we have discussed thus far may not be typical, and therefore, the model may be fitted to nonrepresentative cases or industries. Additional case studies are necessary to determine whether this model can be generalized to other industries.

Similarly, the model assumes that all industries have the same predictive attributes. Like other research in criminological prediction, what holds true for one sample may not hold true for others.[38] It is possible that different models may be required for different industries. Additional case studies of organized crime infiltration in various industries will indicate whether other variables must be considered for efficient prediction models in different types of markets.

Third, a "base rate" problem may hamper the design of a prediction model; the proportion of businesses that have problems with organized crime infiltration may be too small to develop an efficient prediction model. Simply stated, the more uncommon an event, the more difficult it is to predict accurately. The base rate for various industries can be determined only through further empirical research.

Finally, the measurement of such variables as "supply," "competitors," and the other predictors shown in the model can be difficult. Factors such as "financial condition," "types of supplier," and "competitive conditions" are nominal or, at best, ordinal measures of a business situation. Therefore, the ordering of these variables involves some creativity on the part of the investigator. Investigators must examine carefully the measurement units employed in scaling predictive factors to guard against the masking of any true predictive relationship based on inappropriate counting or measurement units.

Despite the limitations noted here, there are two major reasons to believe that such a prediction model may form the foundation for a more useful approach to the investigation of organized crime. First, a model with few predictive factors, as described in Table 11.1, may well include all the important factors. Criminological prediction models have been found, generally, to have a limited number of important predictor variables. In fact, Gottfredson and Gottfredson maintain that little predictive accuracy is gained by the inclusion of large numbers of variables in a prediction model.[39] Therefore, a six-variable model does not necessarily oversimplify the situation.

Second, the prediction model does not necessarily have to predict business conditions conducive to organized crime infiltration with a high degree of accuracy to be useful. For example, probation and parole prediction devices have found models with relatively low predictive efficiency to be useful in distinguishing "high-risk" groups of offenders from "low-risk" groups. In this way, supervision or release decisions can be based on something more rational than "unguided discretion."[40] Likewise, the classification of high-risk and low-risk markets may be useful to both regulators of industry and investigators of organized crime, even if precise prediction of organized crime activity within individual businesses is not possible. An analog to this procedure has already been attempted in case-screening techniques developed for use by police. The Rochester, New York, Police Department developed a system called "Early Case Closure" in which information was gathered to assess the "solvability" of robberies and burglaries. By directing their resources toward crimes with the best chance of solution (and by spending *less* time on cases with little chance of solution), the department was able to improve significantly its clearance rates for those crimes.[41] A similar effort was undertaken by the Stanford Research Institute and Police Executive Research Forum. They developed a model for screening burglary cases, based on factors associated with the crime. Applying the system retrospectively, they were able to predict whether a burglary case would be solved 85 percent of the time.[42] In a similar way, industry regulators and police officials can reduce the amount of time spent on dead-end investigations that invariably occur in proactive and regulatory enforcement, with the use of a prediction model like the one proposed here. A regulatory or police agency could use such a model as a screening device in its jurisdiction. Investigative resources could be focused on those markets identified as "high risk" for infiltration, and perhaps less time would be wasted on investigations that do not lead to prosecution.

The true value of a model to predict the infiltration of legitimate businesses by organized crime will not be realized, however, until additional empirical investigations are conducted in different types of businesses. It has long been held, for instance, that organized crime has infiltrated certain businesses in the fish, linen supply, and trucking industries. These might be useful starting points for the application and refinement of a model to predict (and thereby prevent) the incidence of organized crime in other industries.

Summary

This chapter presented a definition of the infiltration of legitimate business by organized crime along with a typology of its two major forms: scams and corruption of a legitimate business. Several case studies of each of these types were offered.

The elements of a model to predict the incidence of organized crime infiltration of legitimate business were isolated, and their applicability to the case studies explained. The utility of such a prediction model for regulatory and police enforcement of business regulations and organized was outlined. The potential of the prediction model as an investigative and crime prevention tool remains to be tested.

CASE STUDY

Read the facts of the actual case that follow. Employing ideas from this chapter, answer the questions that follow.

The Immigration Scam

Legal entry status is provided to fewer and fewer immigrants in many countries, due to difficult economic times in much of the industrialized world. This has led to a progression of efforts to immigrate illegally through a series of scams that invite infiltration by organized crime.

Undocumented immigrants under tow by the Coast Guard near San Diego hold up signs asking to be admitted to the United States. Nearly 700 people were found to be aboard three ships. Organized crimes groups have emerged to "guarantee" safe, but illegal, entry into the United States. *(John Gibbins, UPI/Bettmann)*

Some who cannot enter legally, attempt to sneak into the country, bear children, and return home, knowing that at least their children will be citizens under the law in some countries, such as the United States. More recently, undocumented foreigners have landed at U.S. airports and claim asylum. Asylum claims by illegal immigrants have risen 900 percent since 1990 to nearly 10,000 per year. Because they are granted a future hearing on their asylum request, and because there is no space to detain them prior to that hearing, the illegal immigrants are permitted to stay in the United States until their hearing. Predictably, they often "vanish" into large cities around the country. Measures to deal with the asylum problem have created new problems. Airlines now face fines for each passenger without proper documentation, but document forgery is becoming more commonplace. A crackdown at JFK airport in New York prompted a significant drop in asylum requests there, but "right now, they're shopping" for weaker links at other international airports in the United States, according to immigration officials.[43]

Organized crime interests in other countries, as well as within the United States, have emerged to "guarantee" a safe, but illegal, entry into the United States. These scams have emerged to provide an illegal alternative to the established immigration application process. For exorbitant fees of thousands of dollars, many of these illegal immigrants end up "destined to lives of indentured servitude in the United States."[44] In some cases, gangs have picked up refugees at airports, encroaching on the turf of the organized crime group that had originally arranged for the passage."[45]

It is estimated that there are as many as 60 brothels in Queens, New York, in addition to cocaine, heroin, and loan sharking operations—all conducted by illegal immigrants. Many of these refugees are attempting to support their families back home, but end up doing so illegally, or else work in legal businesses that do not pay them minimum wage due to their illegal status. Many of these refugees become victims of a cycle from which there is no clear escape: work very hard for little money, engage in illegal activity for more money, or return home to the poverty that led them to leave in the first place. The profile of a prostitute in Jackson Heights, Queens, illustrates the point:

> She earns $25 for every 15 minutes with a man, plus tips. But the brothel keeps 40 percent of her earnings. She came to Queens illegally a year ago, washing floors for $150 a week, not enough to support herself and her three children in Cali . . . she has been a prostitute for only three months and earns $300 or more a night, enough to pay tuition for her children in Colombia and to hire a live-in maid to care for them. Like most of the other eight women in the house—from Columbia, Venezuela and Peru—she wants to go home. She will work only for one year and return."[46]

In other cases, federal immigration officials in Los Angeles claim that Chinese smugglers posed as relatives to obtain custody of Chinese youths illegally brought into the United States. Then, they were held for ransom. Two teenagers said they were bailed out of a detention hall while awaiting their asylum appeals, and were held until their families in China paid.[47] In Boston, reputed members of the Fuk Ching gang were indicted for extortion, robbery, prostitution, and smuggling Chinese immigrants into the United States.[48] These cases offer examples of the exploitation of the legal and underground immigration systems by organized crime interests.

Case Study Questions

1. What circumstances of the illegal immigration "market" place it at "high risk" for infiltration by organized crime?
2. How would you change the current handling of illegal immigrants in the short term to reduce their number and exploitation of the system?
3. Given the motivations of the refugees, and the problems of enforcement at international borders, what would you propose as a long-term solution to the illegal immigration problem?

Endnotes

1. Edward J. De Franco, *Anatomy of a Scam: A Case Study of a Planned Bankruptcy by Organized Crime* (Washington, D.C.: U.S. Government Printing Office, 1973).

2. David Heilbroner, *Rough Justice* (New York: Dell, 1991), pp. 187–188.
3. Ibid.
4. Martin Mayer, *The Greatest-Ever Bank Robbery: The Collapse of the Savings and Loan Industry* (New York: Scribners, 1990).
5. Henry N. Pontell and Kitty Calavita, "White-Collar Crime in the Savings and Loan Scandal," *The Annals*, 525 (January 1993), pp. 31–45.
6. U.S. Comptroller General, *Failed Thrifts: Costly Failures Resulted from Regulatory Violations and Unsafe Practices* (Washington, D.C.: U.S. General Accounting Office, 1989).
7. Kitty Calavita and Henry N. Pontell, "'Heads I Win, Tails You Lose': Deregulation, Crime and Crisis in the Savings and Loan Industry," *Crime & Delinquency*, 36, no. 3 (July 1990), p. 309; and Kitty Calavita and Henry N. Pontell, "'Other People's Money' Revisited: Collective Embezzlement in the Savings and Loan Insurance Industries," *Social Problems*, 38 (February 1991), pp. 94–112.
8. Pontell and Calavita, "White-Collar Crime in the Savings and Loan Scandal," p. 39.
9. Kitty Calavita and Henry N. Pontell, "Savings and Loan Fraud as Organized Crime: Toward a Conceptual Typology of Corporate Crime," *Criminology*, 31 (November 1993), pp. 519–548.
10. Mayer, *The Greatest-Ever Bank Robbery*, p. 210.
11. National Advisory Committee on Criminal Justice Standards and Goals, *Report of the Task Force on Organized Crime* (Washington, D.C.: U.S. Government Printing Office, 1976), p. 213.
12. For interesting summaries of the Pizza Connection case, see Ralph Blumenthal, *Last Days of the Sicilians: The FBI Assault on the Pizza Connection* (New York: Times Books, 1988); Shana Alexander, *The Pizza Connection: Lawyers, Money, Drugs, Mafia* (New York: Weidenfeld and Nicolson, 1988); and Donald Baer and Brian Duffy, "Inside America's Biggest Drug Bust," *U.S. News and World Report*, April 11, 1988, pp. 18–29.
13. Herbert Edelhertz and Thomas D. Overcast, *Organized Crime Business-Type Activities and Their Implications for Law Enforcement* (Washington, D.C.: National Institute of Justice, 1990).
14. President's Commission on Organized Crime, *The Edge: Organized Crime, Business and Labor Unions* (Washington, D.C.: U.S. Government Printing Office, 1985).
15. Edelhertz and Overcast, *Organized Crime Business-Type Activities*, p. 27.
16. Ibid., p. 54.
17. Ibid., p. 114.
18. New York State Organized Crime Task Force, *Corruption and Racketeering in the New York City Construction Industry* (New York: New York University Press, 1990).
19. Ibid., p. 84.
20. Ibid.

21. Ibid., pp. 84–85.
22. Ibid., p. 85.
23. Ibid., pp. 48–51.
24. Ibid., pp. 57–58.
25. Ibid.
26. Peter Reuter, Jonathan Rubinstein, and Simon Wynn, *Racketeering in Legitimate Industries: Two Case Studies* (Washington, D.C.: National Institute of Justice, 1983), pp. 10–12.
27. Ibid., p. 13.
28. Ibid.
29. *People v. Boyce Campbell*, Cal. Superior Court BA 025490, cited in Theodore M. Hammett and Joel Epstein, *Prosecuting Environmental Crimes: Los Angeles County* (Washington, D.C.: National Institute of Justice, 1993).
30. Donald J. Rebovich, *Dangerous Ground: The World of Hazardous Waste Crime* (New Brunswick, NJ: Transaction, 1992), p. 102.
31. Ibid., pp. 103–104.
32. Reuter, Rubinstein, and Wynn, *Racketeering in Legitimate Industries*, pp. 22–25.
33. Ibid., p. 31.
34. Ibid., p. 33.
35. Joseph L. Albini, *The American Mafia: Genesis of a Legend* (New York: Irvington, 1971), p. 265.
36. Dwight C. Smith, "Paragons, Pariahs, and Pirates: A Spectrum-Based Theory of Enterprise," *Crime & Delinquency*, 26 (July 1980), pp. 358–386.
37. Don M. Gottfredson, Leslie T. Wilkins, and Peter B. Hoffman, *Guidelines for Parole and Sentencing: A Policy Control Method* (Lexington, MA: Lexington Books, 1978); and Frances Simon, *Prediction Methods in Criminology* (London: Her Majesty's Stationery Office, 1971).
38. Kevin N. Wright, Todd R. Clear, and Paul Dickson, "Universal Applicability of Probation Risk-Assessment Instruments: A Critique," *Criminology*, 22 (February 1984), pp. 113–134.
39. Michael R. Gottfredson and Don M. Gottfredson, *Decisionmaking in Criminal Justice: Toward a Rational Exercise of Discretion* (Cambridge, MA: Ballinger, 1980).
40. Gottfredson, Wilkins, and Hoffman, *Guidelines for Parole and Sentencing*; and Jay S. Albanese, Bernadette A. Fiore, Jerie H. Powell, and Janet R. Storti, *Is Probation Working?: A Guide for Managers and Methodologists* (Lanham, MD: University Press of America, 1981).
41. Peter B. Bloch and James Bell, *Managing Investigations: The Rochester System* (Washington, D.C.: The Police Foundation, 1976).
42. David Greenberg, *Felony Investigation Decision Model: An Analysis of Investigative Elements of Information* (Menlo Park, CA: Stanford Research Institute, 1975).

43. Bruce Frankel, "INS Getting Cagey in Cat-and-Mouse Game," *USA Today*, August 6, 1993, p. 10.
44. Ibid.
45. Ian Fisher, "A Window on Immigrant Crime," *The New York Times,* June 17, 1993, p. B1; and "Chinese Smuggling," *USA Today*, September 1, 1993, p. 3.
46. Ibid., p. B8.
47. "Smuggled Youths," *USA Today*, August 23, 1993, p. 3.
48. "Chinese Smuggling," *USA Today*, September 1, 1993, p. 3.

12

The Future of White-Collar Crime

We love justice greatly, and just men but little.
— *Joseph Roux (1886)*

This survey of the nature, extent, causes, and response to white-collar crime has answered some questions, but it has raised many others. As one contemplates the future of white-collar crime in America, the answers to five fundamental questions lie at the foundation of any long-term solutions to the problem.

Five Fundamental Questions

The complexity and scope of white-collar crime produces recommendations for change that are usually scattered and poorly focused. It is possible to organize most important proposals for change into five categories. Indeed, more consideration is sorely needed to answer these five questions about white-collar crime:

1. Is greater public indignation required for an effective response?
2. Is more or less regulation of business and government a solution?
3. Are prosecution targets selected appropriately?
4. Will a principled approach to sentencing make a difference?
5. Is there a need for a new personal and corporate ethic?

This chapter establishes the importance of these questions, and how the answers to them lie at the heart of the future of white-collar crime in America.

Greater Public Indignation?

Citizens are very concerned about crime in the streets. Opinion polls have documented increasing fear of crime as the number one concern of most citizens in America.[1] Most of this fear is focused on street crimes, due to the nature of these random, violent events, which are often committed by strangers. White-

Covered bodies of victims in Bhopal, India, who died from a leak at a pesticide plant reflect a few of the nearly 1,000 deaths that resulted. Public indignation and the debate over more versus less regulation of business and industry has been fueled by such catastrophes. *(UPI/Bettmann)*

collar crime lacks this immediacy in the public mind, because it seems less of a direct threat. Harm is often delayed or diffused, and its effect is unclear (as in environmental cases, for example). In the savings and loan scandal, for instance, the huge financial losses will be paid by the government, and ultimately by the taxpayers. Although the public becomes the eventual victim in cases like these, the time, distance, and diffusion of harm among American taxpayers do not have the immediate impact that rape, robbery, and assault have on their victims.

In fact, the white-collar crime draws most attention when it mimics street crime. An example is the Bophal incident in India, where people were killed instantly due to toxic emissions. Or consider the case in Virginia where a fertility specialist inseminated women with his own sperm and tricked others into believing they were pregnant.[2] When white-collar crimes such as these resemble street crimes of violence and theft, the public becomes the most aroused.

A number of investigations of public attitudes toward white-collar crime, noted in Chapter 6, have demonstrated significant concern about the issue. Nevertheless, most of the public debate still centers on what to do about street crimes, rather than white-collar crimes. It is an important question, therefore, to ask to what extent can or should public indignation about white-collar crime be magnified?

If more public concern about white-collar crime existed, perhaps the government would begin to collect national statistics regarding its nature and extent.

This is something now done for street crimes, but as shown in Chapter 6, there is no national effort to assess the true extent white-collar crimes. Therefore, contemporary discussions about what to do about white-collar crime can never get past the fundamental issue: "Is the problem getting worse, better, or remaining constant?"

The savings and loan scandal, Iran–Contra, BCCI, the House of Representatives banking scandal, and telemarketing frauds, among many others, continue to make news on a regular basis. Whether this is helping to promote public indignation, or merely adding to a general numbing or cynicism of the public, is not clear. What *is* clear, however, is that white-collar crimes continue to occur, resources are devoted to investigating and prosecuting them, and many offenders are being punished. It remains to be seen whether the public ultimately will reach its level of tolerance for this conduct and demand changes to the same extent as we have seen for street crimes in recent years.

To Regulate or Deregulate?

It has often degenerated into an ideological debate over the proper role of government in society. Will greater regulation of business and government reduce corporate and individual misconduct, or will more regulation incur unnecessary compliance costs and ultimately harm the economy? This is not an ideological debate, however, because it can be resolved with empirical evidence. Does regulation make society safer? The answer is clearly "yes." Will *more* regulation make society *more* safe? That answer is not so obvious.

Consider the case of the Foreign Corrupt Practices Act, discussed in Chapter 5, in the Lockheed case study and NAPCO critical thinking exercise. This law was passed to criminalize what was seen as undesirable payments overseas to sell American products. Both these case studies make clear that the impact of the law is debatable, compliance is confusing, and the use of law to change the targeted behavior may not be effective.

On the other hand, consider the case of the savings and loan scandal, discussed in Chapter 11. The scandal was the result of a deregulated industry that was bankrupted due to high-level officials taking advantage of government deregulation to enrich themselves at the expense of their customers. The motives for the deregulation can be defended as an effort to promote investment and growth in a struggling industry. The result was one of the largest frauds in American history. The savings and loan scandal provides a clear illustration of the need for some degree of regulation and the dangers of deregulation.

The question that remains is, "What *level* of regulation is required to ensure public safety without placing undue burdens on business and government?" The answer to this question is not clear. Although one can cite numerous violations that resulted from absent or unenforced regulations, many companies still manage to market products and services without violating the law. Perhaps the answer lies in examining more closely how organizations make decisions within certain industries. Instead of looking at gross levels of violations or misconduct, as past surveys have (see Chapter 6), perhaps it is more important to compare the decision-making processes of violating versus nonviolating corporations and agencies. Such an inquiry would ask questions such as, "Why are certain industries more criminogenic than others in generating misconduct?" and "How do companies in businesses with high rates of violation manage to operate within the limits of the law?" Such comparisons of the internal processes of similar organizations, operating in similar environments, may provide useful clues regarding the genesis of corporate misconduct.

Selection of Prosecution Targets?

It has long been argued that the targets of white-collar prosecutions are selectively chosen, leading to charges of unfairness, discrimination, and political influence in the adjudication process. White-collar crime prosecutions are especially vulnerable to this criticism due to the proactive nature of many of these investigation and prosecutions, unlike the reactive approach common to conventional crimes (see Chapter 8).

How certain targets or industries are selected for investigation and prosecution is often arbitrary, depending on the leadership of the enforcement agency and the priorities of their political leadership. This is largely unavoidable because law enforcement and prosecution agencies are agencies in the executive branch of government whose leaders are appointed by the chief executive and whose priorities typically follow whatever directives are submitted to them by the chief executive. In the Iran-Contra scandal, discussed in Chapter 4, President Bush pardoned former Secretary of Defense Caspar Weinberger less than two weeks before his trial (and just prior to Bush leaving office in January 1993). Bush also pardoned five other indicted or convicted men in the scandal. His actions wiped out all the pending cases of Lawrence Walsh, the independent counsel appointed to investigate the incident.[3] Walsh had led the Iran–Contra investigation for six years, and the power of the chief executive to oversee and ultimately undo such a prosecution is made very clear in this incident.

It has been argued that greater reliance on congressional (versus executive branch) investigations on the federal level, or legislative investigations on the state level, might be a way around the executive branches' monopoly on choosing prosecution targets. Although Congress can and does engage in investigations, it often appears that these investigations are no less politically motivated, and the larger number of politicians involved breeds unfocused investigations that often play to the media rather than to the problem at hand. Granting the fact that some congressional investigations are useful, the prerogative for prosecution of any wrongdoing uncovered still lies with the executive branch of government (see Chapter 8).

The short-term remedies for perceived unfairness in the selection of prosecution targets are two: (1) greater public demand for action against white-collar crimes of concern and (2) using the power to vote to obtain chief executives that reflect the wishes of the public regarding white-collar crime. It can be seen that the issue of better target selection for prosecution depends on an aroused and informed public, as noted in point 1 just presented. A long-term remedy might be greater reliance on longer-term investigations of problems by bipartisan commissions that rely on outside experts to help diagnose problems more objectively. This would also help to remove the process from the political machinations of the day to the extent possible. Although the impact of such commissions in the past has been mixed, these commissions can be very effective in identifying which areas *should* be of most concern and thereby focusing more accurately public and political debate to a specific agenda for change.

A Principled Approach to Sentencing?

The criminal justice process has for too long focused almost exclusively on some combination of fines, probation, and incarceration to deal with offenders. Likewise, the civil justice system has employed monetary penalties almost exclusively to compensate victims. It can be argued that these approaches are old, and not very effective, and that a large dose of creativity needs to be added to sentencing law violators. In addition, it is often not clear whether we are trying to punish, deter, reform, or achieve some other purpose with these sentences. The result is a confusing combination of unspoken objectives that often conflict, are not clear to the offender, frustrate the public, and do not serve adequately as a guide for sentencing future cases.

Congress enacted the Sentencing Reform Act in 1984 to provide "certainty and fairness in meeting the purposes of sentencing" and to avoid "unwarranted sentencing disparities" among similar defendants who commit similar crimes.[4] To accomplish this objective, the act created a U.S. Sentencing Commission to create detailed guidelines that would prescribe appropriate sentences for federal offenders. These new guidelines were implemented in 1987 for both white-collar and conventional crimes.

Ironically, the Sentencing Commission adopted no guiding philosophy for its prescribed sentences. This has made it difficult to "meet the purposes of sentencing," because no purposes were ever stated, other than uniformity and proportionality. Instead, a purely empirical approach was taken, and the guidelines were developed based on past practice (through an analysis of 10,000 prior federal sentences). What the guidelines have instituted, therefore, is a prescription for the future that merely codifies past practice. Distinctly lacking in this approach is the answer to the question, "What do we *expect* these sentences to *accomplish*?" There is disagreement regarding which theory of punishment should be adopted, but Kip Schlegel argues persuasively that a single theory should be chosen to guide sentencing decisions or, as others argue, different philosophies of sentencing ought to be ranked in order of importance.[5] Without an underlying philosophy, there is no way this question can be answered, and results have been predictable.

White-collar is viewed as "serious" under the guidelines, and the result has been white-collar offenders receiving sentences that are both longer and more likely to involve incarceration.[6] The commission that developed the guidelines failed to consider their impact on prison populations.[7] It has been argued that the guidelines transfer power to the prosecutor because the offense charged virtually dictates the sentence.[8] This replaces unguided discretion at sentencing with unguided discretion at plea-bargaining.[9]

Questions also have been raised about inequitable treatment of organizations versus individuals under the guidelines.[10] Most significant is the fact that the guidelines may not be accomplishing even their limited purpose—to reduce disparity in sentences. One study has found disparity in sentences still exists by race and by geographical location.[11] Another found disparity may exist among co-defendants based on information they share with authorities rather than on their relative culpability.[12]

Sentencing guidelines were adopted for organizations (versus individuals) in 1991, as noted in Chapter 9, and they provide for "organizational probation" that can place corporations under court supervision and also make restitution, reorganize, or perform specific tasks. Other than this provision, the federal sentencing guidelines attempt to guide the present by institutionalizing past practice with a more careful eye to wide variations in sentences. An explicit philosophical objective must be tied to sentencing if uniformity in purpose and result is to be achieved. Greater use of court-ordered "corporate rehabilitation" and mandated changes in corporate decision-making and oversight procedures might be employed successfully, for example, but only if the high rate of corporate recidivism, noted by every investigator of the subject (see Chapter 6), is regarded as a paramount philosophical objective. Likewise, corporate decertification or license suspension might be effective, but only if incapacitation is viewed as an important purpose of sentencing. Depending on the philosophy of sentencing employed (explained in Chapter 9), therefore, the sentences imposed and their impact will differ markedly. Greater public debate is needed regarding our *expectations* of white-collar sentences before the sentences themselves will become more just and more predictable.

A New Personal and Corporate Ethic?

Greater public indignation is closely tied to the need for a new personal and corporate ethic. We are generally outraged only by things that appear immoral and shocking. As long as white-collar crime is viewed as "another way to do business," and white-collar offenders are those "unlucky enough to be caught," these offenses will continue, due to their failure to arouse moral indignation.

Ethical questions never go away, we just fail to consider them. Consider the issue of ethics in government during the last two decades. After the Watergate affair (described in Chapter 4), there were many recommendations for change, resulting in the Ethics in Government Act of 1978, signed by President Carter. It was designed to "preserve and promote the integrity of public officials," requiring the attorney general to investigate certain types of alleged wrongdoing. After the HUD scandal, the Iran–Contra affair, and questionable fees received by members of Congress, President Bush established the President's Commis-

Workers attempt to build a containment dam around a chemical waste dump near La Marque, Texas. The EPA called the dumpsite the most dangerous in Texas. Better selection of prosecution targets and the debate over the need for a new personal and corporate ethic becomes manifest through such disasters. *(Walt Frerck, UPI/Bettmann)*

sion on Federal Ethics Law Reform. This commission's recommendations resulted in the passage of the Ethics Reform Act of 1989 (amending the 1978 Ethics in Government Act), which changed rules for outside income, gifts, and travel, as well as instituted a pay increase for federal officials.[13] Acknowledging the continuing public concern over misconduct by government officials, President Clinton signed an executive order in 1993 titled, "Ethical Commitments by Executive Branch Employees." This order includes rules designed to prevent those in government service to use it for purposes of personal enrichment later on. It prohibits senior appointees from lobbying in their agencies on behalf of foreign governments for five years after leaving government service. The same prohibition applies to trade negotiators for five years after their government employment ends.[14] These new rules were added to those of the earlier ethics acts. This executive order "may help address the concerns of the average American" arising out of the conflict-of-interest investigations of the 1980s.[15] On the other hand, these prohibitions and penalties display the continual one-sided approach taken toward ethical conduct and law violation. That is to say, ethical conduct is promoted almost entirely through the threat of legal penalties. The problem with this approach, of course, is that it overlooks the low odds of apprehension, the sluggish nature of such prosecutions when they do occur, and the likelihood of subversion of the entire process (as seen in the Iran–Contra pardons). As Sally Simpson found in interviews with corporate managers, they "do not, for the most part, think in deterrence terms."[16] Therefore, it is not surprising that changes in the laws and penalty structures usually have little impact on rates of misconduct.

It can be reasonably argued that ethical violations are occurring much faster than ethics legislation designed to prevent them, and that earlier prohibitions do not seen to affect subsequent conduct. The spate of scandals in business and government documented throughout this book offer evidence that rule changes have little effect on behavior. The ethical approach to white-collar crime, explained in Chapter 7, argues for ethical training as an integrated part of the educational process. The ability to make ethical decisions in the face of competitive and often conflicting demands is a skill that remains largely untaught and unlearned. The result is a society where a premium is placed on expedience, efficiency, and cost-benefit, with a corresponding failure to understand the more important principles of personal ethics and social justice. Until the accumulation of knowledge, income, and power are seen as secondary to knowing what to do with them, unethical and illegal conduct will continue to characterize a disturbing number of business and government transactions.

Summary

Five fundamental concerns will guide the future of white-collar crime. The need for public indignation, finding a proper level of regulation, nonarbitrary selection of prosecution targets, a principled approach to sentencing, and the need for a new personal and corporate ethic all will have dramatic impacts on the extent and response to white-collar crime. This book has organized the study of white-collar crime into a coherent typology, classified its causes, related what we know about its nature and extent, and described the response of the adjudication system to it. The case studies cited throughout the book are a testament to the scope of the problem, but only after consideration, public debate, and consensus on the five questions posed in this chapter will long-term solutions be forthcoming.

Endnotes

1. Jay S. Albanese, *Myths and Realities of Crime and Justice*, 3rd ed. (Niagara Falls, NY: Apocalypse, 1990), Ch. 1.
2. "Fertility Fraud," *USA Today*, September 8, 1993, p. 3.
3. Marjorie Williams, "Burden of Proof," *Washington Post Magazine*, April 11, 1993, p. W6.
4. 28 U.S.C. Sec. 991(b)(1)(b).
5. Kip Schlegel, *Just Deserts for Corporate Criminals* (Boston: Northeastern University Press, 1990); and Paul H. Robinson, "A Sentencing System for the 21st Century?" *Texas Law Review*, 77 (1987), p. 7.

6. Ami L. Feinstein, Samia Haddad, Thomas W. Izzo, and Michael B. Lilley, "Federal Sentencing," *American Criminal Law Review*, 30 (Spring 1993), p. 1095.
7. Dale G. Parent, "What Did the United States Sentencing Guidelines Miss?" *Yale Law Journal*, 101 (1992), p. 1773; and Chip J. Lowe, "Modern Sentencing Reform: A Preliminary Analysis of the Proposed Sentencing Guidelines," *American Criminal Law Review*, 25 (1987), pp. 54–55.
8. Edward M. Shaw, "Plea Bargaining White-Collar Offenses under Federal Sentencing Guidelines," *New York Law Journal*, May 25, 1990, p. 1.
9. Robert G. Morvillo, "Sentencing Guidelines Issues, Six Years Later," *New York Law Journal*, October 5, 1993, p. 3.
10. Steven Walt and William S. Laufer, "Corporate Criminal Liability and the Comparative Mix of Sanctions," in *White-Collar Crime Reconsidered*, ed. by Kip Schlegel and David Weisburd (Boston: Northeastern University Press, 1992), pp. 309–331.
11. Theresa Walker Karle and Thomas Sager, "Are the Federal Sentencing Guidelines Meeting Congressional Goals? An Empirical and Case Law Analysis," *Emory Law Journal*, 40 (1991).
12. Antoinette Marie Tease, "Downward Departures for Substantial Assistance: A Proposal for Reducing Sentencing Disparities Among Co-Defendants," *Montana Law Review*, 53 (1992).
13. Joseph C. Bryce, Thomas J. Gibson, and Daryn E. Rush, "Ethics in Government," *American Criminal Law Review*, 29 (Winter 1992), pp. 315–342.
14. Executive Order No. 12,834, 58 Fed. Reg. 5911 (1993).
15. David K. Bowles and Joann M. McCartney, "Conflicts of Interest," *American Criminal Law Review*, 30 (Spring 1993), pp. 523–544.
16. Sally S. Simpson, "Corporate-Crime Deterrence and Corporate-Control Policies," in *White-Collar Crime Reconsidered*, ed. by Kip Schlegel and David Weisburd (Boston: Northeastern University Press, 1992), p. 303.

Index